W9-BNF-589

BraveHearts

The Against-All-Odds Rise of Gonzaga Basketball

Bud Withers

TRIUMPH
BOOKS
CHICAGO

Copyright © 2002 by Bud Withers

No part of this publication may be reproduced, stored in a retrieval system, or transmitted, in any form by any means, electronic, mechanical, photocopying, or otherwise, without the prior written permission of the publisher, Triumph Books, 601 S. LaSalle St., Suite 500, Chicago, Illinois 60605.

Library of Congress Cataloging-in-Publication Data

Withers, Bud.
  Bravehearts : the against-all-odds rise of Gonzaga basketball / Bud Withers.
    p. cm.
  Includes index.
  ISBN 1-57243-499-6 (hard)
    1. Gonzaga University—Basketball. 2. Gonzaga Bulldogs (Basketball team)
  I. Title: Brave hearts. II. Title.

GV885.43.G66 W58 2002
796.323'63'0979737—dc21

                                                        2002026623

This book is available in quantity at special discounts for your group or organization. For further information, contact:
Triumph Books
601 South LaSalle Street
Suite 500
Chicago, Illinois 60605
(312) 939-3330
Fax (312) 663-3557

Printed in the United States of America
ISBN 1-57243-499-6
Interior design by Patricia Frey
All photos courtesy of Gonzaga University except where noted otherwise.

Contents

Foreword

Over the past 25 years, college basketball has seen staggering changes. There have been vast increases in media and fan interest, unbalanced spending on athletic facilities, top talent leaving college early for the pros, and the explosion in importance of the NCAA tournament. An NCAA tournament has become the college game's Holy Grail and has served to skew expectations for the "big boys" and the "little guys" alike. For a school from one of the power conferences, falling short of an NCAA bid is seen as a failure, and for a school from a smaller conference, like Gonzaga, a loss in the conference tournament usually means staying home from the "Big Dance" and being largely ignored.

College basketball is a game of resources. The schools from the power conferences have more television exposure, more media coverage, better facilities, and more money, which all translate into advantages in recruiting and in hiring and retaining the very best coaches in the game. In addition, schools from the power conferences wield more influence over scheduling, enabling them to duck quality little guys, or to play them only at home. All together, there are powerful obstacles to overcome for a school from a smaller conference to compete favorably on the national stage, and the odds are against any such school consistently winning big.

Gonzaga has defied those odds and has created a blueprint for true success. Zag basketball has proved that a smaller school can win, and win consistently over time, without sacrificing its principles and ideals. With outstanding leadership from the top down, Gonzaga's substance has triumphed in an age of style, and its coaches understand that recruiting quality people that can play is more important than recruiting pure basketball talent. Gonzaga has been a great story for the media because the Zags have been so successful on the court, despite being from a small school in a picturesque but somewhat remote location. But the real story behind Gonzaga basketball is not the wins; it is how the wins are achieved. Gonzaga wins with people, plain and simple.

I have had the pleasure of watching Gonzaga basketball up close and getting to know its players and coaches. I have not seen a more committed, focused, and knowledgeable staff in America than Mark Few and his staff. Few recruits players he would not only enjoy coaching but, more important, would also enjoy being around. Gonzaga recruits only those kids that will fit into its style of play and its principled way of doing things, and there is a keen understanding of team dynamics and the importance of not just working hard but of *working hard together.*

For a basketball person, watching Gonzaga practice and play is a true pleasure. The Zags are innovative, disciplined, and well drilled. Gonzaga's players play hard all of the time—not just when the spirit moves them—and competing on every play is a habit. At Gonzaga, winning is clearly important. However, in my judgment, winning at Gonzaga is not the primary goal. Rather, winning at Gonzaga is a by-product of doing things the right way. Simply put, Gonzaga does it the right way, and as a result, Zag basketball is a model program for all of us to follow.

—Jay Bilas
ESPN college basketball analyst

Preface

*Every March as the NCAA tournament cranks up and mil-
lions of Americans eagerly fill out office pool brackets, I am
asked the same question: why is this event so popular? Why
would CBS commit $6 billion to it at a time when college
basketball is being plundered every year by players leaving
early for the NBA or not even showing up to pretend to go to
college for a year or two? Why do we sit rapt in front of TV
sets day and night during those first two days from high noon
until well after midnight?*

The answer, in a very real if simplistic sense, is this: Gonzaga.

Am I biased as I write this because my friend Bud Withers has written an up
close look at the success of the "Little Program That Could"? Sure. But think
about it. What draws us to the NCAA tournament year in and year out is wondering not so much which power school will end up with the trophy when the
Final Four is over but which *non*-power school will light up the event that first
weekend with an improbable upset.

Gonzaga certainly wasn't the first little program to grab the national spotlight.
All of us who follow college basketball can reach into our memory banks for

names like Richmond—which beat Auburn (with Charles Barkley), Indiana (coached by what's-his-name), Georgia Tech, and second-seeded Syracuse during an eight-year run. There was Coppin State over South Carolina; Valparaiso over Mississippi (remember Bryce Drew?); Hampton over Iowa State; Princeton over defending national champion UCLA; and, most memorably perhaps, Princeton again, although *not* over Georgetown. Many people still think of that 1989 game between the 64th-seeded Tigers and the top-seeded Hoyas as the tournament's greatest upset.

Georgetown won the game, 50–49, with a large assist from a scared referee who swallowed his whistle on a clear foul on the game's last play. But Princeton won the nation's heart by coming so close and giving hope to every underdog team that has ever taken the court in the NCAA tournament.

During these past four seasons, Gonzaga has become the symbol and the beacon for all those teams. Not only did the Zags make it to the round of eight in 1999, but they also put a real scare into Connecticut, which went on to win the national championship. Then, to prove they weren't a fluke, the Zags came back and reached the Sweet 16 as a low seed in the next two years. To me, the greatest stat you could find going into last year's tournament was that only three teams in the field had made it to the Sweet 16 during at least three straight years: Duke, which was the defending national champion; Michigan State, which was the 2000 champion and had been to three straight Final Fours; and Gonzaga.

We all know what happened in last year's tournament. We know that the basketball committee, overloaded with representatives from power conferences, chose to ignore its own criteria and stick Gonzaga with a No. 6 seed. Then, when Wyoming pulled the first round "upset," they all went around and said, "See, we told you."

Baloney. Gonzaga got "Gonzagaed." An inspired Wyoming team cast in an underdog role played great basketball and won the game. One and out—that's the beauty of the event. But to say that the committee was right to pass Gonzaga over as a No. 3 or, at worst, No. 4 seed is ludicrous. Does that mean the committee was wrong to make Duke a No. 1 seed, since it was beaten in the round of 16? No; you seed based on the regular season and then see what happens. The committee didn't do that.

But none of that diminishes what Gonzaga has done these last few years. Dan Monson and Mark Few have coached superbly and the players have proven their toughness and their talent with the way they have performed. In an era when every big-time program is overloaded with players whose only goal is to get to the NBA, it is a joy to see a successful program that is largely made up of youngsters who won't play in the NBA—but probably will graduate.

I've enjoyed every minute of Gonzaga's success. I look forward to next March to see who will get Gonzagaed next.

—John Feinstein

Introduction

The final, fatal seconds were ticking away, and the searing reality was settling in on the players from Gonzaga. The most successful basketball team in the history of the school was done, just like that, a victim of its own perplexing inability to execute the most basic act in the sport: shot-making.

It couldn't find the mark, and now the school president, Father Robert Spitzer, had to. In the empty moments of a 73–66 loss to Wyoming, Spitzer fumbled for an epitaph, something to say in a shattered locker room.

Just as 29 victories in the 2001–2002 season was uncharted water for the Zags, so was this performance in the NCAA tournament. Just as Gonzaga had cashiered teams like Stanford and St. John's and Virginia in recent seasons, now it was mourning the death of its own dreams. Now it was left to ask the unanswerable questions.

What would cause a team known for its nerveless outside shooting to hit 26.8 percent in an NCAA-tournament game? Were the Zags merely assuming the role played inevitably by every big-time program—that of the prey rather than the hunter? (And is there glory even in that suggestion?)

Did they linger too long over the injustice of being dealt a No. 6 seed by the NCAA basketball committee, a group often given to taking care of the lordly programs of the game rather than its working class? Were they—and Spitzer much preferred this hypothesis to the thought that somehow the Zags were dragging the heavy burden of expectation on their shoulders—sapped by the mile-high altitude of Albuquerque against a team that plays and practices in the 7,200-foot aerie of Laramie, Wyoming?

Guard Kyle Bankhead ran to a crushed Dan Dickau, put an arm around him, and tried to offer words of consolation. As they always do, the Zags then gathered on the floor and extended applause in the direction of their cheering section, giving as they had gotten. That has become a tradition, but one usually played out with the overarching theme that Gonzaga probably took it as far as it could be taken. This time there was no such rationale, no comfort to be found in the NCAA bracket, only the cataclysm of a first-round defeat.

And Spitzer had a couple of minutes to help them find perspective. In his heart of hearts, he knew they didn't want to hear this, but they needed to hear it anyway.

"You've been the greatest ambassadors we could ever have had," he said. "We're so happy with you. We're so grateful for you. Thank you for one of the most amazing years Gonzaga has ever had. It's not the number of wins, but who you are. This is the thing to see about yourself. We're just totally grateful."

So shortly removed from a game, so far distant from the next one, the Zags could assimilate only part of what Spitzer was saying. They would always remember, after all, how a team thought capable of the Final Four was ousted without a victory. But just as Spitzer tried to tell them, they would come to know they were part of something much greater than an unexpected loss in the NCAA tournament.

~ ~ ~ ~ ~

At times like this, it had become de rigueur among sportswriters who had boarded the Gonzaga bandwagon in late season to author summary stories forecasting where the Zags might be going the next season. In 1999, after Gonzaga's headlong run to the Elite Eight of the NCAA, the conclusion was that the Zags would be returning to the ranks of the peasants of the game, an assumption seemingly validated when the coach, Dan Monson, left for Minnesota months later.

But in a year, Gonzaga was back in the Sweet 16 under coach Mark Few on the strength of victories over Louisville and St. John's. After a loss to Purdue, the laptops clacked with outlooks for 2000–2001 that were no rosier than the previous year's. Of course, Gonzaga returned to the Sweet 16 the following March, joining Duke and Michigan State as the only programs with ongoing success at that level.

Turns out the writers weren't the only skeptics. Monson remembers his future wife, Darci, attending a gathering of friends to watch a road game on television in 1998, when the Zags had the West Coast Conference (WCC) player of the year, Bakari Hendrix. A former Zag who also won that honor, Jeff Brown, was among those in the group.

"Is Bakari Hendrix that good?" Darci asked Monson. "Jeff Brown said, 'You better enjoy it now, because once Bakari Hendrix leaves, this program is going to go right back to normal.'"

Monson's reaction: "We all felt that way."

A year later, after the Zags had brought down Minnesota, Stanford, and Florida to reach a game against eventual national champion Connecticut to go to the Final Four, Monson had to say good-bye to one of the favorite Gonzaga players of all time, guard Quentin Hall.

"Coach," Hall told Monson in his clipped Bahamian accent, "as long as Casey Calvary is here, you will be fine. But then you better go find another job."

The success is always going to end at Gonzaga, but it never does. It's always going to depart with Hendrix or Calvary or Richie Frahm or Matt Santangelo or Dan Dickau, but it always regenerates to flourish again, firing up cold winter nights in Spokane, Washington, with a new cast to uplift and embrace.

In the spring of 2002, Gonzaga, a Jesuit-based Catholic school, teased the opening of a $119-million campaign for endowments and capital projects with this question: "Why Gonzaga?"

The question had already been asked by an ever-swelling number of college basketball fans in the United States and beyond: Why Gonzaga? How did a little school that made its first appearance in the NCAA tournament in 1995 come to shake the figurative shoulder of the game to attention? Why does a school with fewer than 5,000 enrollment in a medium-sized city surrounded by hundreds of miles of mines and forest and farmland grab the imagination of college basketball, so that somebody wearing a Gonzaga T-shirt in Paris or London or Zurich might be recognized in a chance encounter?

Why, in a sport where the watchword is *upheaval*, does Gonzaga endure to do it again and again and again? How does it leap from one of college basketball's backwater conferences to such a place of preeminence every March?

It is worth remembering that the infrastructure of college basketball does not lend itself easily to such an emergence. In six "power conferences"—the Big East, Big Ten, Southeastern, Big 12, Atlantic Coast, and Pac-10—there are 68 teams, any one of which can make the NCAA tournament with nothing more than a fifth-place finish and a couple of notable nonconference victories.

Then there are the worthy programs from lesser conferences—Temple in the Atlantic 10, Utah in the Mountain West, Cincinnati and Marquette in Conference USA, plus a host of others. And in the wings are a whole panoply of Creightons, Butlers, Valparaisos, and Tulsas.

Surely, Gonzaga's rise to the top of the West Coast Conference hasn't been as treacherous as, say, somebody's in the Big Ten. But it has become clear that domination in the WCC means little in the way of favors from the Division I basketball committee on Selection Sunday.

In terms of sustained, recent success in the NCAA tournament compared to a modest March history before that, there is only one word for Gonzaga: *unprecedented*.

No, Gonzaga doesn't have a market cornered on becoming America's favorite underdog in the NCAAs. Several Midwest teams—Ball State, Kent State, Butler, Indiana State with Larry Bird in 1979—have burst forth with how'd-they-do-it performances. But these have been mostly one-year phenomena.

Others have found an illicit recipe for instant success: Cleveland State exploded to the Sweet 16 in 1986, and then its coach, Kevin Mackey, was caught in a crack house. Ten years later, Massachusetts went to the title game, but its entire run was vacated in NCAA records for violations.

For any sort of vague parallels to the Gonzaga phenomenon, you have to look at Georgetown, Seton Hall, and Tulsa. Thirty years ago, John Thompson began building a power at Georgetown, but he did it in an urban setting, at a school that would soon become part of the powerful Big East. Seton Hall's first NCAA appearance was in 1988, and a year later it played in the title game, but it also had a vast talent pool near its gym and the lure of the Big East. Tulsa is a closer mirror, identical to Gonzaga's two Sweet 16s and Elite Eight over a longer stretch of time (since 1994), but it had a bit more history with three unsuccessful appearances in the NCAA in the mideighties.

Much of the uniqueness of Gonzaga's run owes its contrast to the transitional nature of the college game today. Sometimes the Zags seem to be doing everything backward. At a time when all the rage is making a fast getaway for the NBA, Gonzaga players often stay a year longer, redshirting as freshmen. At a time when coaches are apt to make the quick hit and move on to a bigger, better-paying job, Gonzaga's stay; Mark Few arrived at the school in 1989 as a graduate assistant and has rebuffed several feelers to climb—that's the conventional wisdom, anyway—the coaching ladder.

If and when Few leaves, the torch will be passed to his top assistant, Bill Grier. It's already in writing.

"In today's world," Grier says, "guys change jobs like the weather. As a player, you get used to playing one way for two or three years. Then the plug gets pulled and all of a sudden, you're playing a new system. That system may require a different type of player, so personnel changes with the type of kid you're bringing in.

"We know what works at our place. We know what kinds of kids work here."

The system has been in place so long, there isn't a lot of need for severe regimentation off the practice floor. Hang around the Gonzaga offices, and you sense a relaxed atmosphere born of confidence in how to do things. It took Few's other full-time assistant, Leon Rice, aback.

"We don't have a lot of staff meetings," said Grier, who has worked alongside Few for 10 years. "Mark and I have been together so long, it's not like we need to sit down and meet and talk about everything we need to do. It was hard initially for Leon. He didn't know what was going on."

Maybe that's the first foundational brick of Gonzaga basketball that America finds so endearing: it's stable. It isn't every guy grabbing to get his; it isn't the knee-jerk assumption that there's a better deal somewhere else. Just as Princeton always captured the imagination because it played the same way under Pete Carril, so does Gonzaga survive the turbulence around it.

Last winter, it got back to Few that Dan Belluomini, the former San Francisco coach who is now a West Coast TV commentator, was ruminating on Few's future if the Washington job were to open.

"Oh, he has to take that," Belluomini said summarily. "How can he not?"

Few is more inclined to wonder, how can they think that way?

"I think they can't comprehend that Gonzaga is a top 20 program," Few said. "It's out of the realm of possibility."

Stability is written all over Gonzaga. It's on the face of Jack Stockton, 74, whose son John went on from the Zags to a Hall of Fame career with the Utah Jazz. Perhaps it's not a coincidence the younger Stockton will play his entire career with one team; his dad grew up in a house on DeSmet Street abutting campus, and when he moved, it was to a home four blocks away.

"That's progress," quips Jack Stockton. "Four blocks in 74 years."

Dan Fitzgerald, the longtime coach who got all this going, would tell you he saw evidence of stability long ago. He remembers a conversation he had with Monson, his number one assistant, when Monson was marveling at the overall achievement one year.

"There's thirteen guys on this team," Fitzgerald said. "Twelve of them have a mother and a father in the house, and the other is a great kid. All we do all day long is coach. We're not putting out a lot of fires. Your energy is not down at the police station."

Of course, one man's stability is another's staleness. Longevity would be a liability if it weren't for the fact that the Zags have an eye for evaluation as well as character.

Jeff Condill, Jack Stockton's partner of 11 years in their off-campus tavern, played for a year alongside John Stockton and became an All–West Coast Conference player himself. He believes there was a legacy handed down even before anybody outside eastern Washington knew about Gonzaga.

"One thing we had, we had good kids," Condill says. "We weren't as successful, but we still knew what it's like to be a Bulldog, be a Zag, and I think that's carried through.

"There are lots of special things about this place. You go out and lace 'em up and compete. You competed 24 hours a day. We're the small school that could— or couldn't. Back then it was kind of on and off.

"These kids have taken that with them. Everybody's gaga—shirts, they wear with pride. Now people are recognizing them in New York and Chicago or Europe: 'Hey, Gonzaga, huh? They got that basketball team.' Before, they wouldn't have a freakin' clue."

To recruit carefully means to take a step toward the exquisite chemistry to which every coach aspires. The Jesuits would point to Psalms 133:1: "Behold, how good and how pleasant it is for brethren to dwell together in unity!"

Father Spitzer likes to use the basketball assist as metaphor for the greater mission of the university.

"The whole idea of service, of offering things up for the common good, the prevalence of the assist on the team, there's a degree of give-it-upness, if you will," he says. "It underlies the team spirit, that there really is a sense of camaraderie and common good that we're seeking in the university.

"It's absolutely wonderful."

The act of simply keeping to its own template puts Gonzaga at a distance from the hurly-burly of some other college programs. Consider only a thin layer of the unease that visited other big-time schools in the 2001–2002 season:

Shortly after the Zags beat New Mexico, the Lobos suspended and then dismissed guard Marlon Parmer. The coach, Fran Fraschilla, said a "cloud" had been lifted from the program. Fresno State, another loser to Gonzaga, played in and out of suspensions to Melvin Ely and Chris Sandy, after guard Tito Maddox didn't return because of dealings with an agent.

Pepperdine, Gonzaga's chief competition in the WCC, succeeded in spite of an early-season, off-court fight between two players. Kentucky's Gerald Fitch and Cory Sears were suspended after scuffling on an airplane.

At Minnesota, the school for which Monson left Gonzaga in 1999, attorneys and judges argued over whether the former coach, Clem Haskins, could be denied a settlement after his part as a central figure in a messy academic scandal of work performed by players' proxies.

Arkansas' own academic malaise was obscured by the strange force-out of coach Nolan Richardson. His departure underscored that no black player who entered his regime from 1990 to 1994 had graduated. Of course, he wasn't alone; it was the same among all players at 36 other schools during that period.

After the season ended, Cincinnati center Donald Little, dismissed from the team a year earlier in two alcohol-related incidents, was arraigned on charges of felonious assault and kidnapping. Authorities said he taped a teammate to a plastic lawn chair and helped burn him with cigarettes and a heated coat hanger—in other words, he chose a novel way to develop chemistry.

"They've maintained their integrity," says Condill of his alma mater. "They haven't sold out to bad kids, or kids that shouldn't be here."

It's a long season, and college basketball is an explosive game. The team still playing with purpose and cohesiveness in March is often the exception. In *David Copperfield*, Charles Dickens could have been thinking about the quest of a college basketball team when he wrote of a "long pull, and a strong pull, and a pull all together."

Once together, always together. For most, to play or coach at Gonzaga is to forge a lifetime of relationships. The place is the mom-and-pop grocery store of college hoops, until you're trying to wrestle away a rebound or defend a three-on-two fast break.

Few met his future wife, Marcy, when she worked at the basketball office at Gonzaga. Ditto for Grier and his future wife, Nicole. When Monson got married, Few and Grier were in the wedding. When Few got married, Monson and Grier were in the wedding. When Grier got married, Few was best man and Monson was in it. And Few's father, a Presbyterian minister in Creswell, Oregon, officiated all three ceremonies.

Teammates of a decade ago Jeff Brown and Jamie Dudley skied together at Aspen last winter. Several more old teammates joined them for a weekend of golf in the spring at Bandon Dunes on the Oregon coast. They e-mail each other regularly. When Grier flew to interview for the Boise State job in March, he got together with former Zag Geoff Goss for dinner—not once, but twice.

"It's a cliché to say it's a family atmosphere," says Rich Fox, the transfer from Colorado eligible at Gonzaga for the 2002–2003 season. "But it's like that."

Sometimes it's a big family. Few is appreciative and protective of the famous—occasionally infamous—Kennel Club, the student booster group. Twice during 2002, he showed up at the line where students were waiting to pick up their tickets with perhaps 25 pizzas. He and his two-year-old son, A.J., handed them out.

Families have spats, and so does Gonzaga, but the Zags' indiscretions tend to stop short of the police blotter. Last year, swingman Alex Hernandez risked expulsion from the team after an ill-timed snit cost Gonzaga a technical foul and very nearly the New Mexico game, followed by another technical against Portland.

Monson recalls another Zaglike contretemps during the 1999 run to the Elite Eight. Mike Nilson, the defensive specialist, would routinely cut hair for his teammates in the locker room, and they became increasingly lax about cleaning up the mess despite Monson's warnings.

After their return from Seattle and the Stanford upset that swept them into the Sweet 16, an untidy locker room so ruffled Monson that he booted them from it for three days, telling them to remove any gear they might need before the biggest game in the history of the program. Then they went out and beat Florida.

Monson also remembers the bigger picture. "Those kids would thank you for everything they got, from a sweat suit to a TV in the locker room," he said. "We were trying to make it better, and they always appreciated that."

Why Gonzaga? Dr. Ken Anderson, a management professor, sits in his office on campus and ponders the question and comes up empty, and if people like him can't explain it, it may be inexplicable. Anderson played for the Zags a generation ago, is the faculty athletic representative, and has spent time as president of the WCC executive council.

What, he asks, if Minnesota hadn't been confronted by its academic fraud in March of 1999, resulting in the suspension of four Gophers on the eve of the first NCAA game Gonzaga would win in its history? Would those players have helped Minnesota carry the day, stunting Gonzaga's rise to prominence before it could start? Who can know?

Another high-profile coach offers his own reason for Gonzaga's success. "I think they've done a really good job," he says. "I don't want to be quoted, but in the profession . . . [they say] what's the best thing about Gonzaga? It's Washington and Washington State."

The struggles at both schools have undoubtedly contributed, but that's a risky conclusion. The year Gonzaga ignited its rise with an appearance in the Elite Eight, Washington was also in the NCAA tournament but failed to sustain it. Moreover, the Zags have developed their own blueprint and only occasionally do they compete with Washington and Washington State for the same players. They have simply done a better job of evaluation and coaching than either of the other Division I programs in the state, and if that's weakness on the part of Washington and Washington State, it could also be ascribed to Stanford or Virginia or any of the other NCAA teams Gonzaga has brought down.

There are no pat answers for Gonzaga, only descriptions of their achievements. The words *mind-boggling* are volunteered by three different coaches—Fitzgerald, former Gonzaga boss Jay Hillock, and Monson's dad, Don, who headed programs at Idaho and Oregon.

"I can't believe it," says Hillock, who coached Gonzaga from 1981 to 1985. "I think they're the most overachieving program, easily, in all of Division I basketball."

Don Monson had good teams at Idaho in the early eighties, including a Sweet 16 team in 1982. He knows the ruts in the yellow brick road.

"For a school this size to be able to get the national attention and go so deep into the NCAAs as they have . . ." he says, trailing off. "I had a great team at Idaho that went deep, but we're talking one-year deals. The Gonzaga story is not a one-year deal. And I see it continuing.

"You see these other teams on TV. I've watched them; I've coached against them. You don't think Gonzaga can play against these guys, and they *can* play with them."

Ultimately, it's about a triangle of faith, a term the Jesuits would like—faith on the part of recruits that they will develop at Gonzaga, faith by the coaches in a system, faith of the school administration that the best way to sustain this supernova is to reward longtime coaches, to keep them in succession like French kings.

There was a turbulent week in March 2002, when the whole Gonzaga phenomenon seemed to teeter. Few interviewed for the vacant Washington position and a week later took his name from consideration. Simultaneously, Grier was interviewed at Boise State and Montana talked to Rice about its vacancy.

Like dominoes, they fell—back into their chairs in the Gonzaga offices. Few said he would have struggled to look Blake Stepp and Cory Violette—players whom he had once sold on the virtue of the Zags over the Pac-10—in the eye.

Grier got excited briefly about Boise State, began plotting who might be on his staff if he were hired, and when he got on a plane to leave, felt something hit him like a wind shear. "All of a sudden," he says, "reality set in and I thought, 'What am I doing?'"

It was not dissimilar for Rice, who was hired full time at Gonzaga in 1999.

"I wake up whistling 'zip-ah-dee-do-dah' that I get to do what I do," he says. "And I think Mark and Billy feel the same way. It's kind of what makes our place so special. We appreciate it and they appreciate us.

"It's Camelot."

Dan Monson is now entrenched at Minnesota, on the brink of reaping the harvest of his exhausting labors to cleanse the Gophers of their academic scandal. Yet he would not disagree with Rice.

He is asked if he misses Gonzaga.

"Oh," Monson says, "every day."

The Culture on Campus

The evening begins with more non-basketball-playing Gonzaga students on the Martin Centre floor than players. Some 25 are there to form a tunnel for pregame introductions for the Zags.

There will not be any high tension on this night, for the opponent is the University of Portland, one of the bottom-feeders of the West Coast Conference. Rather, it's an excuse for the Kennel Club to pursue its raison d'être and spend a couple of hours mocking the opponent and giving love to the Zags.

Some 1,050 are members of the Kennel Club, a student cheer group not officially under the aegis of the university. There are those who would say that's a good thing. Membership in the group requires $15, which buys a T-shirt and—just maybe—some beer when there are leftover proceeds. One of the recent T-shirts featured the mascot bulldog and, owing to the stars floating around his head, it appeared that he had attended one of the club's pregame functions.

Club members sit together at the games, a large clot of red, blue, or white—depending on that year's shirt—and ride players, bait officials, and generally try to forget they have an engineering exam the next day.

Former coach Dan Fitzgerald invented the group and named it. Since then, it has grown into one of the most recognizable elements associated with the university.

Neil Tocher, a Montana product, was president for the 2001–2002 season. In the house he shares with students near campus, the decor might be described as early Busch Light.

"The Kennel Club is one of the reasons I came to Gonzaga," he says.

He adds that the Kennel Club used to be notorious for "about 50 guys that would get extremely drunk and go to the games and cause a lot of problems." Knowing that, he has tried to balance the club's hedonistic bent with some restraint, because he likes what the athletic department has done for the group. Students get 1,000 tickets to the games, plus leftover faculty and staff allotments, and he has had the perk of a personal relationship with athletic director Mike Roth and the basketball coach, Mark Few.

"Things just exploded this year," he says, referring to a website devoted to the club.

To be in the Kennel Club means when Eastern Washington fans chanted "Ov-er-rat-ed" at the Zags in 2000, the Gonzaga rowdies responded with "Nev-er rat-ed." To be in the club means that when Loyola managers spread folding stools in a circle during timeouts, you chant "Kum-ba-ya, kum-ba-ya." To be in the club means deciding when to break into the singsong refrain of "It's all ov-er," to symbolize the death of the opponent's chances. Sometimes that can be adapted to the occasion, such as when Gonzaga led Portland 29–4 in 2001, leading to "Sin-gle dig-its," or "Up by twen-ty"—and thirty, and forty, as would be the case in this game.

Unofficially, club members are expected to ply friends at Santa Clara or San Francisco for inside intelligence on their players.

"We look for girlfriends' names; we look into history," says another Kennel Club officer, Steve Churney. "Somehow, somewhere, we get the tidbits."

A lob pass from Blake Stepp to Ronny Turiaf for a raging slam sends the Kennel Club into a froth. Moments later, Stepp finds Anthony Reason for a second one, and the crowd goes wacko. The game is over well before the club is chanting "Up by for-ty," with 14:04 left. They're mostly bored the rest of the way, at least until they realize there's a possibility of free hamburgers (which the students sometimes get if the team reaches a certain number of three-point shots). Then, with five minutes left, they chant, "We want Wen-dy's."

The evening ends with Reason's selection as player of the game and another tunnel of students formed to usher the team back to the locker room.

It's definitely collegiate, as well as collegial.

"You go, you have fun," says 2001–2002 student body president Cathy Smits. "It's kind of a rowdy crowd, but it still maintains school spirit. Not every Kennel Club member drinks; not every Kennel Club member goes to every party."

Still, the university casts a wary eye to the club, hoping it can display a measure of self-control.

"Unfortunately," Smits says, "there are some things with the organization that aren't the best. So I think the university is trying to work with the students to make it better."

~ ~ ~ ~ ~

Gonzaga University sits on 108 acres by the Spokane River, half a mile from the downtown core of a city of 195,000. The school was founded in 1887, two years before statehood in Washington, as a frontier boarding school for boys. Joseph Cataldo, a missionary who extended Christianity to American Indians in the area, started it with the encouragement of Spokane's early civic leaders.

The school is named after the 16th-century Italian Jesuit saint Aloysius Gonzaga, a descendant of a noble Renaissance family, who died at 23 attending to the sick in plague-stricken Rome in 1591. He was designated the patron saint of youth in 1726.

The trademark twin spires on "St. Al's" church, often associated with Gonzaga, are in fact an anomaly as great as the Zags' residence in the elite of college basketball. The church is a separate entity from the university, even as it is an enduring symbol of the campus.

Father Robert Spitzer, 50, is a Gonzaga grad who came most recently from the faculty at another Jesuit school, Seattle University, to the president's office at GU. He is not put off by the notion that some people know Gonzaga only for its basketball, citing the accomplishments of a final-four debate team in 2001 and consistent high marks for GU's schools in fields like business, accounting, engineering, and law. *U.S. News and World Report*'s annual catalog of America's best colleges has placed Gonzaga among its top comprehensive regional universities in the West for 13 of the past 16 years.

It's a private school with about 5,000 students, a little more than 3,000 of them undergraduates. Full-time undergraduate tuition was $18,300 in 2001–2002.

The university espouses a commitment to go beyond intellectual teachings to development in spiritual, intellectual, social, and physical pursuits. About half the students are Catholic, and a degree requires three courses in religious studies, one each in scripture, Christian doctrine, and applied theology. Gonzaga basketball players say the campus ethos regarding Catholicism is non-judgmental.

"No expectation, nothing further," said Jeff Brown, a three-time All–West Coast Conference player in the early nineties. "I still remember the public school kid, taking my first religion class taught by a Father. I remember thinking, 'What do I call this guy?' Call him Father."

Vice president for student life is Dr. Sue Weitz, a smiling, gregarious woman whose background was mostly with public schools before she came to Gonzaga two decades ago.

"It was a concern to me," says Weitz, who was Presbyterian. "My father was pretty anti-Catholic. I was so welcomed."

There's an unmistakable feeling of community and high-spirited camaraderie, born partly of the cozy enrollment number and surely not damaged by the success of the basketball program. Between frequent hellos to student acquaintances and faculty members, Weitz points to a display in the central dining area where the cook staff bakes small cakes available to every student, to be picked up and devoured during the month of his or her birthday.

In the middle of campus is the Crosby Student Center, converted from its original use as a library. Outside it is a statue and just inside is a room of memorabilia dedicated to the life of Harry Lillis Crosby.

He was born in 1903 in Tacoma, Washington, before his family moved to Spokane. As a boy, he would clamor for someone to read to him the "Bingville Bugle," a youth feature in the *Spokane Chronicle*, and "Bing" was born. He would become one of America's most beloved singers and actors in the mid-20th century, and his family one of Gonzaga's major benefactors.

The overwhelming percentage of students who shuffle daily past the Crosby statue are white, a fact not lost on Gonzaga administrators who have tried to bring more diversity to the population. A faculty member recalls an introductory address in the late nineties by Spitzer's predecessor, Father Edward Glynn, whose tenure was brief due to a power struggle with the board of trustees.

Glynn had been at Gonzaga a generation before and had come most recently from St. Peter's College in New Jersey. "I'm reminded of what lovely people you are," Glynn, who pushed hard for diversity, told the faculty. "The problem is, you're all white."

In the 2001–2002 school year, 76 percent of the student body listed itself as Caucasian. Some 5.5 percent were Asian or Pacific Islander, 3 percent were Hispanic, 1.5 percent were American Indian or Alaska native, and 1 percent was listed as black. Two percent identified themselves as international, and 11 percent declined to give information.

Spitzer has pushed diversity as well, and figures show the mix has increased at least slightly since he took over. All minority listings were slightly lower in 1999–2000 than two years later, albeit with a greater 17 percent rate not reporting.

The effort toward a more multicultural university includes scholarships for racial or ethnic minorities, a recently created vice presidential position to encourage diversity, and the establishment of Unity House on campus. There is also a one-credit-hour course for freshmen called University Pathways, in which perhaps half the curriculum includes diversity awareness.

"Spokane is such a tough place for diversity to be a piece of cake," says Gonzaga registrar Jolanta Kozyra, who says she knew of a prospective female student from Chicago who chose not to attend GU because she couldn't find a hairdresser who specialized in African-American styles. Indeed, although Spokane has a relatively robust metropolitan population of 420,000, the percentage of blacks was only 1.6 in 2000, compared to 91 percent white.

Gonzaga point guard Winston Brooks came from a heavily African-American area of Richmond, Virginia, but time at two junior college outposts helped him adjust to the reversed racial mix.

"When I left to go to school at 18, that was like the first white people I'd been around," he said. "I didn't have any problems with it. To me, we're all human.

"Here in Spokane, I have so many friends of different colors and races. It's a whole new atmosphere to be in."

The city that surrounds the Gonzaga campus grew up around the labors of fur trading, lumber, mining, and, in 1881, the Northern Pacific Railroad. The intersection of those industries gave Spokane a meteoric population boost, from mere hundreds in 1880 to 20,000 in 1890 and to 100,000 some 20 years later, rivaling the biggest cities in the nation.

Lewis and Clark reached the area in 1804, and a few years later, the Hudson's Bay Company of fur traders established themselves near the falls at the Spokane River, a position that gave the city its first name, Spokane Falls. Late in the 19th century, Spokane was the hub for an explosion of gold, silver, and lead mining nearby.

The bacchanals of the Kennel Club may have come by their diversion naturally. Four years before Prohibition swept the nation, Washington voters approved in November 1914 state Initiative No. 3, which banned the sale and manufacture of liquor in the state. It didn't, however, do away entirely with drinking, allowing import permits to be obtained from county auditors for either two quarts of hard liquor or 12 bottles of beer every 20 days. According to Don Duncan's *Washington: The First Hundred Years*, there were 34,000 of those permits gobbled up in Spokane County, which had only 44,000 registered voters.

The biggest employer in the area is the Fairchild Air Force Base. Kaiser Aluminum is the largest manufacturer, and there are a growing number of electronics-related companies. Housing is cheap; the median home price is $104,200, less than half that in Seattle and below that of other inland cities like Boise, Idaho, and Tri-Cities, Washington.

The urban core was gussied up by a world's fair in 1974. The sporting ethos includes the 12-kilometer Bloomsday Run, annually attracting more than 50,000 participants, and Hoopfest, a three-on-three summer basketball tournament that has drawn as many as 5,600 teams.

Don Kardong, a 1976 Olympian and longtime chief of the Bloomsday Run, notes that Spokane "is sometimes described as not being a very good spectator-sport town. But one thing that GU basketball showed is if you have a good product, it's going to create a mania.

"It's the perfect kind of Spokane story, in a way, this overlooked team—Spokane always feels it's overlooked by western Washington. It's kind of the ultimate underdog moving up the ladder, that's pushed everybody's hot buttons."

Spokane's climate is more Midwestern—without the humidity—than West Coast, to the surprise of a lot of outsiders who figure it for the drippy, gray weather of Seattle. Spokane's annual precipitation is only 17 inches.

~ ~ ~ ~ ~

On the Gonzaga campus an oft-debated issue—as it is at a lot of Catholic institutions—is that of academic freedom versus the religious imperative.

David DeWolf, a Gonzaga law professor who has been active in the debate, describes the opposite camps:

"The liberal attitude, in kind of caricature, is that to be a Catholic university, you have to be a university first, and what a university is, is defined by what other universities say it is," he says. "And essentially, whatever is left over gets to be Catholic.

"I'm more of the conservative variety: to be a Catholic university, you have to be Catholic first, and you need to make it a place that you wouldn't need to look up in some catalog someplace to find out what's Catholic about it."

Let the arguments begin.

"It's polarized the entire campus," says theology professor Mark Alfino, who has debated both DeWolf and Spitzer on the issue. In his joust with Spitzer, Alfino insisted, "It is a weak faith that does not welcome reasons, challengers, even rascals and rogues. That's why it is a strong faith that embraces academic freedom."

The controversy descends from the papal encyclical *Ex Corde Eccesiae*, which prescribed a sort of Catholic vision for universities. A fundamental part of it is a provision that theologians at those schools essentially need to be answerable to their local bishops. With liberal theologians, that does not universally sit well.

In 2000, the Women's Studies Club at Gonzaga—recognized by the university but not part of it—invited a speaker from Planned Parenthood. Spitzer got wind of it and had the invitation rescinded.

Two years later came a bigger firestorm. This time, the Women's Studies Club sought to sponsor a play called *The Vagina Monologues*. After considerable debate, Spitzer decided to allow the presentation to take place at the West Coast River Inn—off campus.

"The Gonzaga ideal is enhancing the whole person," says Cathy Smits. "So there's a fine line. How do we educate the whole person and still give them information on these issues that aren't affiliated with or don't coincide with the Catholic faith?"

7

In his debate with Alfino, Spitzer, himself a professor of philosophy, argued that among legitimate options for the university is a stance between sponsorship and rejection—nonassociation.

"He thinks there's something between censorship and academic freedom," says Alfino, "and I don't think that makes a lot of sense."

Responds DeWolf, "There are a lot of people who teach here and go to school here who view Gonzaga's Catholic identity as sort of an interesting historical resource, but one that doesn't have much to do with the day-to-day operation of the place.

"My attitude about it is, if you're going to run a Chinese restaurant, it ought to be recognizably Chinese."

The success of the basketball team seems to have introduced another dynamic to the discussion. Enrollment is up dramatically at Gonzaga, and almost everybody seems to agree that basketball has something to do with it. Does the mere fact that some students have been attracted by basketball bring a measure of secularization to a school whose administration has tilted toward conservatism?

Apart from basketball, meanwhile, there are side issues.

"People seem to want Gonzaga for their kids," says Alfino, "although they don't necessarily want Catholicism. They want that ethos of a Catholic campus even though their kids weren't religious.

"This is a heck of a place, and nobody wants that ethos to go away. There's no polarization on that. But some people feel that there's already something wrong with wanting the ethos without the religion."

~ ~ ~ ~ ~

You can look, but you won't find an athletic dormitory on the Gonzaga campus. While high-level basketball demands much from those who can take part—sequestered hours of practice, days on the road—there appears to be a genuine connection between the Zag players and the rest of campus.

A general university requirement mandates that students live in dormitories their first two years at Gonzaga. It's almost impossible not to be part of campus culture.

"It's not the type of campus where you have a training table," says former player Jeff Brown. "I'm having my morning Cheerios across from the guy who lives across from me in the dorm. It's a close campus where everyone knows everyone."

A lot of Gonzaga players eat at the main dining area on campus. Last year, Ronny Turiaf helped a Zag cheerleader, Travis Millspaugh, get elected activities vice president for 2002–2003 by wearing one of his campaign T-shirts.

"They're supportive of us as students," says Cassie Lavalle, activities vice president for 2001–2002. "It's not necessarily that they're the basketball team and we're the students. They had intramural championships, and Germayne Forbes and Ronny Turiaf were there, cheering on their friends. It was kind of funny to see the role reversal."

It has become tradition at Gonzaga at season's end, when the last shot has been launched and the final horn sounds—usually, that's in the NCAA tournament—for the players to huddle and then applaud the fans. Those frequently include people like Tocher, who traveled 30 hours in a motor home to see the Wyoming loss at Albuquerque, or Churney, who did a 27-hour road trip to Tucson for the opening rounds in 2000.

"We show support," says Brooks. "Most basketball teams think they're above everyone. We're there on the ground with everyone else."

Because of the emotional closeness on campus, GU students don't tend to feel they're rooting for a phenomenon as much as a person when they're cheering on the basketball team.

"I study with Zach Gourde," says Smits. "That's a connection that makes the hype that much more exciting and real. It's not our school pride, it's pride in our friends."

Gonzaga players are there at the annual president's reception the Sunday before classes begin. It's a dressy event at which all GU athletic teams appear to help welcome new students and their parents.

The patrons at Coffeehouse, a campus offering that features small local or student musical groups, often include players like Gourde, Kyle Bankhead, and Cory Violette.

In the spring, after the basketballs are put away, Gonzaga players have an intramural softball team, which must be the biggest in captivity: 6'11" Richard Fox plays first base, 6'9" Dustin Villepigue is in right field, and the 6'8" Violette is the Zags' version of Rey Ordonez at shortstop.

Consensus is that academically, the Zags don't differ much from the rank-and-file students. Faculty members seem to vouch for them, as do their classmates.

"I'm a pretty keen basketball fan," says Alfino. "There are folks here who probably aren't. But in general, I think the campus is pretty supportive of the basketball program. We've got basketball players with relatively good character, and they're articulate, actually something representative of the ethos of the school.

"These are pretty neat kids. They're real religious, respectful, and they don't talk a lot of smack. More than just the public story, I think that's true."

His philosophical foil, DeWolf, agrees with him on this one.

"There's something about the team," DeWolf says, "that reminds people of what college athletics is supposed to be."

There is the inevitable segment of faculty that casts a jaded eye toward basketball. But it seems to be based on a fundamental distrust of athletics as part of the university rather than anything specifically related to hoops.

"There are a lot who are opposed to this level of intercollegiate athletics, although they've been quieter in the last few years," says mathematics professor Dan Hughes, a season-ticket holder and 25-year veteran of the faculty. "That's there. It's always been there, especially in times of budget crunches."

"It's part of life," says fellow math prof Bill Carsrud, a faculty member for 31 years and another big fan. "Now there's a lot more faculty that are interested."

One of the reasons basketball appeals to faculty like Hughes and Carsrud is the same one that endears a lot of people to Gonzaga: personal relationships.

"I always have some of those students in my classes," says Carsrud, "whether it's Cory Violette in a calculus class or Dan Dickau in a stats class. That makes it a lot homier."

Says Violette, "It takes a different breed of guy to go to school at Gonzaga. It's very study-oriented. I mean, college kids party—you're not going to find a school that doesn't do that—but when the winter rolls around, it's real quiet on campus. You're not going to have the same amount of anonymity you have at a big school. But I like that."

It seems that there are fewer academic nooks and crannies at Gonzaga in which the basketball player could hide. For one, there is no football team on campus; the Zag basketball team is the biggest, hottest, most visible thing going. Second, average class size is much smaller than at a major state university, numbering between 20 and 30. Says Ken Anderson, the faculty athletic representative who played at GU a couple of decades ago, "There's no ubiquitous general studies major."

That doesn't mean Anderson hasn't found himself playing defense more than he would like. He has had to rationalize some recent graduation percentages for men's basketball that are lower than the Gonzaga student body at large as well as the rate of the athletic population there.

"I've answered more questions about graduation rate in the last 12 months," sighs Anderson, "than I did in the previous 60."

The NCAA releases an annual survey of graduation rates based on a timetable of six years. Thus, the report it issued in 2001 reflected the freshman class that entered in the 1994–1995 school year, a group whose statistical "window" closed in 2000, six full school years later.

That report showed 33 percent of the freshmen on scholarship entering Gonzaga in 1994–1995 having graduated by 2000. Of course, it's a tiny control group of only three.

The NCAA also includes four-class rates with its annual figures, showing the ratings not only of the latest class but also of the previous three combined with it. Gonzaga's graduation rate for the four freshman classes entering from the fall of 1991 through 1994 was at 36 percent for a group that numbered between 11 and 15.

Gonzaga's four-class rating was the same in the survey of 2000 for those freshmen entering from 1990 through 1993. In both years, their numbers were higher for black basketball players than for minorities and whites combined—60 percent (three of five) in the 2001 survey and 100 percent of a small group of black transfer students also included as a separate control group.

Graduation rates for the GU student body overall in the two years reflected by the 2000 and 2001 surveys were each 63 percent, while the athletes' percentages overall were 65 and 73 respectively.

Such rates, and the means of calculating them, have been a sore point for a lot of universities, Gonzaga among them.

"In our opinion, it's the crazy way the NCAA calculates it," says Anderson. "It's not a graduation rate, it's a volatility rate or a churning rate."

"It's awful," says basketball coach Mark Few. "It gives a totally inaccurate reflection of what's going on at a program."

Sometimes the control group is so small that it can yield deceiving numbers. Of course, if the numbers are consistently small, it's more trend than aberration.

The classes that followed the 1994 enrollees bumped Gonzaga's graduation rate up. While only one of three freshmen entering in 1994 graduated from GU, the three who followed the next two years—Matt Santangelo, Richie Frahm, and Axel Dench—all earned diplomas, giving the Zags a respectable 67 percent rate over three classes.

Basketball programs across the country have been more vulnerable to looking bad in the survey than any other athletic programs. First, more basketball players leave school early for a shot at the National Basketball Association—a factor that has rarely affected Gonzaga—and they count negatively unless they graduate in six years.

Moreover, basketball is the most volatile of college sports in its player movement, one in which freshmen often contribute early, leave when they don't, or create other players' departures when they do.

Transfers are thus endemic to the sport, and they're poison to the NCAA graduation survey. Each instance of the cavalcade of players who have left the University of Washington for Gonzaga has counted against the Huskies— including, a decade ago, Jeff Brown and Eric Brady, each of whom won various all-academic honors at Gonzaga.

Another quirk: walk-on freshmen—although they may win scholarships, flourish in school and on the floor, and graduate on time—don't figure in the count. Gonzaga had one high-achieving group that entered school in 1989, but they didn't help the survey released in 1996 because several were walk-ons.

A 36 percent graduation rate is fodder for those who think basketball erodes the Gonzaga academic reputation. The program's defenders could counter with a couple of arguments: first, the improved level of the program has increasingly meant that Zag seniors may have professional opportunities, in the NBA or overseas, and a player usually pursues those without his degree, especially if he didn't spend a year redshirting.

"No question, that's hurting us a little bit," Few says. "It's the caliber of kids we've been getting. As soon as the season gets over, those agents or tryouts want them right now, and I don't have a problem with kids making that choice. They've got a small window of time from when they're 22 to 30 when they can get paid to play basketball."

12

Second, that same higher standard of basketball means it takes a better player to meet it, and those who fall short may seek a place where they might figure to play more.

For instance, when the 2006 survey comes out, don't expect the Zags to look good. That class originally consisted of guards Germayne Forbes and Jimmy Tricco and forward Jay Sherrell, all of whom transferred out, mostly to find a level at which they could play. Tricco went first, to Duquesne.

What happened to the three-man class that entered in 1994? Mike Leasure was a valued sub on the 1999 Elite Eight team, then graduated and became a policeman. Forwards Phil Ball and Keith Kincaid left the program after it became apparent to both sides that they weren't going to be major contributors; thus, they count against Gonzaga's graduation rate. Ball ended up at Christian Heritage in El Cajon, California, getting a degree at the NAIA school. "It wasn't really the best fit for me and I really wasn't the best fit for them," Ball said. "I always look back at my experience at Gonzaga as valuable, but it just wasn't a good fit. San Diego was a great fit."

"When he left," Anderson said of Tricco, "his GPA was closer to 4.0 than it was to 3.5. He's going to count against us."

Few spends appreciable time in the off-season dogging former players to fulfill remaining credits to get a degree. And he says the Zags may try to improve the graduation rate among high-level players by encouraging them to attend summer school and complete work by their final semester, or at least be close. Duke University has recently had success doing this, using it as a counter to justify early departures for the NBA draft.

Gonzaga dean of admission Philip Ballinger says he has discussed with upper-level administrators the subject of whether the accelerated pace of the basketball team could, or should, lead to separate admissions standards.

"There's been a decision up to now: no separate standards," Ballinger says. "So the same kinds of things we would apply to a legacy applicant or an applicant with special circumstances, those kinds of things are used to look at marginal athletic recruits as well. But no separate standards."

He says he hasn't yet sensed an intrusion of the basketball program on those standards.

"I haven't been given an application yet of a kid who is clearly not a Gonzaga kid," Ballinger says. "But I'll know when that happens."

~ ~ ~ ~ ~

Steve Churney is behind the bar of one of the most famous watering holes in the West. Every time the name John Stockton is mentioned, it seems that a reference isn't far behind to the tavern his father, Jack, co-owns.

It's Jack and Dan's, at Hamilton and Sharp, no more than 10 minutes from the farthest corner of the Gonzaga campus. The place has no direct connection to Gonzaga, but that's like saying Augusta has no direct connection to the Masters.

Breaking for an interview, Churney pours himself a draft, deposits tomato juice into it, and takes a seat at the bar.

"I'm a senior," he says by way of introduction. "I'll have a fifth year. I academic-redshirted."

The place is rich in Gonzaga lore. Like much of the goodwill spread by the basketball team, however, it isn't seen so much as felt. There is little in the way of memorabilia—no souvenir T-shirts or mugs—just the redolence of former players who worked the bar or who came in to catch a game on TV with their buddies.

Former guard Jamie Dudley had a job here, and so did sharpshooting guard Richie Frahm, and so did his teammate, sell-out defensive stopper Mark Spink. This is where Few had his weekly get-togethers with Jud Heathcote, the former Michigan State coach and longtime eastern Washingtonian—"Tuesdays with Jud."

It's Gonzaga's "Cheers." It began as a butcher shop, recalls Jack Stockton, and just after Prohibition ended in the early thirties, it was Louie's Snappy Service.

"My understanding is, if you wanted a bucket of suds—that's what they called it—they'd fill up kind of a little bucket and take it to you on a motorcycle," said Stockton.

After that it became Joey's, named after a boxing coach at Gonzaga. For continuity's sake, it stayed Joey's for 14 years after Stockton and Dan Crowley shook hands on a partnership in 1962—just as it has remained Jack and Dan's although Crowley's interest was bought out in the early nineties by Jeff Condill, a former Zag teammate of John Stockton.

"It's a special place," says Condill. "A lot of business gets done in here, a lot of neighborhood concerns. School concerns get hammered out in here."

Condill can come up with a healthy list of professionals who have worked the bar as Gonzaga students—a neurosurgeon, cardiologists, lawyers, and engineers.

Churney's field isn't yet established. For now, his aim is to save enough money to tour all 30 major league baseball ballparks.

If his association with Gonzaga hoops wasn't already a matter of record as a result of his work with the Kennel Club, he became enshrined one night last February. He worked the bar until 2:00 A.M. at Jack and Dan's, hurried home to change clothes, and then waited in line outside for the next day's distribution of tickets to the long-awaited Pepperdine game.

But then, that kind of devotion is relatively common on the Gonzaga campus. Smits, the former student-body president, planned to go home to Wenatchee in central Washington for spring break in 2001, when she discovered that a woman near campus was donating two plane tickets and hotel accommodations for the Zags' opening-round NCAA games in Memphis.

Smits had a job as a hostess at a Wenatchee restaurant, but she put her name into the drawing anyway.

"Cathy," said the caller late that afternoon, "you're going to Memphis."

She called the restaurant the next morning on her way out of town. "This is the chance of a lifetime," she said. "I can't pass it up."

The restaurant decided it couldn't pass up a chance to fire her. Like any red-blooded Zag, she'll tell you the experience was well worth it.

2

Stuffed Birds, Inflated Dreams

Before there was a $6 billion contract between CBS and the NCAA, before anybody outside of Spokane knew about Gonzaga, there was still an accepted way to play at the school.

The year was 1961. College basketball was just coming out of the point-shaving malaise that infected teams from the East to the Midwest. The NCAA tournament featured only 24 teams, and Gonzaga was 34 years removed from playing in its first one.

But the Zags had the most decorated player in their history, a 6'1" guard named Frank Burgess. In his final game, at Idaho, he had a chance to nail down the nation's scoring championship, needing 31 points. That was only a point below his average.

He kept passing the damn ball.

In the locker room at halftime, when Burgess had only 12 points, head coach Hank Anderson went off.

"If I wanted a passer," boomed Anderson, "I'd have somebody else out there. I want a shooter."

So Burgess shot, and he shot, and he shot. He finished with 37 points, and indeed, he did claim that scoring title, finishing with 32.4 points a game.

Go through the Gonzaga record books, and Burgess claimed just about everything else, too. Even without that landmark season, he would have the school scoring record, which he had established in 1960 at 28.9 points a game.

Burgess is Gonzaga's career scoring leader at 2,196 points, compiled in three years. He is the single-game leader, having put up 52 against California-Davis. He made more field goals than any other Zag, and more free throws. He coholds, with Geoff Goss, the record for single-game free-throw accuracy with 15 straight.

He shot the ball more than any other Zag—1,780 times. But he also got to the foul line 727 times in his three years and hit 596 of those—both school records—suggesting that Anderson was right about who ought to be shooting the ball.

Frank Burgess is in his office in Tacoma, Washington, now, testifying for the defense. He is a U.S. district court judge, appointed by President Clinton in 1994.

"What the hell are you doing?" he remembers Anderson asking him that night in Moscow, Idaho.

"He wanted me to win that thing. Everybody else did, too. Well, I was trying to do that. But they were trying to stop me, doubling and tripling me."

Gonzaga's basketball history can hardly be called illustrious. Its past 20 years might best be described as a gradual upward ascent on a graph, with the occasional dip or plateau, culminating in the madcap success ignited in the late nineties.

It has been only since 1959 that the Zags have played an NCAA Division I schedule. But it's fitting that the era would begin with Burgess, because he represents the high achievement on the floor and off that often characterizes Gonzaga's players.

He laughs at the notion that an emphasis on being a student-athlete might be a latter-day phenomenon.

"If they think that's new now," he says, "I got news for them. Forty years ago, Father Morton [Edmund Morton, then university president] said the very same thing to me."

~ ~ ~ ~ ~

Burgess was born in rural Eudora, Arkansas, as the nation was in the throes of the Depression in the midthirties. His dad worked at a cotton-processing warehouse, and his mother cared for eight children.

Burgess could play basketball. But he didn't always want to.

"It was kind of hard to convince him to play," a high school classmate, Nathan Crawford, told the *Arkansas Democrat-Gazette* in 2001. "He had no interest in playing. He was more interested in studying."

But Burgess could be enticed. Without outdoor lights on dirt courts, he and his friends once got in trouble for creating illumination by firing up used automobile tires.

Burgess produces a framed diploma from Eudora Colored High School. Everything was separate then—black and white schools, black and white schedules, black and white state tournaments.

He had 61 points once in a tournament game. He went for 40 the night that Eudora upset heavily favored Magnolia in a state quarterfinal game.

An older brother entered the air force, but Burgess decided to go to Arkansas Agricultural, Mechanical, and Normal College, now Arkansas–Pine Bluff. The coach who recruited him died over the summer before his freshman year, however, and his successor, Leroy Moore, came from Oklahoma with what seemed an endless procession of players from that state.

"I got the feeling he thought nobody could play ball but folks from Oklahoma," Burgess says. "It seemed like he was playing favorites."

Burgess stayed at Arkansas AM&N a season, and then he followed his brother into the air force. It had always held a fascination for him. In the South, a certain status was conferred to servicemen. He would make a career of it.

He was first assigned to Scott Air Force Base in Belleville, Illinois. He learned communications technology, but his most obvious skill was basketball. Stationed at Hahn Air Force Base near Koblenz, Germany, he then found himself having to balance the desires of two commanders.

One didn't care for athletics. "The other was a big guy who said, 'You will play,'" Burgess says.

And he did. He put up some big numbers—games of 40 and 50 points in the air force. But as time passed, he found himself assigned a lot of menial jobs, and in the meantime, he was getting correspondence from colleges inquiring whether he had considered getting out.

Among the curious was Mel Porter, whose father owned a dry-cleaning business near the Gonzaga campus and who had graduated from Gonzaga himself. Porter tried to interest not only Burgess, he also wrote to Anderson.

"Who are they?" Burgess asked. "Where is that?

"I hadn't been but five miles west of the Mississippi."

Burgess opted out of the military after a 31-month tour and began screening college choices. He was shown the University of Kansas by future Los Angeles Lakers star Bill Bridges, and he considered others, including Southern California. He also thought about a return to Arkansas AM&N, at least until a dean told him there'd be no scholarship for him later if he shunned AM&N this time around.

Gonzaga was holding a hole card. An NCAA rule provided that transfers to independent schools, which GU was, would not have to sit out a year. Those transferring to conference-affiliated colleges were required to wait a season before playing.

Moreover, Burgess was a small-town guy and Gonzaga was a good fit. Burgess was most impressed, however, by what he heard from Father Morton.

"He probably never even realized it when he said it," Burgess said. "But when I was looking at other schools, it seemed like everything was basketball, basketball, basketball. When I was introduced to him, it was about athletics, but he made it clear to me, you're also here to get an education.

"That was so unusual, that somebody was concerned that I could do something maybe a little different from bouncing a ball."

Until the air force, Burgess had not played on a mixed, black-and-white team. The landmark court decision of *Brown v. Board of Education* was not rendered until 1954, a year after his high school graduation, and societal acceptance of blacks was hardly universal. It was not uncommon for sports teams traveling to Southern states to be asked to house blacks in a different hotel.

"If you call Washington, D.C., the South, it happened there, too," Burgess said.

In 1961, he says, he was seated at a restaurant with two other blacks whose menus caused them to do a double take. A tuna sandwich was nine dollars.

Burgess asked to see the menu of a white at another table.

"They had a regular menu," Burgess said. "If you think the price is too high, you're gonna leave. They accomplished their mission."

Burgess got a similarly chilling welcome to Spokane. He remembers the campus as having perhaps only five black students, but that wasn't the problem; his life was centered mostly on basketball and home, because he had come out of the air force married with twin six-month-old daughters.

Hank Anderson and the Gonzaga trainer had canvassed the area bordering campus for a rental house for Burgess before he arrived. They put a deposit down, and when Burgess flew in, they stopped by the dwelling to have the landlord show the place.

Burgess noticed the landlord addressing the trainer rather than him.

"Why don't you tell him?" the trainer said. "He's going to be the one living here."

At that point, the landlord said he had taken a deposit from another party, "and if he doesn't take it, he [Burgess] can have it."

"Let's go," Burgess said.

It wasn't the only evidence of racism. Years after he had left Gonzaga, Anderson told him he had suggested to the father of Mel Porter, his conduit to the school, that he invite the Burgesses over for dinner to welcome them to the community.

"He said, 'Well, he couldn't do that,'" Burgess said. "That was against how he felt the races should be. Here's a contrast between a father and a son—just the opposite."

It can't be said that Burgess' seasons at Gonzaga were banner years for the program; the only winning season of the three came in 1959–1960, when the Zags went 14–12. But they were playing a stepped-up Division I schedule for the first time. In Burgess' senior year, that included trips to Detroit, Providence, St. John's, and Xavier, all defeats.

"We were in way over our heads," said Anderson. "But to get publicity, we'd take as many games like that as we could. The fact the kid was leading the nation and we didn't play all setups . . ."

Anderson's recollection of Burgess: "He was a great one, just a great one. He could thread that net from anyplace."

Burgess' name is all over Gonzaga's list of 40-point games, from an era a generation before the three-point shot. He has seven of the Zags' thirteen best games of all time, one of the most memorable an effort of 42 points in a blowout victory in 1960 against Seattle University in its heyday with standout Eddie Miles.

He shot an excellent 48.8 percent in his career. He never had a season of shooting less than 80 percent from the foul line. His career rebounding average was 7.6 a game. Burgess was named a second-team All-American by both the Associated Press and *The Sporting News*.

But he clearly had more than basketball on his mind. He was drafted in the third round (27th overall) by the Los Angeles Lakers in 1961, but he opted to go to the fledgling American Basketball League, a forerunner to the American Basketball Association.

"At that time, there weren't too many places for a black athlete to go," Burgess said.

He spent a year with the Hawaii Chiefs and then qualified for Gonzaga Law School. "It wasn't a hard decision to just go on and do something else," Burgess said.

He had a private law practice and was a U.S. magistrate for 12 years before his appointment to the U.S. district bench.

Burgess casts a long shadow. A younger brother, Robert, found that out when he decided to follow Frank to GU in the early sixties.

"He came to Gonzaga for about a minute," Frank Burgess says. "Things didn't suit him. He was coming in as a freshman when I was a senior. He thought too much was expected of him because of me. He had a little animosity about that. I don't know why he would transfer that to me, but he did for a while."

~ ~ ~ ~ ~

Well before anybody knew much about Gonzaga basketball, the school won some recognition for two sports—football and boxing. It won a national boxing title in 1950.

The school lists its first year of basketball as 1907–1908, with a 9–2 record accompanied by the notation: "No coach." In those days, coaching assignments were fleeting, lasting one or two years.

Gonzaga thus had 10 coaches until 1920, when it attracted a "name"—he was Charles E. "Gus" Dorais of Chippewa Falls, Wisconsin, and, as was typical of the Zags then, he was much more acclaimed for his football exploits than for those in basketball.

Dorais was a 5'7", 145-pound starting quarterback at Notre Dame from 1910 to 1913, captaining the Irish in 1912. His years in South Bend paralleled those of end Knute Rockne, who would later coach five unbeaten teams in 13 seasons with the Irish, becoming one of the legendary names in American sports.

In a storied upset of Army in 1913, Dorais and Rockne are credited with popularizing the forward pass. Dorais led the Irish to three straight unbeaten seasons and became the first consensus All-American at Notre Dame in 1913. In 1954, he would be inducted into the National Football Foundation Hall of Fame.

Legend has it he lost a coin flip to Rockne for the Notre Dame coaching job, and Rockne's career was launched in 1918. Dorais coached a year under Rockne as "first assistant" in 1919 and then moved out to Gonzaga in 1920.

Naturally, Dorais coached everything at Gonzaga, but the primary emphasis then was football, which the school would sponsor until 1941. With a student body of a mere 200, Gonzaga rose to national stature, going undefeated in 1924. One of the student managers during Dorais' tenure was Bing Crosby, who would become a legendary singer and actor and Gonzaga's most beloved alumnus.

Dorais was less successful coaching the basketball team. He did, however, have a 16–7 season in 1925–1926, his last at Gonzaga, giving him a 41–48 record in five years. Dorais then departed for the University of Detroit for 17 seasons, later coached the Detroit Lions, and subsequently won selection into the Gonzaga Hall of Fame.

Basketball continued to be a spotty proposition at Gonzaga, evidenced by an inexplicable 0–2 record under Claude McGrath in 1937–1938. Ah, perhaps it wasn't so inexplicable; a year earlier, reported the *Gonzaga Quarterly*, "In mid-season Captain Herman Brass left school to continue his engineering studies at an Eastern university. His loss was a distinct blow to the squad. Up until the time he left, Brass was the most consistent and aggressive member of the Bulldog quintet."

McGrath was adept at keeping his job; he began with eight straight losing seasons before going 16–13 in 1941–1942. In the April after that season, McGrath, a product of Spokane's North Central High School and a football letterman at Gonzaga, entered the service as a first lieutenant.

Much of McGrath's military duties centered on organizing an outstanding Second Air Force football team, part of a league founded to raise money for the war effort. The team played on New Year's Day 1943 in the Sun Bowl.

McGrath would return after 45 months in the service to reassume his jobs as Gonzaga athletic director and basketball coach. Until then, athletics was hit-or-miss; the Zags had four different basketball coaches bridging McGrath's two tenures.

Jack O'Brien, a former Spokane city councilman and a manager for the basketball team, one night found himself suiting up for Billy Frazier, the first of

McGrath's successors. He recalls a core of five "pretty doggone good players" and then a second string, of which he was a part, used primarily for scrimmages. It was a game against Spokane's Whitworth College that was going to be his shining moment.

"They had built a new gymnasium, kind of a college center, and they invited the Gonzaga basketball team to come out and play the dedication game," O'Brien says. "Whitworth didn't have much of a basketball program, and by the middle of the second half, we were so far ahead, we put in the second string—and that included me."

Suddenly, O'Brien's big chance materialized before his eyes. There was a defensive rebound by one of his teammates, and O'Brien leaked behind Whitworth's defense. The long pass found its way into his hands, and he launched himself for what would be his first college basket.

But the floor was still slick in the new facility. O'Brien's legs went out from under him, and he skidded on his backside into a hardwood base at the end of the floor, creating a terrible crash.

"It didn't hurt me any," O'Brien says. "But it sure raised hell with the paneling on that stage."

No, the shot didn't go in.

As for the Zags, they played games in a cramped facility at the east end of what is now the school's administration building. It has long since been converted to a theater.

O'Brien remembers the arena having a trapdoor in the ceiling, which opened into an attic accessible from the third floor of the building. It was also an entrée into a delightful prank perpetrated in the late thirties by his brother-in-law, John Fahey, a history student at GU.

There was an animal museum on that third floor, and one night, Fahey and a buddy sneaked a great stuffed bird out of its case and brought it to the trap door. In those days, the timekeeper signaled the end of each half with the blast of a blank cartridge from a pistol.

As the first half of the game drew to a close, the pistol report was followed by the crash of the bird and a huge gasp from the crowd. The pranksters were caught—but it must have been worth it.

By 1946–1947, McGrath had returned from the war, and the Zags had their first sustained run of success since their infant years. They went 20–9 that season, followed by 24–11 and the school's first postseason appearance in history—the National Association of Intercollegiate Basketball tournament (now the NAIA) in Kansas City. That team was led by Rich Evans, Jack Curran, and Frank Walter, numbers 8, 16, and 17 on the Zags' career scoring list.

McGrath bowed out after the 1949 season for private business, his tenure (12 years) and his victories (129, against 131 losses) each third in Gonzaga history.

That ushered in L. T. Underwood, for whom Hank Anderson holds no great affection. Anderson remembers him as a former Kentucky player who had grandiose ideas about how the program should be run.

"It just about broke Gonzaga," Anderson says. "He had to fly everyplace and stay at the best hotels. When I went there, we had to ride the bus and the train. We were really pinching nickels and dimes. Gonzaga was having a tough time financially not just with athletics, but keeping its doors open, period."

Underwood lasted only two years, long enough to put up a school-record number of losses in a season (22) that stands today.

~ ~ ~ ~ ~

You could say Hank Anderson brought Gonzaga into the modern era of basketball. When he took over in 1951, the program was small-time in almost every way, including staffing.

"I was the only paid official in the athletic department," he says. "I was the athletic director and the basketball coach. I had student help for freshman basketball coach and trainer."

Anderson is a native Oregonian who went to the University of Oregon in 1940, a year after the Ducks won the first NCAA basketball championship. He played with several of the "Tall Firs," as that team was known.

He did three high school coaching stints in Oregon, spliced by some service time at the end of World War II, and came to Gonzaga from Grants Pass, Oregon. The move was hardly a financial bonanza.

"I think I was making $6,500 at Grants Pass," Anderson says. "I was making $6,000 at Gonzaga. You taught a lot of classes along with it."

Gonzaga was still an NAIA school, playing a steady diet of Whitworths, Puget Sounds, Pacific Lutherans, Central Washingtons, and Eastern Washingtons (Eastern was still decades from its own foray into Division I).

It became Anderson's passion to get the Zags into Division I. Upon his arrival, they were in a no-man's-land both competitively and in scheduling. They would play 10 or 12 games annually against NAIA competition, but they would also take on Division I programs like Washington State and Seattle.

The cross-competing was a problem unto itself. NAIA schools were allowed to play freshmen, while those in the NCAA were not until 1972–1973. Then there was the occasional beneficence of coaches like Washington State's Jack Friel, who allowed the Zags to use their freshmen against the Cougars.

As an independent, the Zags had no ration of 12 or 14 conference games around which Anderson could build a schedule. It was a hand-to-mouth existence, and never mind his salary.

From 1952 through 1955, Anderson had an excellent player in Jerry Vermillion, an NAIA All-American whose 1,670 rebounds puts him 760 in front of the runner-up on the school's career list. But Gonzaga hovered around the .500 mark into the late fifties, and Anderson convinced his bosses the program had to change.

"We wanted the NCAA," Anderson says. "I drove it. They were just happy. Before I went there, they had lost money with their football and spent an awful lot of money on basketball."

In the 1958–1959 season, Gonzaga began playing primarily a Division I schedule. Anderson would usually supplement games against Northwest teams with a trip east for five or six days, in which the Zags would routinely take their lumps but score a guarantee of $2,500 or $3,000 that helped keep the program afloat.

"The university was backing me," he said, "as long as it wasn't costing them any money."

Gonzaga was thinking big in another way in the late fifties. A friend of Anderson, Jim McGregor, had coached at Whitworth from 1950 to 1953 and then gone overseas. McGregor would occasionally tout a player whom Anderson might entice to come to Gonzaga.

One of those was the biggest Zag in captivity, Frenchman Jean-Claude Lefebvre.

"He was about 7'3"," Anderson said, "and weighed about 340."

That's huge today. Then, it was gargantuan. *Sports Illustrated* was so dumb-struck, it did a piece in its December 9, 1957, issue—Anderson still has it—with an accompanying photograph showing Lefebvre shaking hands with the most famous Zag, Bing Crosby.

"Still the biggest guy I've ever seen," said Frank Burgess, who produces a clipping from the *Spokane Spokesman-Review*. It was the kind of loopy photograph common to that day—Burgess and Lefebvre pictured at the opening of a bridge in Spokane.

Unfortunately, Lefebvre was more conversation piece than force. He wore size-22 sneakers, which had to be specially built by a shoe company. He had only modest experience at basketball before coming to the United States and the Zags had him for only the 1957–1958 and 1958–1959 seasons before he returned to his homeland to prepare for the 1960 Olympics.

Asked if he was at all skilled, Anderson is diplomatic. "No," he said. "I would say he had a real good attitude and was willing to work."

To hear Anderson tell it, Lefebvre was afflicted with a disease often known to big men—he wanted to play on the perimeter.

"One particular game, we were playing at Stockton, the University of Pacific," Anderson says. "They had a little guard that scored real well."

Ahead by two points, the Zags got instructions from Anderson to watch out for the guard. Lefebvre took it to heart.

"Jean-Claude took off after him outside like a big, raging bull and fouled him," said Anderson. The guard obliged by missing both free throws.

Afterward, Anderson asked Lefebvre, "Why in the world would you foul somebody shooting that well?"

"Well," Lefebvre said, "it was time for him to miss."

Anderson's quest to push the Zags to a higher profile involved more than merely going Division I. Just as it is now, scheduling was a fundamental albatross, fueling Gonzaga's urge to join a conference. "It was just becoming ridiculous," said Anderson. "How were you gonna get 25 or 26 games?"

In 1963, Gonzaga became a charter member of the Big Sky Conference, joining Idaho, Idaho State, Montana, Montana State, and Weber State. In 1970, Boise State and Northern Arizona would make it an eight-team league.

Shortly after the Big Sky was born, Anderson had his best teams at Gonzaga, going 56–21 in a three-year stretch. They were led by a 5'7" guard, Billy Suter, who ranks number 11 on the Gonzaga career scoring list, and by 6'4" forward

Gary Lechman, a physical player who averaged 23.1 points in 1967 and is number 2 to Vermillion among GU career rebounders. Anderson calls him "the best inside man I ever had."

In just its third and fourth years in the Big Sky, Gonzaga tied for the league championship, with Weber State in 1966 and with Montana State in 1967. The first of those seasons coincided with the Zags' move into Kennedy Pavilion, the same gym that would host them for only a few more years. At last the Zags were leaving behind the days of playing in the antiquated Boone Avenue gym and the headaches associated with the off-campus Spokane Coliseum.

"We never had a home court," Anderson says, "which makes it that much tougher to win ballgames."

The well went dry for Anderson just after those cochampionship years. The Zags endured four straight sub-.500 conference seasons, and after a 14–12 year in 1971–1972, Anderson's 21st at the school, he resigned and left for Montana State. Gonzaga's longest-tenured coach won 290 games and lost 272 at the school.

Controversy surrounded the process of replacing him. His assistant, Rich Juarez, wanted the job, and so did Adrian Buoncristiani, an assistant coach at Cal–Santa Barbara. In a 5–4 search-committee vote, Buoncristiani got the nod. One insider says a committee member whose vote might have kept it deadlocked missed the meeting.

Buoncristiani, who stood 5'6", had grown up in San Francisco and attended St. Ignatius High School. One of his first acts was to hire Dan Fitzgerald, one year his junior, as assistant coach. Fitzgerald, also a product of St. Ignatius, would stay two years and then return to succeed Buoncristiani in 1978.

Buoncristiani's record was numbingly average—he went 13–13 three straight seasons—but Fitzgerald says it wasn't for lack of trying.

"I know how hard Adrian worked," Fitzgerald says. "He absolutely killed himself to make that thing go. It almost drove him to the nuthouse."

Shortly after Fitzgerald took over, Gonzaga made a move to end its 16-year membership in the Big Sky and enter the West Coast Athletic Conference. It was logical; unlike their conference brothers, the Zags had no football team, and the WCAC, as the West Coast Conference was then known, featured private Catholic schools.

During the lame-duck season between the Big Sky and the WCC, at some outpost in the Big Sky, Fitzgerald cackled at an official: "You'll be here next year. I'll be in Malibu."

He was right, of course. But for much of the next two decades, Gonzaga's map would still include a lot of backwater as well as the beach, and the driver for that wild ride was Fitzgerald.

3

The Godfather in Exile

Sitting there in a hole-in-the-wall tavern a mile from downtown Spokane, Dan Fitzgerald is rolling. The temptation is to say it's because it's St. Patrick's Day, and in a green polo shirt, he's an Irishman in his element, but that would be wrong. This is the usual Fitzgerald—"Fitz" as he is known by everybody around Gonzaga—spinning stories as long as you'll listen, reeling off the yarns of his lifetime.

This is the godfather of Gonzaga basketball, the guy who hired the good coaches, who set down a standard of play and of behavior, who had a lot to do with establishing the basketball culture at Gonzaga—a way of playing and going to class and conducting oneself.

Ask him about a certain player a generation ago who's now 40 with three kids, and Fitzgerald invariably will preface his recollection with, "Amazing story . . ."

Coach against a nun in a full habit? Fitzgerald did it. Sleep in his car on long trips while recruiting for the Zags? Fitzgerald did it. Grab life by the throat and battle and claw for every blessed basket and every inch of stature available to Gonzaga basketball? Fitzgerald did it.

Oh, yes, he also got the school on NCAA probation.

~ ~ ~ ~ ~

He was born in San Francisco's salty Mission district in 1942, the middle of three brothers. His dad co-owned a bar. He smoked at 12, boxed in a Catholic Youth Organization program, and survived.

"Just your average dysfunctional household," Fitzgerald says. "Some people had it better; a lot of guys had it a lot worse."

He was around basketball early at St. Ignatius High School. The two-time NCAA-champion San Francisco Dons, with Bill Russell and K. C. Jones, used to practice there. It was a golden age of Bay Area basketball, what with USF–Santa Clara going to the 1952 Final Four, Pete Newell building toward a 1959 national title at California, and the Cow Palace hosting Ohio State's national championship over Cal in 1960.

But Fitzgerald was going to be a baseball player, a pitcher and first baseman. He started at Santa Clara, dropped out of school with the intention of signing a pro contract, then realized he was vulnerable to the military draft and ducked into San Francisco State, majoring in English. Through his older brother, Jim, a skeptical Fitzgerald took a teaching and coaching job at St. John Vianney High in Los Angeles.

"Hell of a story," Fitzgerald says. The Murphy family of Murphy Oil offered to donate several million dollars to the school, with the condition that everything in the place would be renamed, signs replaced, stationery redone.

"I'm in there with the priest," Fitzgerald says. "I'm 24 now, I've got all the answers. I invented not only the game but the ball and the air."

Fitzgerald expressed dismay at some aspect of the transition. "Damn it, Fitz," the priest admonished him. "Give me $8 million and I'll name it after you."

It was at this school that Fitzgerald matched wits against a nun, who in the retelling over the years became Sister Mary Basketball. Fitzgerald's junior varsity team was scheduled to play at Bishop Montgomery, whose coach was sick.

"The guy's not there, and out comes the nun, in the full deal," Fitzgerald says. "You gotta be kiddin' me. I've got about 12 pages of notes and every offense known to mankind."

The nun won. "On the Harbor Freeway," Fitzgerald says, "I'm about to throw guys out of the goddamn bus."

Fitzgerald moved on to Mitty High in San Jose and then became freshman coach at Santa Clara in 1971. When Adrian Buoncristiani got the Gonzaga job in 1972, Fitzgerald followed him to Spokane, but after a couple of pedestrian years there, Fitzgerald was ready to get out of coaching. He went to work for Converse shoes, but Carroll Williams of Santa Clara lured him onto his staff shortly after.

In 1978, Buoncristiani left Gonzaga after a six-year run, and the Zags came looking for Fitzgerald. Today, Fitzgerald revels in boxing the ears of the Gonzaga administration, a tradition he says began back then.

Fitzgerald was told by others that he had the job. But Gonzaga athletic director (AD) Larry Koentopp called, and Fitzgerald was led to think the deal was sideways.

"Can you send a resume and some recommendations?" Koentopp asked.

Fitzgerald complied, leaning on people like Hubie Brown and John Wooden for help.

A Zag official called Fitzgerald back. "This is how little they know," Fitzgerald says. "The guy says, 'Do you know all these guys?'"

That brought Fitzgerald to Spokane, where he might have thought he was playing in a Richard Pryor–Gene Wilder comedy.

When he was in Spokane for his interview, Fitzgerald stayed with Stew Morrill, who had played at Gonzaga during Fitzgerald's assistant-coach years there. Morrill, later to become head coach at Utah State, had assisted Buoncristiani and in fact was driving Buoncristiani's car.

"We're driving down Division, freezing," Fitzgerald says. "I said, 'Stew, there's something wrong with this. The two guys that are interviewing are driving to the interview in the guy that got fired's car.'"

What Fitzgerald recalls about the interview is that Gonzaga officials expressed concern about his ability to manage the game.

"We understand you can recruit," somebody said. "Can you coach?"

Fitzgerald leaned forward and said, "I'm a lot better coach than this place deserves."

Fitzgerald, who says he was making $22,000 at Santa Clara, remembered to ask the next day what he'd make as the new Gonzaga head coach.

"Eighteen thousand," Fitzgerald says. "They got no money. I said, 'Gimme a bed and I'll put it in the locker room.'"

With that began a whirlwind era of Gonzaga basketball. Fitzgerald hit the ground running, signing five recruits in seven days. He insists his recruiting budget was $700. Two zeroes there.

"Things were so screwed up it was unbelievable," Fitzgerald says. "At that time, there was talk of the school closing. Financially, it was just a disaster."

Morrill left for Montana to join Mike Montgomery's staff, and Fitzgerald hired an assistant named John Dybvig. Koentopp, who was also the baseball coach, left his athletic director post just three months after making the basketball hire, and by the summer of 1978, Fitzgerald had the dual role of AD and basketball coach.

Dybvig left after only a year and Fitzgerald hired Jay Hillock.

"What we did was unbelievable," Fitzgerald said. "No help, just playing our ass off."

Fitzgerald went hard. He's one of those four-hours-of-sleep-a-night people, and a lot of nights, he made do with less. Three times, he remembers making the 1,200-mile drive to Los Angeles to recruit, sleeping in his car. He worked and willed the program to victories, even as it seemed victory was somehow secondary.

Fitzgerald always seemed almost surprised by success, as if it couldn't be happening as a by-product of such spare resources. Execution was the standard, and winning tagged along as an innocent companion.

Mulling over that eccentricity, Fitzgerald says, "I don't think I ever coached to win—from the standpoint that we've just got to win games. Probably in a reverse way, that if we do these things, we're gonna win."

When Fitzgerald thinks about the five best games his teams ever played, he'll note that four of them were losses. Indeed, he doesn't attach any particular reverence to the 1995 Gonzaga team that was first in school history to make the NCAA tournament, calling it—in a spasm of shocking deprecation—"maybe our eighth- or ninth-best team."

~ ~ ~ ~ ~

Fitzgerald's first year as head coach was Gonzaga's last as a member of the Big Sky Conference. He was approached by Gonzaga president Father Bernard Coughlin, who proposed an entry into the Western league of Catholic schools, the West Coast Athletic Conference (now the WCC). It was a natural.

"I said, 'Hey, Father, I'd like to play St. Al's [the grammar school next to GU] 26 times and go to the regionals,'" Fitzgerald says. "'We're going to get our brains beat out. But as president, if you can get us in there, you've got to.'"

Years later, in 2002, when the NCAA bracket was announced, the West Coast Conference drew attention as the reason Gonzaga was assigned only a No. 6 seed. Committee chairman Lee Fowler cited 12 victories by the Zags against teams with a 200 ranking or lower in the Ratings Percentage Index computer.

But it was a far different conference back when Gonzaga joined. Jawann Oldham and Clint Richardson played for Seattle University. Mark McNamara was at Santa Clara. Before the NCAA gendarmes got to San Francisco and the school closed down the program, the Dons trotted out players like Bill Cartwright, James Hardy, Winford Boynes, and Quintin Dailey. Portland had hell-for-leather teams led by Darwin Cook, Jose Slaughter, and Rick Raivio.

Rivalries in the league simmered, especially among the California members. Many of the coaches were salt-of-the-earth guys like Portland's Jack Avina, who grew up poor and seemingly had a leg up on operating a basketball program the same way.

Avina remembers his team playing a game at Seattle in the seventies, followed by a recruiting trip.

"We were invited to a postgame party in Seattle," Avina says. "I got in a Mustang to go back with five of the cheer girls and drove down to Portland with them. I got to my house about 12:00, drove all night, and ended up in Gridley, California, right above Sacramento. It was understood—that's the way we had to operate.

"Gonzaga had less money in those days than we did."

Avina recalls Fitzgerald's inventiveness in establishing the Gonzaga program.

"Whenever I dealt with Fitz, I was always looking in my back pocket," Avina laughed. "Not that he's dishonest, it was just that he was looking at every angle.

"It was a standing joke among the coaches in the league: we never knew how many scholarships Fitz had. You'd walk in to scout a game, and Jay and Joe Hillock would be in the upper gym with a whole bunch of guys, working them out."

Fitzgerald's impact at Gonzaga was immediate. The Zags went 16–10 in that final Big Sky year, the first winning season since Buoncristiani went 14–12 in 1972–1973. It was also the most success Gonzaga had seen since the midsixties, when the program was 56–21 in three seasons under Hank Anderson, glory years of Zag hoops unmatched until the turn of the century.

"Now we're on our feet," said Fitzgerald, recalling his first season. "We're really pretty good."

Fitzgerald set about to add some "name" opponents and found the going as difficult as Gonzaga does today. He called Al McGuire, the legendary Marquette coach.

"Nope," McGuire said. "I don't play anybody that's gonna be 17–10. I don't want to be one of the 10, and I sure as hell don't want to be one of your 17."

McGuire proposed a one-for-none deal. One appearance by Gonzaga in Milwaukee, no strings attached for Marquette.

"It's something I won't do," Fitzgerald said. "I'll play you two for one."

"I know what you're gonna do, you son of a bitch," said the street-schooled McGuire. "You got no money. You're gonna come back here and play Wisconsin-Milwaukee on Thursday, and with a minute and a half to go, you're gonna be tied. Now the media's gonna be on my ass. Then you're gonna play us on Friday night, and with three and a half minutes to go, we're gonna be tied.

"Call Ray."

Fitzgerald did call Ray Meyer at DePaul. The Blue Demons were nearing the end of their glory days under the icon Meyer, who consented to a two-for-one deal with Fitzgerald in 1980. Gonzaga would win the third meeting in Chicago, but it might have been the first one, won by DePaul, 74–56, that surprised Meyer most.

In the days before the shot clock, Meyer figured the Zags might come out and hold the ball against his hugely talented team.

"We were gonna," Fitzgerald told Meyer. "But we need to get our mind-set for the next level—that hey, we're OK here."

Fitzgerald's first key recruit just after he got the Gonzaga job was Carl Pierce of Oakland. Pierce had started college at Santa Clara when Fitzgerald was there, and had been booted from the team for a poor attitude.

Fitzgerald drove to the Bay Area and, indulging a whim while motoring across the Bay Bridge, turned around at Treasure Island. He retraced his route, headed for Pierce's old home, and found Pierce's mother receptive. She pointed Fitzgerald toward El Cerrito and a Safeway store, where her son handled boxes in a warehouse. Fitzgerald ferreted him out and convinced him to enroll at Gonzaga, and Pierce became a second-team all-league selection two straight years.

Fitzgerald's next acclaimed player was point guard Don Baldwin, a first-team all-league pick in 1981. His achievement more familiar to longtime Gonzaga fans is that he was the player who kept John Stockton from starting as a freshman.

"This sounds almost sacrilegious," Fitzgerald says. "There are people at GU that would tell you Baldwin was the best point guard ever there."

Stockton came to the Zags from a Spokane high school and, truth be told, they had little inkling what kind of player they had. Decent college player? Yes. First-round NBA draft pick, most prolific passer in professional history, a member of the NBA's all-time top 50 team? No way. Gonzaga's primary recruiting competition for Stockton was Idaho, coached by Don Monson, father of future Zags coach Dan Monson.

Stockton was not particularly athletic, but he had deceiving speed. He couldn't jump much, but he had huge hands. He wasn't the strongest guy around, but he was smart, tough, and supremely competitive.

Jeff Condill knows how competitive he was. Condill, who played both guard positions, had just transferred west from Southern Illinois–Edwardsville, and he recalls the prevailing atmosphere generated by Stockton, who was two years older.

"He had a feeling that this is my team, my gym, and nobody's coming in here to threaten it," Condill said.

Stockton blocked Condill's first shot in a pickup game, and they locked gazes. Later, they warred over Ping-Pong in Stockton's basement in the late hours until Stockton's wife would tell them to hold it down.

"Ping-Pong, to lawn darts, to doing work on the basement," said Condill. "Who was gonna saw a board in half in the least amount of strokes? I'm not kidding—15, 15½. Back and forth, here we go."

Some of Stockton's competitiveness was forged playing with his older brother, four years his senior, and his friends.

"He just learned ways to beat 'em," said Jack Stockton, John's father. "They didn't give him any slack at all.

"He had a ball under his arm all the time. I can remember him dribbling the ball in the basement with the lights off. 'What have I got down there?' Any team he ever turned out for, there was no doubt in his mind he was gonna make it. He always said he was gonna be an NBA player."

Fitzgerald remembers DePaul's Meyer marveling at Stockton when Gonzaga played in Chicago during Stockton's freshman year.

"Ray, I know this is nuts," Fitzgerald said. "There are days in practice I think he's faster with the ball than without it."

Hillock, Fitzgerald's assistant then, is now director of pro personnel for the New York Knicks, living in Vancouver, Washington. In his office is a photograph of Stockton, chest to chest with Magic Johnson, palming a basketball in one of those oversized hands.

Somewhere in the alchemy that turned out John Stockton was a supernatural metabolism.

"At the '84 Olympic camp, he had the lowest heart rate," said Hillock. "They thought he was dead."

By the time Stockton was done, he had made two all-conference teams and become the conference player of the year and an academic All-American. Even as his senior year developed, however, there was considerable doubt about him as a professional.

A breakthrough took place at the 1983 Far West Classic in Portland, where Stockton was named Most Valuable Player, even as the Zags lost by 20 to Oregon in the semifinals and ended up finishing third.

"That night, I see him," Fitzgerald said. "I said, 'You'll get drafted. For sure, you'll go in the first five.'"

Rounds, Fitzgerald meant.

Stockton's team went only 17–11 his senior year and finished fourth in the WCC, hurt by injuries. Fitzgerald begged to get him invited to NBA camps in Lewistown, Montana, and Portsmouth, Virginia. Then he got on the phone to NBA scouting maven Marty Blake to try to cadge an invitation to the major NBA tryout in Chicago.

"No, no," Blake said.

"Marty, he's good enough," Fitzgerald pleaded. "You've got to get him to Chicago."

Hillock recalls Stockton catching a break simply because the 1984 Final Four was in Seattle. A replacement was needed for an unavailable player at the coaches All-Star Game.

"I don't want to take anything away from John," Hillock said. "If it hadn't been in Seattle, he wouldn't have been invited. He played very well."

Stockton later starred at the NBA camp in Portsmouth. He was opening eyes. Fitzgerald called his friend Les Habegger of the Seattle SuperSonics, the former Seattle Pacific coach.

"We'll take him in the second round if he's there," Habegger said.

By this time, Blake had come through with the berth in Chicago. The question now was, should Stockton accept it?

On a three-way phone conversation among Fitzgerald, Stockton, and his agent, Jim White, Fitzgerald weighed in.

"John now knows he's going to be in the second round," Fitzgerald says. "I said, 'I don't think you should go to Chicago. I think it's a mistake.'"

"Two months ago," Stockton replied, "we were begging Marty Blake to go to Chicago. We should go."

"Screw Marty Blake," Fitzgerald shot back. "How can you help yourself?"

Fitzgerald's fears were unfounded. By now, Stockton's momentum could not be stemmed, as he proved in Chicago. Stockton tracked down Fitzgerald at a Seattle motel after the camp.

"Fitz, it's John."

"How'd you play?"

"Well, I think I played OK. Detroit sat down with me today and said they'd take me first. Phoenix said they'd take me first."

But Utah, itself unsure of what it might have in Stockton, did the most homework. Fitzgerald recalls a conversation with Frank Layden, the czar of the Jazz.

"How's he handle money? How's he get along with black kids? Does he have a girlfriend?" Fitzgerald remembers Layden asking. "Other teams hardly did anything."

Even at that, Hillock is convinced that even the Jazz somewhat fell into the player sometimes acclaimed as the best passer in NBA history.

"I talked to Frank yesterday, and they thought they were drafting a backup to Rickey Green," Hillock says. "Had John not been a first-round pick, they might have cut him, because he wasn't ready."

But that round-five pick of December became a first-round choice in the spring, and for almost a generation John Stockton would subtly, stoically spread the message of Gonzaga basketball.

~ ~ ~ ~ ~

Well before Stockton had left Gonzaga, Fitzgerald had vacated his seat on the bench but remained as AD. His was not a style that lent itself to a Ray Meyer–like tenure.

"I go to the president," Fitzgerald said. "I say, 'I can't do this.'"

As it turned out, neither could Hillock. Fitzgerald went 35–19 in his first two years in the new league before passing the baton to his assistant in 1981. Hillock struggled to a 60–50 record in four seasons, each year finishing around the middle of the WCC. But his real conflict was internal.

One night after a game, Fitzgerald was doing a routine booster function, and he noticed Hillock wasn't there. Eventually, Fitzgerald tracked him down at an old Spokane hangout called the Hub Tavern.

"I can't coach," Hillock said.

Today Hillock says, "We just couldn't win. I just couldn't get over it. I just couldn't handle it. I'd come out of a junior college where I'd won 62 games [in three years]. I just couldn't get it out of them."

The timing was all right for Fitzgerald, who knew he didn't want to be a full-time athletic director. So he took back the coaching job in 1985, and a year later the Zags won 18 games.

Fans that boarded the Gonzaga bandwagon in the late nineties surely were unaware that the Zags had some history, particularly on Fitzgerald's watch. In his 15 seasons at the school, Gonzaga won 18 or more seven times, including four years of 20 victories or more in the nineties.

He seemed to have the thing going. He didn't recruit so much as he got in the living room and challenged. He had a handful of questions he would slip into the conversation to learn more about a potential player.

Who's your favorite player? "If you said Darryl Dawkins," Fitzgerald cracked, "you and I would probably separate."

In front of Mom and Dad: how do you like your high school coach? "If the dad said, 'He doesn't let him shoot,' that's a bad sign," Fitzgerald said.

Can you sit on the bench? Doug Spradley, a two-time all-league player in the late eighties, handled that one best. "I can sit on the bench," Spradley responded. "But I'm not gonna."

If you don't get a scholarship, what will you do? "A lot of guys said, 'Oh, I'll just go someplace for an education,'" Fitzgerald said. "The guys that wanted basketball all said, 'I'll go to junior college. I'm a Division I player.'"

Always, Fitzgerald stresses, it was on a shoestring. He says longtime trainer Steve DeLong was getting his athletic tape in a tradeout arrangement. The combination coach–athletic director was making $72,000 in 1997, he recalls. The recruiting budget in 1995—the year of Gonzaga's first NCAA tournament appearance—was $8,000.

How can that possibly be? Until Bakari Hendrix in 1997, Gonzaga didn't have an All–West Coast Conference player from the state of California.

"There was a reason," Fitzgerald said. "Why would a guy come up here and not play for Carroll Williams or Dick Davey [at Santa Clara]?"

"Try this," Fitzgerald says. "You know how we got to Portland, the men's and women's team? On the bus, for a Division I game. And kicked their ass, too."

Fitzgerald recalls being proud of Gonzaga's homemade recruiting video one year, before he ran into Eddie Fogler, coaching for Dean Smith at North Carolina. Fitzgerald got hold of Carolina's video.

It began with a wagon rolling slowly down a cobbled road, clackety-clack, clackety-clack, and a figure of an old settler bent over. A hoary voice says, "This is tobacco road. This is the road for your future." Another figure comes down that road and says, "I'm a United States senator, and I'm a Tarheel." A captain of industry comes next and says, "I'm a Tarheel." And then with a resounding whoompf, a basketball is slammed through a hoop. And Michael Jordan says, "I'm a Tarheel."

Suddenly, Fitzgerald wasn't so impressed with the Gonzaga video.

But if lack of money limited the Zags, it also provided a rallying point. As long as there were competitive souls on the staff, there was a thunderous pride in overcoming the odds. Once, Portland athletic director Joe Etzel ran into Fitzgerald's aide, Dan Monson, at a high school game.

"You guys sleeping on the floor still?" Etzel asked.

"Hey, we haven't done that for a while," Monson said.

Says Fitzgerald, "It pissed Dan off. I used to say, 'You can be poor, but you don't have to be bush.'"

~ ~ ~ ~ ~

Whatever your opinion of Dan Fitzgerald—and there are varied ones—there can be little debate over this issue: he knew how to hire.

True, there were exceptions. After he worked with Jay Hillock, he hired Jay's brother Joe to his staff—and eventually fired him.

"He and I have had a falling-out," says Jay Hillock. "I sided with my brother. I still respect [Fitzgerald] as a coach. He was a hard worker who had great practices."

41

In the late eighties, Fitzgerald had an opening on his staff, created when he fired Bill Evans. The choice was between Dan Monson, son of former Idaho and Oregon coach Don Monson, and John Wade, an assistant at Eastern Washington.

Wade made sense. He was a black coach, and the Zags hadn't had a diverse staff. He knew the state of Washington, and having coached in nearby Cheney, he wouldn't be surprised by anything in Spokane. He was more experienced than Monson.

But Monson had his own hole card. He was friends with Mike Peterson, who was head coach for the Gonzaga women's program, and through that relationship, Monson had worked the Zags' basketball camp.

"He works his ass off," Fitzgerald says. "He's my kind of guy. I loved what he did in camp. He'd be out all night, but he was the first guy on the floor working in the morning."

At the celebration of the 50th Final Four in Kansas City in 1988, Fitzgerald received an award from the National Association of Basketball Coaches. He set up shop in a hotel to interview Wade and Monson.

"Poor John comes in, and he's just awful," Fitzgerald says. "Dan comes in nervous as hell and does a great job."

Fitzgerald went with his instincts, and Monson became his top assistant.

"I'm sure a lot of people think I got him the job," said Don Monson. "That's not the case at all. I never talked to Fitz.

"All I know is, Dan Fitzgerald gave my son a chance to be a head coach. He and Dan [Monson] were very good together. My Dan challenged him a lot, whereas other guys didn't challenge Fitz. Then Fitz kept giving him more and more responsibility. Dan did a lot of scouting and defensive setup."

In 1989, Fitzgerald needed a graduate assistant and turned to Mark Few, a preacher's son from Creswell, Oregon. Few would have an immediate impact as primary coach of a group of players who redshirted the 1989–1990 season but would later have a monumental effect on the program.

Few stepped into a full-time assistant's job when Joe Hillock left a year later. That pointed the Zags to another Oregonian, Bill Grier, to fill Few's restricted-earnings post. It wasn't hard unearthing Grier; he was head coach at Few's old high school in Creswell.

The four of them—Fitz, Monson, Few, and Grier—would form the brain trust that mapped Gonzaga's ascent from the school-that-almost-could to the program that snatched the attention of the world of college basketball.

The Gonzaga campus seamlessly mixes the old and the new.

The Martin Centre, originally known as the Kennedy Pavilion, opened in 1965. It seats 4,000.

John Stockton's physical credentials didn't seem to portend a great player, but former Zag coach Dan Fitzgerald says there were times when Stockton seemed faster with the ball than without it. His game kept improving after he joined the NBA—the Utah Jazz guard was named to the NBA's list of its 50 best players of all time.

Dan Fitzgerald, head coach through much of the eighties and nineties, began laying the foundation for the Zags' recent success when he stepped up recruiting and hired Dan Monson and Mark Few as assistants.

Those who saw Jeff Brown in pickup games doubted whether he could play, a fear he dispelled by winning all-league accolades three years in a row.

Bakari Hendrix, a 6'8" pivotman, led Dan Monson's first Zag team to a 24–10 record against stepped-up competition in 1997–1998, winning West Coast Conference player-of-the-year honors.

The irrepressible Quentin Hall, a native of the Bahamas, was a key early recruit for Dan Monson and his staff.

AP/Wide World Photos

Dan Monson, who led the Zags to 52 victories and an Elite Eight appearance in his two years as head coach, was known for his hard-charging, motivational style.

Gonzaga's mascot, Q the bulldog.

Casey Calvary was a force early and late against Florida in the 1999 Sweet 16, slamming home a basket here and later tipping in a shot for the biggest single play in Gonzaga basketball history.

"The partnership was really tremendous," said Fitzgerald. "Don't get me wrong; it wasn't all peaches and cream. I mean, I'm probably very demanding, in the sense that you're gonna coach. I said, 'I don't care about recruiting.'"

Fitzgerald says the word *recruiting* as if it's distasteful, which, in today's often-slick, sometimes-sleazy era, it is.

"I never hired guys that played for me," Fitzgerald says. "I didn't want clones. The other thing is, I believe you have to coach first. There are three things: coaching first, recruiting second, and scheduling and management third. You bring in the five best players in the country, and if you don't coach 'em, you're not worth a damn. We had six kids make all-league that walked on. Unbelievable."

As the nineties wore on, Fitzgerald, still doing double duty as coach and athletic director, began to show signs of wear. The Zags finally cracked the NCAA tournament in 1995, following their first tournament appearance in history in the NIT the previous year. One day Monson said, "This is getting big enough, you can't be worrying about cross-country."

Fitzgerald admits, "I was just exhausted. It's probably harder to [act as both AD and coach] in a place without resources. You do one of two things: you screw everybody else, or you screw your own team."

At the same time, Monson, seasoned now under Fitzgerald, began to get feelers for his first head-coaching job. It made sense for Fitzgerald to try to grease the skids for Monson to replace him as coach.

He approached the Gonzaga president, Father Coughlin, with a proposal: "I'll stay two more years and then I'm the AD."

You could say the notion was not immediately met with acclaim. The president balked.

"Look," Fitzgerald said. "Do you think I was here 20 years to give it to some yahoo?"

Fitzgerald banged on administrative doors, talking to the president of the board of trustees, cajoling vice presidents. There was some sentiment to take the search national rather than simply name Monson as the coach-in-waiting.

Fitzgerald says he couldn't hold back against one administrator whom he won't name.

"Here's why you don't have a national search," Fitzgerald said. "One, you don't have enough money. And two, you're so dumb, you'll hire the guy with the best tie."

Finally, Fitzgerald wore them down. The Gonzaga brass decided that Dan Monson would apprentice two more years under Fitzgerald and take the head-coaching position after the 1996–1997 season.

Today, a lot of people trace the rise of Gonzaga basketball to the hard-charging Fitzgerald.

"My feeling is, his name is not mentioned often enough for all the success Gonzaga has achieved," says Dan Belluomini, a TV commentator and former coach at San Francisco. "It's like they forgot about him."

Says Avina, "I do think he set the groundwork for that whole program."

As planned, Fitzgerald stepped down from coaching after the 1996–1997 season, leading a 15–12 team. Nobody would have guessed his other title would evaporate so soon thereafter.

~ ~ ~ ~ ~

It is a little-known anomaly in Gonzaga's rise to prominence: all the while the Zags were rattling the cages of the Big East, SEC, and Pac-10 in the NCAA tournament, they were on NCAA probation.

Aha! Cars provided to players by overzealous boosters? Proxies taking tests on campus? Improper loans cosigned for power forwards with evil intentions?

Count on Gonzaga to do things in its own quaint way, including getting put on probation.

The news began dribbling out mere months after Fitzgerald had finished coaching the 1997 team: a Gonzaga staffer discovered that the West Coast Conference had been sending the school reimbursement payments for WCC basketball games but that the checks never found their way into university accounts.

The language in the NCAA report was at once cold and confusing:

> From December 1981 to June 1997, the director of athletics was the sole signatory on a local bank account in the name of "Gonzaga University Athletics," which was maintained as a private account and was not disclosed to anyone outside the athletics department. From August 1990 through June 1997, the director of athletics misappropriated $199,874 of university money by depositing it in the private account. Approximately

$178,874 of this amount was derived from at least 105 checks made payable to the university and sent to the director of athletics for appropriate distribution . . . the director of athletics acknowledged depositing other university-owned checks, allegedly of lesser amounts, in the bank account during the years 1981 through 1990, but the enforcement staff was unable to locate records identifying those checks and/or amounts . . .

It is important to note that the director of athletics also deposited personal funds into the private account. He contends that in order to recover the portion of the deposits that were personal without revealing the existence of the private account, he would pay his athletically related expenses out of the account and then obtain reimbursement from the university for those same expenses. He contends that he only used the misappropriated funds to supplement the university's athletic program. However, in part because he routinely destroyed the bank statements for the private account, only limited documentation exists as to how money in the account was spent.

The case must have been a head-scratcher for the NCAA committee on infractions. On one hand, it was clear that Gonzaga's—and Fitzgerald's—bookkeeping was a mess and in violation of NCAA rule. On the other, it wasn't as though Gonzaga basketball players were cruising campus in late-model SUVs.

The NCAA investigation discovered Gonzaga had provided basketball players approximately $400 a year to host recruits making official visits to the university; had provided $1,500 a year in meals to prospective players on recruiting visits; and had purchased in 1989, and maintained through 1997, a used car costing $8,800 for recruiting purposes for the basketball program and others at the school. At the same time, the committee concluded that Gonzaga didn't violate NCAA legislation regarding limitations on recruiting expenditures.

While the committee might have been nonplussed over Fitzgerald's intentions, it could not overlook his mismanagement. First, it allowed an exception to an NCAA bylaw mandating a four-year "statute of limitations" on violations before the inquiry was made, ruling that Fitzgerald's actions "constituted a pattern of willful violations on the part of the institution."

The NCAA nailed Gonzaga for the dreaded "lack of institutional control" and for "unethical conduct," due in part to Fitzgerald's "provision of false and misleading information to the institution in order to prevent detection of misappropriated revenues" and "failure to disclose information to an outside accounting firm retained by the institution to conduct annual NCAA-mandated fiscal control audits."

Gonzaga attempted to mitigate the damage. It put Fitzgerald on leave early in July 1997; issued letters of reprimand to three staffers, including two basketball coaches, for failure to report the violations in a more timely fashion; required athletic-department members to attend a compliance seminar; and developed a document on proper fiscal procedure.

Among other penalties, the NCAA hit the Zags with a four-year probation without serious sanctions. It demanded an audit, tighter controls on fiscal procedure, and measures designed to educate. And it slapped a "show-cause" addendum on Fitzgerald, requiring that any NCAA school that might hire him in the probationary period lasting until June 5, 2002, explain itself before the committee on infractions to determine whether his duties should be limited.

Dan Fitzgerald resigned on December 22, 1997.

Late in 1998, he appealed the findings, stating, "I spent 25 years in intercollegiate athletics, and at no time did I ever knowingly violate the rules. An athlete never received an extra benefit, nor did our teams ever gain an unfair advantage."

The appeal was denied.

~ ~ ~ ~ ~

In Spokane, Fitzgerald is part hero and part pariah. Some people believe he was only trying to prop up a threadbare basketball program, giving it what everybody else had. Others think what he did was unconscionable.

He hasn't been back to Gonzaga, won't go near the place where he spent almost two decades of his life.

"Yeah," he says. "It's hard to stay away."

To this day, he maintains he didn't think he was doing anything wrong.

"I made some bad decisions," he says. "You'd have to be arrogant or an absolute moron if you didn't recognize that. The thing that stunned me is that it was an NCAA violation. Stunned. I mean, I went, 'What?'"

Fitzgerald falls back on the hypothesis that reasonable people conclude that if his methodology was lousy, his morals were untainted. The mess never would have happened, he contends, if the Gonzaga administration had funded the program more heavily.

Fitzgerald would like what Jarrod Davis, his all-league guard of the early nineties, says.

"We weren't getting shit," Davis insists. "I think it was just a way for Fitz to get by."

Jay Hillock, now estranged from Fitzgerald, was quizzed by investigators years after he had been at Gonzaga.

"They were trying to get me to kick him on his way down," Hillock says. "I couldn't do it. Like I told him when they were trying to bury him: I didn't learn accounting from him, I learned the flex [offense].

"I don't think he ever stole money. Did he probably stash it for basketball? Yes."

Fitzgerald says he had the backing of Mike Gilleran, the WCC commissioner.

"Mike Gilleran wrote them [school officials] a letter," Fitzgerald says. "He said what you've got is an employee that made a big mistake. Stay with him. And if anything else shows up, get rid of him and then punish him."

What will forever gnaw at Fitzgerald is the protracted period when he didn't know his fate, when he wondered whether they were for him or against him. When they offered to reassign him within the university.

"If they had fired me 30 seconds after they found out, I'd have some respect for them," he says. "But to go through what I went through, the expense of it . . . and then to offer me a job back. I said, 'There's not enough stamps for me to lick.'

"Did I make some bad decisions? Hell, yes. My reasons were good; my means were bad. I would never, ever do it again knowing the consequences—and certainly knowing it would be an NCAA violation."

Fitzgerald adds a tantalizing footnote: "To think I was the only horse that knew where the hay was . . . you'd have to be pretty naive to think that."

Within the athletic department?

"Well, no, within everybody. Within the university."

It would be logical that Fitzgerald would leave town, in search of his own Elba. Instead, he decided to take a charge, just as he used to ask his players to do, and stuck around in Spokane.

"I really thought about that," he says. "You know what's interesting? For the most part, the acceptance in town has been terrific."

He drops a small bombshell.

"I would definitely get back in," he said. "I just don't know. It's also not gonna be Resumes 'R' Us."

Fitzgerald can see himself on a variety of benches: he could provide wisdom to a young college coach in need of a seasoned mind next to him. He could be a short-term bridge at a program that eventually wants to hand the job to a younger man.

"I'd go to high school," he says, "if it was the right situation."

But he's 60 now, and the market is not desperate for senior coaches with some baggage. Even those who established the culture that brought Gonzaga to prominence.

4

Three's Company

The skeptics told them it would never last. No way the relationship could endure. They were trying to do something that couldn't be done. They were foolish for even attempting it.

It worked.

A major part of the genesis of Gonzaga basketball in the early nineties could be found in a modest home on the north side of Spokane, on Wiscomb Street. There, Dan Monson, Mark Few, and Bill Grier lived together, three blithe, young, ambitious hoopniks who couldn't wait to see where the game they loved might take them.

"Everybody would go, 'How could you do that? All day in the office together and then go home? . . .'" Monson says. "It was just like it was different in the office."

It was, and it wasn't. In the office, the three assistant coaches to Dan Fitzgerald talked help-side defense and flex offense and dreamed about what sort of player could make the Xs and Os come to life. And then they'd go home and talk help-side defense and flex offense. It was a basketball family.

Monson owned the place. Few paid rent, and Grier, the restricted-earnings coach making $5,000 a year, chipped in a little less. Of course, Grier contributed in other ways. He was the Felix Unger of the household, cooking and keeping the place spotless.

"Extremely anal," Few observed.

Grier was also something of a ladies' man. He would entertain his guests by cooking dinner and showing them the garden out back, while his housemates rolled their eyes.

Somehow, they survived each other. Maybe they realized they needed each other. Maybe they sensed a necessity for a brotherhood against the mercurial ways of "Fitz," their head coach.

But it worked, and it worked well. Even on Wiscomb Street, there was chemistry in Gonzaga basketball.

"It was awesome," Grier remembers. "That's so unique in college basketball. We were all young and energetic, and that's what we loved. I wouldn't have wanted to do it any other way."

~ ~ ~ ~ ~

Dan Monson was a coach's kid who didn't want to coach. Or so he thought. Which was fine with his dad, Don, former head coach at Idaho and Oregon.

"I never really encouraged him to be a coach," said Don. "I encouraged him to be around athletics. He was a very average athlete, a better football player than a basketball player, a good, competitive kid."

Dan was bright, with an excellent memory, a facility for concentration and for getting good grades more easily than his two sisters. His thing was math. As his father was doing stints as a high school basketball coach in eastern Washington, Dan would sit in the stands with his mother as a preschooler and quickly total up how many baskets their team was ahead or behind.

In the early eighties, Dan was headed quietly to a major in business at the University of Idaho, where Don was finishing a successful run as head coach. At the end of his sophomore year, he realized he was moving toward a point of no return in upper-level business classes and had a personal epiphany: what he felt an urge to do was teach. Coaching was just another form of teaching.

Dan used to have Sunday dinner at his folks' house. He sat down with them one spring day with butterflies in his stomach. He was scared.

"Dad, I want to talk to you about something," he said. "I really want to be a coach. I want to change my major."

The senior Monson, whose gruff exterior is legendary, eyed him. "Are you doing it because it's what you want to do? Or because it's what I do?"

"It's what I want to do."

Don Monson got up and gave his son a big bear hug.

Dan got his first job at Oregon City (Oregon) High School, teaching and coaching the JV basketball team. It was a year that gave him pause regarding his future.

"I really didn't like coaching that first year," he said. "It was three o'clock, and you'd just done six algebra classes. You'd already 'coached' for six hours and you didn't feel like going to practice."

On the plane ride to the Final Four in Dallas in 1986, he and his father got out an NCAA guide and targeted 25 schools to canvass for a graduate-assistant coaching job. Some 23 coaches responded, including Bob Knight, then the coach at Indiana, who said he didn't have an opening but would try to help him if nothing else worked out.

It did, shortly. Dan and his mother, Deanna, were relaxing by the pool at their hotel in Dallas when they ran into Gene Bartow, then the coach at Alabama-Birmingham. They had met at the Great Alaska Shootout in 1984, when Don Monson's Oregon team played there. Dan asked Bartow what his son Murry was doing now, and Bartow seemed surprised that he remembered the name. Murry Bartow, later the head coach at UAB, was himself working for Knight at Indiana.

"That's awesome," Monson said. "I'd love to do something like that."

"Really?" Bartow responded. "Write me about it when you get back."

Soon, Dan Monson had his first college job, at UAB. He felt good about it; he had reached out and gotten it himself rather than relying on his dad's connections.

Don Monson decided to drive Dan to Birmingham from Eugene, a journey interrupted by a few casino stops.

"We got to Reno the first night," Don recalls. "Next day, we got to Vegas. I said, 'Man, we better start driving pretty soon.'"

"It was good bonding," Dan says. "He did most of the driving; I did most of the sleeping."

Dan Monson stayed at Alabama-Birmingham two years, the first one an excellent learning experience because Bartow was short one full-time assistant. Monson experienced the full range of coaching responsibilities.

His next job would be fateful both for him and for Gonzaga basketball.

While a college student, Monson used to organize his father's basketball camps at Oregon. He had a minor in computer science, and he computerized the whole operation before a lot of schools were doing that.

Later, in the middle of his hitch at UAB, he got a call from Mike Peterson, who was head women's coach at Gonzaga. Peterson had been a women's assistant at Oregon, after which the senior Monson helped him land the Gonzaga job.

Peterson encouraged Dan Monson to work Gonzaga's camps. Word was out around the Zags that an assistant to Dan Fitzgerald, Bill Evans, might not be long for the program, and it wouldn't hurt for Monson to get to know Fitzgerald.

Monson considers the time after his Alabama-Birmingham stint to be the most daunting of his career. He had few connections; he hadn't played college basketball, so there was no network to lean on.

But Evans indeed departed. Monson triumphed over John Wade, the assistant from Eastern Washington, even as Joe Hillock, Fitzgerald's number one assistant, was lobbying for Wade.

"When you interview with Fitz, you don't know," Monson says. "He did all the talking. Mike Peterson really helped me. And Fitz's wife, Darleen, and I always hit it off. One thing about Fitz, he's really close to his daughter and his wife, and when they like someone or don't like them, it's very influential with him."

Dan Monson was off to Spokane. For what he would bring—and whom—it would be a defining moment for the Gonzaga program.

~ ~ ~ ~ ~

Mark Few grew up in Creswell, Oregon, a town of 2,500 only 10 miles south of Eugene. He played point guard on a top-rated high school basketball team a generation ago. Like Gonzaga, the school's nickname was the Bulldogs.

He was good enough to be a small-college athlete, but he dislocated a shoulder playing football as a senior at Creswell. The shoulder continued to trouble him during his freshman year at NCAA Division III Linfield College in

McMinnville, Oregon, where he had hoped to play point guard in basketball and infield in baseball.

With a college career in sports a diminishing prospect, Few decided to spare himself the private-school tuition and transferred to the University of Oregon. Initially, he wanted to play baseball, but that dream died along with the program; the financially strapped Ducks became the only school in the Pac-10 to drop the sport.

An opportunity in coaching came quickly. He was approached by his high school coach about helping at Creswell, and at 20, he joined on. He dabbled in that and would later get his first paid coaching job at the school in 1986.

Before that, he was a gym rat around the Oregon campus, becoming good friends with Oregon guard Greg Bell and Olympic decathlete Tim Bright. He worked Oregon basketball camps in the summer, where he befriended Dan Monson as well as his future assistant at Gonzaga, Leon Rice.

"We met," Few says, recalling the introduction to Monson, "and just kind of hit it off."

They played in golf scrambles on the McKenzie River organized by the Oregon basketball program. As much as Few loved to coach, he loved to have fun. He was passionate about golf and liked to fish, although Bright says his affinity for fly-fishing would come later.

"He'd use bait and spinners," says Bright, who has stayed close to Few. "He'd tease me about throwing those fake flies out there. He'd give me a hard time about fly-fishing."

It isn't hard to imagine Few pulling up stakes and taking a flier on a chance offer at Gonzaga. He was footloose in his twenties, frequently joining Bright on his worldwide travels.

At the 1988 Olympic Trials in Indianapolis, a couple of days before he was to compete, Bright got an unexpected call from Few and another friend.

"Come and sleep on the floor," Bright said. "It'll be great."

They did, and Bright excelled. Now, he says, "I keep threatening to call up when he gets to the Final Four and say, 'Hey Mark, I need a place to stay.'"

Few went to Seoul for the 1988 Olympics and also joined Bright as he competed on the European tour a couple of times. They were young and looking for a good time, but as Bright recalls, "Anytime we'd get carried away a little bit, he'd drag me to church or I'd drag him to church. It was important to stay grounded."

At the same time, Few was doing stints at Creswell and Sheldon High in Eugene as an assistant coach before getting a call from Monson in 1989. Gonzaga needed a graduate-assistant coach.

Few jumped, despite the hardships.

"I think I was paid $1,500 my first year," he says. "I taught weight training, tennis. I had to take out a student loan just to pay room and board. You're basically working about 20 hours a day."

Why do it? "You're single, you're young, you want to coach."

~ ~ ~ ~ ~

Bill Grier knew Few, after a fashion. Living in Cottage Grove, Oregon, another 10 miles south of Creswell, he would read about the exploits of the Creswell team in the little local paper, the *Cottage Grove Sentinel*.

Few's team was the rage of its AA classification; Cottage Grove, playing a level higher with Grier as its point guard, was just getting by.

"We knew who each other was," Grier says.

Grier went on to Central Oregon Community College in Bend and, like Few, saw his college plans sabotaged, although for a different reason. A state budget crunch caused by failing tax levies cut sports programs there, and he transferred a year later to Southwestern Oregon CC. He had a sniff of interest from schools like Linfield and Willamette but, like Few, he opted for the cheaper tuition at Oregon and fell into the same little coaching coterie with Monson and Few, working camps, keeping an ear to the ground for vacant jobs.

In the late eighties, he assisted at Cottage Grove, then he moved to Few's old high school, Creswell, for the 1990–1991 season. Meanwhile, the Gonzaga staff was still in a state of transition; two years into Monson's time there, Fitzgerald had decided against retaining Hillock.

"When he let Joe go, it was really, really hard on me," said Monson. "I felt he [Fitzgerald] had brought me to get players, and we didn't get it done in time."

But the pipeline to the Eugene area kept flowing. Monson and Few moved up on Fitzgerald's staff, and they knew enough to go get Grier. Of the bare-bones life of the graduate assistant (GA), Few told Grier: "It's a struggle financially, but I love it."

When Monson approached Grier, there wasn't a lot of waffling. Was he interested? "In a heartbeat," Grier replied.

Grier remembers making about $5,000 his first year at Gonzaga, more than Few had. He was dead set against taking out any loans, so he simply scraped by, living the threadbare life of the GA.

"I'm so grateful to Dan," Grier says. "He really took care of me from a financial standpoint. He charged hardly any rent. He was always buying me dinner. Mark would buy me lunch. If it wasn't for those two, I don't know if I could have done it financially."

~ ~ ~ ~ ~

Fitzgerald, Monson, Few, and Grier. "Fitz" was the yin and they were the yang. The head coach and his three assistants—all a generation younger—could hardly have been more different, yet they found themselves pulling in the same direction.

Sometimes they wondered. A lot of times they wondered. It seemed that the program was so steeped in a just-get-by, avoid-the-hangman attitude that it would never achieve anything significant.

In the eighties, Gonzaga had four fourth-place finishes in the West Coast Conference and a couple of fifths. The preconference schedules were uninspired, peppered with Eastern Oregon, Western Montana, Whitworth, and Whitman. The sum of it was 16- and 17-victory seasons—occasionally a little more or less—that were always respectable but nowhere near groundbreaking.

It drove the young lions crazy. They couldn't understand the attitude that fostered that culture. And they couldn't understand Fitz.

Few remembers the prevailing feeling: "Look, this is the worst job in the league. All you've got to do is stay out of last place. You don't want to be in first place, because when you're in first place, that creates expectations."

The reaction of the young assistants? "Screw that."

Fitzgerald was a complete paradox. He was the consummate competitor. But almost more than winning, he seemed to revel in the struggle, as if victory would somehow diminish the nobility of the fight to get it. Winning everything would make it appear that it was too easy. Besides, winning would raise the expectation that winning ought to be possible at Gonzaga. It was more fulfilling to work long hours, to fight the good fight but to embrace the limitations. They were your friends, because they kept you in a comfort zone.

Says Monson, "I remember Fitz in those late nights used to tell us, 'You'll never win the league. It's the worst job in the league.' Then he'd give you the reasons: 'Everyone's in a better city, a better facility. Now you can catch lightning in a bottle and win the league tournament, but as long as you're here, you're never going to win a league championship.'"

It is Monson's view that the long years of battling programs with greater resources, the nights of sleeping in a car, had taken their toll on Fitzgerald.

"The place had beaten him up pretty good," Monson says. "The assistants before us had gotten beaten up. We came in not understanding that attitude. We were a good combination. He would keep us beat up, but we would keep him thinking that things could get done here."

One of the goals at the start of every year was simply to have a winning season. To this day, Monson and Few exchange phone calls when their teams have clinched a winning season. Last year in January, when the Zags had dispatched Loyola Marymount to run their record to 16–3 on the way to a No. 6 national ranking, Few got the routine phone call from a teasing Monson at Minnesota: "First of all, congratulations on a winning season. That's always our number one goal."

They loved working for Fitz, and they hated it. He gave them jobs, and he gave them significant responsibility. He also gave them hell.

"My first year, I was trying to figure it out," Grier says. "I was kind of entertained by it all. For Fitz, it was new blood, somebody to hear the same stories those guys had heard for two or three years."

For the young assistants, the makeover had to begin with recruiting. Gonzaga was not in the practice of beating other schools for players.

"The mind-set at the time was, why would a kid go to Gonzaga if he could go anywhere else?" says Monson. "They did a great job of developing players. If I brought anything to the table, it was a young, brash, don't-know-any-better attitude—that 'No, why would we want this guy, nobody else does?'

"I didn't listen to the Fitzy 'You're-so-stupid-you-don't-understand-how-this-works.' Right away, we got a couple of kids that other people wanted."

Unfortunately, as often happens in recruiting, they didn't turn out to be players. But by then, Few was on board, and he relished recruiting even more than Monson had.

"He took it to a whole 'nother level," Monson says. "Mark wouldn't recruit a kid unless the Pac-10s were in on him. The more schools, the better for Mark. He's still that way. That's what makes him as good as he is."

Fitz, on the other hand, couldn't understand it.

"Why are you wasting your time on that kid?" was a phrase the assistants heard more than once. Even Monson wondered what Few was thinking in the mid-nineties when the Zags were chasing Matt Santangelo, the guard from Portland, right along with Stanford and the Oregon schools.

"I was, 'Wow, I'm with you, buddy,'" Monson says. "'Knock yourself out, but . . .'"

Nobody would tell you working for Fitzgerald was easy. In keeping with his notion that the beauty of the race was in the struggle, they worked long hours, often senselessly, analyzing the game to death. There was always something else that needed to be reviewed. They studied video and studied it some more. If there wasn't something to do, something else was unearthed.

"We'd literally watch the jump ball seven times," Few said, "and its alternate possessions."

In Grier's first year, Fitzgerald assigned him to scout a couple of Division II games.

"He wanted to know what they did on a jump ball, for crying out loud," Grier says. "There's one jump ball in the game."

Fitzgerald had a habit: at some time during a game, he would see something that suggested victory or defeat, fire up out of his seat, and pronounce: "Ball game!"

His assistants swear that one night, Fitzgerald jumped off the bench after the Zags lost the opening tip and proclaimed, "Ball game!"

When a game ended, the staff would troop to Fitzgerald's office to watch video over beers, sometimes until the sun came up. "Paper route," he called it, when they'd be there until the morning newspaper was being dropped on doorsteps around Spokane.

"Then he'd want to go somewhere and get breakfast," Few says.

Today, both Monson and Few have mostly adhered to a vow they made long ago as assistants: don't bother watching video immediately afterward. Forget it until the next day.

Watching video, Fitzgerald would have the remote control in hand, hit the rewind, and accidentally allow it to run too far. That would result in him picking up something else he had missed the first time, and they'd watch those plays again. The task increased exponentially. Even today, when the Zags are viewing video and misplaced fingers allow it to rewind too far, somebody will say, "Oh, Fitzy."

Everything needed to be dissected. When they were on the road and the game had to be reviewed, Fitzgerald had a standing rule about the kind of hard-core tavern where they were headed: "No broads, no bands." Only basketball.

Mornings, Fitzgerald would convene staff meetings. They might last from 8:30 to noon.

"He'd put recruits on the board," Few says. "'What do you think about this guy? How good is he?'" A day or two later, they might be discussing the same thing.

They learned to deal with Fitzgerald's abiding skepticism and his biting criticism. Fitz could brook no perceived lapse in preparation by his assistants.

Grier remembers the first Division I scouting assignment, for a game against Portland. The Pilots had a lumbering center who didn't look to shoot, so Grier's conclusion was the Zags could play off him outside 10 feet. Jeff Brown, the Gonzaga big man, took it to the extreme, stationing himself under the basket on the other Portland post player, and Grier watched in horror as the Pilot big guy lofted up a 16-footer that went in.

Fitzgerald leaped to his feet. "I'll tell you what," he roared. "You really missed on that guy!"

They jousted; they warred; they debated. The younger coaches introduced some newer principles to the system, and Fitzgerald would counterbalance with his traditional ways.

He viewed warily the concept of weak-side help, harping instead on the tried-and-true standby of on-ball defense. One day in practice, the three assistants were all screaming, "Help side! Help side!" when Fitz's whistle sounded.

"You guys are so f——ing dumb!" he barked at the three of them. "F—— help! Guard the ball!"

By 1993–1994, the talent level had been upgraded, and the preseason forecasters recognized it. Gonzaga was widely picked to win the WCC, which was just about the worst thing anybody could do to Fitzgerald.

"We tortured Fitz with that the whole preseason," Monson says. They tried to tell him it only reflected a perception of the ability level at Gonzaga, but it didn't matter. "It drove him crazy," says Monson.

The Zags breezed into the league schedule and won their first six. Then they ran afoul of an upset at Loyola Marymount.

"We didn't have to go watch film, but we had to go eat and have beers with him," says Monson. "Mike Peterson was in town with his women's team. When somebody else was there, he would just kill the assistants: 'My assistants were so stupid. They thought we had enough talent. They talk about all this talent we had. I told them how dumb they were. This team is not gonna win three more games. This is the worst team I have ever had.'"

The next day, Gonzaga went to Pepperdine, which had been a kingpin in the league until then. The Zags won, 70–48, and sure enough, they went on to go 12–2 and win the WCC regular-season championship, just as the predictions had said from the beginning.

Referring to the assistant coaches, Few says, "There were halftimes we'd go into an opposite room from the players and go, 'Let's sell life insurance. It's a heck of a lot easier than going through this for $24,000 a year.'"

Deep down, Fitzgerald appreciated them; it just didn't always shine through. He entrusted Monson with considerable scouting and defensive responsibilities, and Few began to blossom as an offensive strategist. Grier would evolve into a defensive specialist, which would later complement Few's offensive strength.

"Fitz relied on Dan in games," says Don Monson. "Dan will always say he got the coaching background from me, but Fitz taught him how to coach. Fitz was a very good coach."

"He was very theatrical," says Grier. "You look back on it, and it was just hilarious. He was sometimes a psychopath.

"But having survived it, I look back on the things he taught me, things about preparation, that have become invaluable."

It wasn't necessarily easy to know that then. Few says after he met his future wife, Marcy, the long hours and frustration over Fitzgerald's peculiarities began to wear on him.

"Dan [Monson] kind of formed a shield," Few remembers. "He'd go out with Fitz every night, which allowed me to do the recruiting and the scouting.

"He'd be kind of a buffer. Rather than make it confrontational, I'd just hit the road. Or in Spokane, I'd dive into individual work and make myself unavailable."

~ ~ ~ ~ ~

Thirty-six years after laboring at Division I basketball, Gonzaga finally broke through in 1995, playing in the school's first NCAA tournament. It was a schizophrenic season that began with 11 victories in 12 games against mostly outmanned competition; six straight losses to open the WCC; then, without warning, 10 victories in 11 games against the league, including the tournament championship.

The team was led by sharpshooting Australian wing John Rillie. He had come over on a touring team and spent a year at Tacoma Community College. After his coach, Ron Billings, was fired, he wanted to leave as well, and the Gonzaga staff was split on whether to take him. Fitzgerald saw something and won out, and Rillie's shooting carried them through the WCC tournament.

"If you guys would just settle down," Monson implored some jittery Zags in the tournament, "John is not gonna let us lose."

Gonzaga met up with Maryland and All-American center Joe Smith in the NCAA tournament at Salt Lake City, a 14th seed against the Terps' No. 3. The Zags shut down Smith but got hurt by others. The athletic Maryland defenders were able to contest Rillie's shots and broke the game open in the second half, winning 87–63.

By this time, Fitzgerald was pondering his own long-term future. Even though the landscape had grown greener at Gonzaga, the fight had been draining. Monson, meanwhile, was ready to pursue some head-coaching opportunities, including the one at nearby Eastern Washington.

"That's a tough job," Fitzgerald said.

"But Fitz," said Monson. "I'm ready to be a head coach. You're going to be here a long time."

"How do you know that?"

"Because I just know you."

Fitzgerald came back the next day and proposed that he coach another five years with the guarantee that Monson would succeed him. Monson declined—too long. Shortly, Fitzgerald dropped the time line to two years, and Monson accepted the idea.

While the certainty of an improved head-coaching job was a boon for Monson, the transition also had its drawbacks. Recruiting was done on the promise that

Monson surely would be a worthy head coach. It also meant that for a year, the recruiting staff was short by one member; in his final season, Fitzgerald wasn't recruiting for a new coach.

Says Monson, "I had to explain: I'm going to be the next head coach. I'm going to be good. You could just see it in parents' eyes—why would we go here? The other schools just killed us with the 'lame-duck coaching.' I almost thought we'd be better off just hiding this from the kids and announcing it in the spring, that you're gonna take over."

Maybe it did kill the Zags in recruiting. But if it did, it wasn't evident on the floor, where the little school was about to do some big damage.

5

Takeoff, and a Splash Landing

Dan Fitzgerald's coaching days were done at Gonzaga, and they had been good ones. In his last six years, the Zags went 55–29 in the West Coast Conference, won one league title outright, and tied for another.

But it didn't take long for Dan Monson's new regime to put a stamp on the program. First off, the nonleague schedule was going to be upgraded; the Wiscomb Street Three were nothing if not blithe and bold.

Monson's 1997–1998 Zags were going to open with a yawner at home against Concordia of Oregon and then fly to the Top of the World Classic in Fairbanks, Alaska, for three high-level games. Before December, there would also be a meeting at Michigan State (when the key parts of the 2000 national-champion Spartans—Mateen Cleaves and Morris Peterson—were sophomores).

For Gonzaga, the time seemed right to step up the schedule. The talent level had never been better. The Zags had 6'8" pivotman Bakari Hendrix, Fitzgerald's first real score in California. He would be WCC player of the year in Monson's first season.

There was Matt Santangelo, a guard from Portland who would contribute the first of three All-WCC seasons. The Zags had gotten him through Mark Few's persistence and a bit of luck recruiting against Stanford.

Fitzgerald had run into Stanford coach Mike Montgomery and tried to get him to tip his hand on the Cardinal's intentions with Santangelo. Montgomery was close to the vest.

"Mike," Fitzgerald pleaded, "Gonzaga's going to beat Stanford on him? I need a favor. If you're going to take him, let me know. I don't have a lot of dough, and we need to get another guy."

Montgomery came through. He called Fitzgerald later to tell him Arthur Lee had committed to Stanford three days before Lee announced it, freeing up Santangelo for Gonzaga.

"He's better than I thought," Fitzgerald said in retrospect. "I thought he was an all-league guy as a senior."

From just across the Columbia River there was Richie Frahm, another Few recruit. The Zags were hung up between him and Ron Grady of suburban Portland, who was being wooed primarily by Monson. Each player knew the other was being rushed hard by Gonzaga, and each knew there was only one scholarship available.

On the day before Grady was due to visit—as it turned out, a delay in his transcript kept him home anyway—Frahm and his mother trekked across the state to the Gonzaga campus and Frahm committed himself to the Zags, with the idea of nipping Grady at the wire.

"I went unannounced," says Frahm. "They didn't know at all. Basically, I beat him to the punch."

Frahm's first season at Gonzaga was Fitzgerald's last, a 15–12 downer that caused Frahm to think about transferring.

"I had higher expectations for my college career," he said. "Basically, I just wanted to go to a bigger school. I made a couple of phone calls. I didn't think it seemed realistic that we could make Gonzaga a powerhouse. I don't know what kept me there. I guess seeing Casey Calvary step on campus."

The parts were coming together. One was Bahamian point guard Quentin Hall, for whom Few was also the lead recruiter. Few first saw him at a high school tournament in Las Vegas. As the former Washington staff of Bob Bender, Ray Giacoletti, and Ritchie McKay was scouting Seattle standout Jason Terry, Hall's team from the Bahamas took the floor.

"This little guy just tore Jason Terry up," said Few. "Ripping him, talking to him, he had 30-something on him. They were pressing all over the floor. They just killed the Washington team."

That led Few to travel to the Bahamas to visit the 5'8" Hall. The scene was like something out of a Steve Martin movie.

"I was wearing a blue suit," Few says. "The school was in a temporary trailer, no air-conditioning. I'm sweating, brutally. Practice is on an outdoor court. There's only one indoor gym on the island. Everybody else is in shorts, and I'm just sweating through my blazer. It was the grossest thing."

In a moment of self-doubt, Few wasn't even sure he remembered what Hall looked like.

"All of a sudden, this big, beaming smile comes up to me," Few said. "I just fell in love with him."

The Zags placed him at North Idaho Junior College because Hall's grades didn't qualify him at Gonzaga. The next summer, the three coaches were at Grier's wedding when they encountered Hall in tears.

There had been an incident in a dormitory at North Idaho, and Hall was off the team. He was certain he was headed back to the Bahamas, his college career finished. But the Gonzaga coaches knew him so well by then, they trusted him, and fortuitously, Leon Rice was right there at the wedding.

Rice was head coach at Yakima Valley Junior College, where Hall transferred on his way to a productive two years at Gonzaga as a frenetic defensive stopper who could also unleash the occasional offensive burst.

From a junior college in eastern Washington, the Zags had 6'11" Jeremy Eaton, who would give them a nice offensive weapon. Eaton's intriguing pastime outside basketball was rodeo steer roping.

Then there was Monson's first recruit as a head coach. He was Casey Calvary, the 6'8" forward from Tacoma and a raw physical talent who had been overlooked by the bigger schools in Washington.

There were things about Calvary that made him perfect for Gonzaga. First, he needed significant refinement on the floor—everything from post moves to shooting—and the Zags' system has always been about development. With a lot of coaching and his own hard work, Calvary would become a second-team All-American.

Second, Calvary was supremely stubborn. Monson was just embarking on his head-coaching career, and what recruiting attention Calvary was getting from other schools centered on Monson's unproven track record. The more Calvary heard rivals tell him Monson was a risk, the more he challenged it.

Still, Monson was a nervous wreck at a golf fund-raiser in Spokane the day Calvary was supposed to be back from his recruiting visit to Colorado State, Gonzaga's chief competition. Calvary was unavailable at the time appointed, and Monson sensed a piece of his future slipping away.

Finally, Monson reached him.

"Well, coach, it's over," Calvary said.

Silence.

"I'm with you."

The coaching change at GU had brought a sense of relief to some players. Few, given the offensive reins by Monson, would allow more freedom on offense, and this was a team that could handle it.

"It was a breath of fresh air," Frahm said. "The flex offense was boring for a lot of our guys. We raised the tempo up. It was a lot more fun and more effective."

It was thus with a formidable arsenal that Gonzaga descended on an unsuspecting field in Fairbanks. Monson's first game against a Division I team was against Tulsa, and it was preposterously easy; Gonzaga won 78–40.

All through the previous off-season, the Zags had treated the Tulsa game as the symbolic launch to a new take-on-all-comers mind-set.

"Every day," says Santangelo, "we were preparing for Tulsa. It really allowed us to improve our workouts. We weren't sure we could compete at that level. It was a whole change in mentality."

The Tulsa coach was Bill Self, who would go on to Illinois and deny Monson's 2002 Minnesota team a spot in the NCAA tournament with a last-minute comeback on the final day of the regular season in Minneapolis.

"I can beat you 10 straight times," Self told Monson a few weeks after that 2002 game, "and it won't add up to as badly as you beat us in Fairbanks."

At halftime, the Zags were ahead 34–10. If this was the curtain-raiser on their foray into big-time basketball, it was a powerful one. Calvary remembers thinking at halftime, "Wow, not only can we play with these guys, we can absolutely murder them."

Gonzaga nipped Mississippi State and put away fifth-ranked Clemson by 13 points to win the tournament. It was the first real sniff of national recognition for the program.

"Once we won the Clemson game," Calvary says, "I was pretty sure we could beat lots of teams around the country."

Monson's first Gonzaga team did everything but get into the NCAA tournament. It tied the school record with 24 victories (since bettered), and it won the WCC regular-season title. But it lost in the WCC tournament final to San Francisco, got snubbed by the NCAA selection committee, and had to settle for a victory at Wyoming in the NIT before a loss at Hawaii.

"They sent us out to Wyoming to lose," says Calvary. "We couldn't get a home game to save our lives."

To this day, Monson isn't so certain that wasn't the better of his two teams. But his second one, mostly intact, set a standard at Gonzaga partly on the weight of the chip on its shoulder from the slight by the NCAA.

"We felt kind of used by the NCAA selection committee," says Frahm. "That might have made us better the next year."

The 1998–1999 team was 10 deep. Axel Dench, an Australian big man, supplemented the front line, a product of Monson's recruitment after his father, Don, had coached in that country and helped the Zags get another Aussie, Paul Rogers.

Other key parts included Mike Leasure, Mark Spink, Mike Nilson, and Ryan Floyd, all of them Washingtonians, most overlooked by everybody else. Floyd was a backup guard from little Harrington in eastern Washington; Spink and Nilson were give-it-up, defense-and-rebounding demons.

"It was like we were going to prove it to everybody and not leave anything to doubt," says Few. "Guys like Frahm and Santangelo were very driven, beyond Gonzaga, very much in tune with their bodies and staying in shape."

Hendrix was gone, but the abundance of mature guards boded well.

Gonzaga opened with a competitive loss at Kansas. What Monson saw afterward convinced him he had a team that wasn't going to be satisfied with moral victories.

"By the time I got in the locker room," he said, "it was destroyed."

The schedule was again daunting. On the same trip in the preseason NIT, the Zags flattened Memphis by 15 points and then lost at Purdue by the same margin, a defeat notable for the irrepressible Hall's yapping at the Boilermaker crowd.

As promising as the Zags were, the preconference performance wasn't seamless. On a late December trip to Texas–Pan American, Gonzaga was down by two, and after two missed free throws by one of the Broncs, a falling Calvary shoveled a desperate pass through the legs of an opponent toward Santangelo, who fired in a three-pointer at the buzzer for a 74–73 victory.

"I don't think many people understand what a fine line it is," says Few. "We played horribly; they were like the 300th-rated team in Division I. I mean, we're done, we're beaten, by the 300th-rated team. It's amazing to think how bad we were in that game, and how good we were against Stanford and Connecticut."

There was no denying the Zags through the WCC schedule and on into the league tournament. They won their first eight in conference, got ranked 25th in the coaches' poll, and—naturally—lost by 16 at San Diego in their next game. They would lose only once more in the regular season, to Pepperdine.

"We stayed so healthy," Few says. "Guys were averaging 28 minutes a game. The chemistry was good. The guys like Nilson and Floyd and Spink were great role players."

The Zags were able to play Hall and Santangelo together. Each had point-guard skills, but each fit in at the wing, too, because they could run and shoot.

Gonzaga took no prisoners in the WCC tournament, winning three games by a combined 59 points, including a 91–66 throttling of the host team, Santa Clara. The Zags hit 18 of 31 three-point shots against the Broncos.

It was Gonzaga's second NCAA appearance, and even in the buildup, it was memorable. GU was seeded 10th opposite 7th-seeded Minnesota, but the meeting was at KeyArena in Seattle, explaining why the Zags were a slight favorite.

On Tuesday, the *Saint Paul Pioneer-Press* broke a story alleging that some Gopher players had had schoolwork done for them and that some of the coaches knew it was happening.

It was awkward for Gonzaga, but it was also fun. "I remember telling a lot of jokes about how we have to do our own homework," said Calvary. "How great it would be to just play basketball and have somebody else do your reports."

On the Minnesota side, the reaction was one giant squirm. Jesse Ventura, the pro-wrestler-turned-governor, even weighed in with his disappointment, saying, "They felt the need to release this story the day before the NCAA tournament. It couldn't have waited until after?"

In other words: scandal, schmandal. How's our transition game looking?

Wednesday, at the routine game's-eve press conference, Minnesota coach Clem Haskins was peppered with questions about the story. Without a lot of success, he kept saying, "Let's turn the page."

That, apparently, was something not many Gophers had been doing.

The next morning at the pregame meal, the Zags got the word—four of the Gophers suspected of wrongdoing in the scandal were ruled ineligible, including starters Kevin Clark and Miles Tarver.

"We're not gonna fall into that trap," Monson vowed to his team. "They're still gonna put five Big Ten players on the floor."

Before the suspensions, Monson had been plotting a triangle-and-two defense, with Clark and forward Quincy Lewis the man-to-man targets. To Lewis' overwhelming regret, he would now be the object of a box-and-one defense, and the one was Quentin Hall.

The little guard became a metaphor for Gonzaga's greater quest, a 5'8" wolverine tormenting the bewildered, 6'6" Lewis—flying at him, bumping him, jamming his penetration, and all the while, jabbering at him. "Telling him he was terrible," Calvary said, "telling him he's never going to make the league."

At one point, Hall bounded into a Gonzaga huddle and told Monson in his clipped Bahamian accent, "Coach, we need to stay in that. It's just really messing with them." Was it ever! On the day he was needed most, Lewis had the worst game of his career, going 3 of 19 from the field for eight points.

"I would hate to have been that kid," Few says. "You've got this little 5'8" chicken hawk on you, and you can't shake him."

Gonzaga blew out of the gate with six three-point baskets in the first eight minutes, and Frahm led the way, firing in 16 points in 12 minutes as the Zags took a 45–26 halftime lead. Already depleted, Minnesota had two players draw three fouls each in the first half and turned to reserve forward John Aune for eight minutes. He had previously played seven minutes the entire season.

The Gophers stormed back in the second half and threatened to make Gonzaga's NCAA stay brief. They got within two, 65–63, with 1:22 left when Frahm caught the ball in the corner. He drained a three, part of his game-high 26 points, and the Zags had their first NCAA-tournament victory.

Referring to the Minnesota attrition, Santangelo said, "Had it been a regular-season game, maybe a team would have had a tendency to relax a little bit. But with the nervousness of being in the tournament, the energy, we were just ready to get on the floor. At that point, we were all just rookies."

As meaningful as it was, as fearlessly as the Zags had played, it didn't dent the national consciousness. It was easy to lay the Minnesota loss at the feet of the four suspended players.

Now the Zags had to worry about Stanford, the Pac-10 champion. As always, the Cardinal was a board-pounding outfit used to having its way inside. But it was a good matchup for Gonzaga, which wouldn't be intimidated or out-quicked.

The offensive plan was to have Eaton, Dench, and Calvary—all capable shooters—draw the Stanford big men away from the basket. As it happened, none would have a very good game offensively, but the space created helped Gonzaga to a 47–33 rebounding advantage, unheard of against Stanford.

It was the slender Spink who symbolized Gonzaga's desire. Banging against the muscular 6'9" Mark Madsen and 7'1" Tim Young, Spink snatched down five rebounds in 14 minutes. Somehow, Hall had eight rebounds to lead the Zags.

"That was one of those games where I don't know if we went in believing we could win," said Santangelo. "I think we believed, but I don't know if we knew we could win or not. As the game wore on, you could just see the belief build."

If Frahm and Hall had been the keys to the Minnesota victory, Gonzaga rode the shoulders of Santangelo in this one. Playing against Lee, who had taken the scholarship that might have been his, Santangelo threw in 22 points and had six rebounds and six assists. Lee, meanwhile, had a game-high 24 points but made only 6 of 18 field goals to get them.

"Santangelo had control of that game," said Few.

It was a terrific game, the intensity heightened by a Seattle crowd of 15,187 that was more than willing to adopt Gonzaga. Even the officials were into it. In the last five minutes, veteran referee Ted Valentine ran by press row and exclaimed, "I think we've got a game goin' on!"

The Zags, ahead by 13 in the first half, fended off every Stanford charge and won 82–74. This was truly a breakthrough victory for Gonzaga, coming against a No. 2 seed that had been to the 1998 Final Four and then returned four seniors who would experience 98 wins in their careers.

"You kept thinking physically and emotionally we were going to run out of gas," said Monson, "and we never did."

Now the train was rolling. In the NCAAs, a first-round victory often gets lost because the second round comes so quickly. But here were the Zags in the Sweet 16, and the national media had most of a week to dote on them.

"That's the greatest week of the year," said Few, who has come to know it intimately. "You finally get time. It's like a normal league weekend."

It was, except for one inconvenience. Monson, irked that the team's new locker room had been left messy, tossed the team from its quarters for the entire week. Players had to carry shoes and workout gear in their backpacks, and they changed in the bleachers at the Martin Centre, giving them, Santangelo says, "a sense that we weren't God's gift."

If it was a psychological ploy by Monson to keep the Zags grounded, it seemed to work.

"It was a nice distraction," said Santangelo. "It took your mind off all the things going on."

The other survivor from Seattle headed for America West Arena in Phoenix, Arizona, was Florida, a No. 5 seed that the Zags considered more beatable than Stanford. The third-seeded team, North Carolina, had been taken out in the first round in a hail of bullets from Harold the "Show" Arceneaux of Weber State.

"We just need to play well," Monson told his team. "And if we do, we'll beat Florida."

Once again, it was a tenable matchup for Gonzaga. Florida's game was a full-court, 40-minute press, but the Zags were deep enough to handle it, and their three-guard attack of Hall, Santangelo, and Frahm gave them ample ball-handling.

Gonzaga's habit of creating a big early cushion continued, as opponents struggled with the Zags' multifaceted attack. GU took a 13-point lead, but Florida chipped it to a 1-point deficit at halftime, and it was heated down the stretch.

With 45 seconds left, it appeared that the Zags had made a fatal defensive error. The Gators set a perimeter screen for big man Greg Stolt, and Nilson left Stolt open. Stolt buried a three-point shot, and Florida led 72–69.

"We were in disarray," Few says.

But the Zags dumped the ball inside to Eaton for a score with 20 seconds left, and the bench screamed for Hall to foul.

"I don't know why I didn't," Hall would explain later. "My mind said, 'Foul, foul,' but my body wouldn't let me."

Instead, he harassed Florida forward Brent Wright, and with 15.4 seconds left, Wright picked up his dribble and tried to protect the ball. As he did, he dragged his pivot foot.

"I don't think the official wanted to call it," said Few, "but it was in front of the world."

Suddenly, the Zags had the possession they needed. Hall tried a 13-foot runner for the lead, but it hit backboard and rim and found the waiting hands of Calvary in the key. Soaring and switching to his left hand after his right was grazed, he slapped the ball up and in with four seconds left.

Nilson, hoping desperately for redemption, described what he was feeling.

"I was so nervous, my heart had dropped down into the bottom of my pants and my hands were dripping," he said. "Everything seemed to move in slow motion. I could see the clock move in tenths of seconds."

Florida's Eddie Shannon raced the ball up court, and the Zags froze as he launched a perimeter shot that fell away.

Occasionally, Few will pull out that tape and be transported into "the greatest moment in Gonzaga history, easily." The footage always brings fresh chills down his spine.

A wild ride got wilder. In the aftermath of the victory, Gonzaga players trooped into the lobby of their hotel, spotted the pool, and made a beeline for it—no matter that they were still in basketball shorts. Fox TV sportscaster Angie Arlati requested an interview with Hall, and the Zags decreed that it wouldn't happen unless she jumped in with them. She did, fully clothed, and conducted interviews in the Jacuzzi.

All it was, was the time of their lives.

"I don't think too many people slept that night," said Frahm. Certainly, Calvary didn't. He was awakened at 6:30 the next morning by a call from the Fabulous Sports Babe, who wanted the next interview.

"We realized how close we were to the Final Four," Frahm said. "How can you imagine that? It was like a trip to Fantasyland."

Gonzaga, which had never won an NCAA game, had now won three straight. Perhaps a more traditional program would have shut down the media and fan attention to greater benefit, but the Zags were new to all this. Besides, how could you deny them?

"No, once you saw how our guys handled the media, from Quentin to Matt, bantering back and forth . . ." Few says. "It was great."

Reality was Connecticut—big, bad, hungry Connecticut. The Huskies, under coach Jim Calhoun, had a huge monkey on their backs, never having been to the Final Four, and this was the team that could do it. They had an All-American forward in Richard Hamilton, a deft if pudgy point guard in Khalid El-Amin, a serviceable big guy in Jake Voskuhl, and a valuable forward who could defend and rebound in Kevin Freeman.

The Zag coaches were sobered, especially at UConn's ability to defend. The challenge was daunting, bigger than anything they had faced. At the same time, says Few, "Hey, we're 40 freakin' minutes from the Final Four."

That Friday night, figuring they had watched all the tape they could stand, the Gonzaga coaches piled in a car with a couple of friends and headed for a restaurant in nearby Tempe to escape the hoopla. Driving back to their hotel, they clicked on a national sports-radio talk show.

"Gonzaga's got no chance," said the host.

Monson was inflamed. In the desert darkness, he had them pull the car to the side of the road and he called the show, trying to convince the producer he was indeed the coach at Gonzaga. The producer wouldn't buy it. Finally, Monson told him what he'd be wearing tomorrow at courtside, and they let him on to state his case.

As it turned out, he had a pretty good one. Gonzaga led 32–31 at the half. The Zags fell behind by six in a taut struggle, but inside the seven-minute mark, they tied it at 53. Neither team was shooting well; baskets out of set offense became a milestone.

Hall was turning in another phenomenal defensive effort while somehow leading Gonzaga in both scoring (18) and rebounding (seven). He simply demonized El-Amin, holding him scoreless from the field in 12 attempts.

"El-Amin was just freaking out," Few recalls.

But El-Amin did hit five of six free throws, including some big-pressure attempts in the closing minutes. Hamilton was a load, leading all scorers with 21 points. What hurt Gonzaga most, however, was three UConn putbacks down the stretch, huge in a game in which scoring came at such a premium and with the Huskies feeling the pressure. Connecticut had a 47–33 edge in rebounds, precisely the margin Gonzaga had held against Stanford.

Finally, it was over. Connecticut prevailed 67–62. Even a five-point spread wasn't indicative of how microscopically close the Zags had come to the Final Four.

The outside shooting that had been so good deserted Gonzaga, as Santangelo went 1 for 9 and Frahm 2 for 11.

"That one definitely haunted me for the summer," Santangelo said. "For someone who was one of the leaders, you struggle so much."

In the locker room, some of them cried. The welter of emotions got to them—the idea that they had come to the doorstep of the Final Four and been turned back, the knowledge that they had experienced something together that they could never duplicate.

There was no immediate realization of where Gonzaga had been and from where it had come. Two sweet weeks were a blur, a whirl of adrenaline and interviews, of pressure and deliverance.

"It still kind of hits you now," Monson says. "Wow, we were this close. Now it hits you way more than it did in those 48 hours leading up to it.

"I think for the first time, the kids were a little tired. It had been a long two weeks with a different spotlight. It was a very emotionally tired team by the time that game came. They did a great job fighting through it."

Ever so gradually, the Zags found perspective. For some, it came as early as the bus ride back to their charter flight home, when Eric the "Fridge" Edelstein, a GU broadcasting major and part-time comic, did his repertoire of zany impersonations.

After all the late nights and early mornings, after the naps in cars on the road, after all the faulty rewinds on the remote control, Gonzaga had arrived.

"This was all new," Few says. "Before this, there were no *Sports Illustrated* articles, or Jim Rome, or anything like that. All of a sudden, that stuff just took off because of all that attention."

Gonzaga would go on to the Sweet 16 again in 2000 and do it again the next year. If the Zags had caught lightning in a bottle in 1999, they did well at preserving it, too. But there never would be anything as good or as golden as it was that March.

~ ~ ~ ~ ~

Meanwhile, the mess at Minnesota was growing. The scandal pervaded the basketball program, encircling tutors who routinely took exams for players. The Gophers' 1997 Final Four records were vacated, and so was the chair of the head coach, Haskins.

Monson was off in Palma de Mallorca, Spain, helping coach at the World University Games, where he was blissfully unaware of Minnesota's daily angst.

When he got back in mid-July, he clicked on his telephone answering machine to find a long list of messages, one from Minnesota athletic director Mark Dienhart.

He wanted to talk about the Gophers' vacancy. Monson was tired, skeptical, and initially unwilling. In his absence, the recruiting burden had fallen to Few and assistant Bill Grier. But Monson consented to a quick flight to Dallas from Los Angeles, where he was scouting high school players in a tournament. He watched Cory Violette of Boise long enough to give this directive to Few and Grier: "We need to offer him."

It was the last game he would scout for Gonzaga. Two days later, Minnesota called back and applied more heat, saying it wanted to fly Monson and his fiancée or attorney back to Minneapolis. Monson's fiancée, Darci, was tied up; she had a couple of wedding showers—her own—to attend.

Monson was a physical and emotional wreck—gassed from the European trip, behind in recruiting, about to get married—and mentally unready to entertain a career move. Still, it was out there—a chance to coach in the Big Ten.

"My thought is, you don't go where the climate is, or the friends," says Don Monson, his father. "You go where the job is. I probably influenced Dan on that. He went back and forth twice. He wasn't going to take it. He said, 'Did you ever regret going to Oregon?' I said, 'Nope.' He said, 'I didn't think you did.'"

Oddly, Monson saw in Minnesota's academic morass a hidden benefit. Not only would the school be patient in allowing him a rebuilding job from its embarrassment, it would require the Gophers to do more than give lip service to academic concerns. They had to be important.

But he waffled. As his attorney, Brad Williams of Spokane, negotiated downstairs, Monson cried in his room. He said he wasn't taking it. The Gophers stopped him from walking away by throwing a couple of hundred thousand dollars more at him. He was still balking when they came through with a clincher that had a subtle appeal: a travel budget that would allow his parents and his sisters' families to visit him.

"When they know the school is buying," he says of family members, "it's different."

At one point, he was talking to himself: "If you turn this down, don't ever be unhappy with the resources at Gonzaga, because Minnesota has everything you've ever dreamed of. Don't call yourself a competitor if you don't want to try to do this."

And he was gone, replaced quickly by Few. Their coach had moved on, but the Zags' uncanny penchant for success in March had not.

6

Mighty Oak, Small Acorn

Is it talent? Coaching? Serendipity? Blind luck? Fool happenstance?

As observers of college basketball try to come to grips with what's happened at Gonzaga in recent years, a lot of theories have been advanced. Most of them have dealt with the confluence of people like Dan Dickau, Casey Calvary, Matt Santangelo, and Richie Frahm at one happy intersection.

There can be no minimizing of their efforts. But if there was a stage set for the turn-of-the-century success, a blueprint handed down, it developed a decade earlier, something like a flower that grew up through a small crack in the asphalt.

In the 1989–1990 season, the Gonzaga program had its worst season in four decades—an 8–20 overall record and 3–11 in the West Coast Conference, GU's poorest showing in history in that league. Half the victories came against these schools: Western Montana, Eastern Oregon, Montana Tech, and Whitman.

But something subtle was going on beneath the surface misery of a 10-game conference losing streak. Off by themselves, sharpening skills for better times, was a whole squadron of reinforcements that would change the culture of Gonzaga basketball. They would never go to the Elite Eight, or the Sweet 16, or even the NCAA tournament, but they would have a hand in establishing a foundation that has endured.

"It's not like we set the world on fire," said one of those upstarts, Matt Stanford. "But in a short amount of time, we did some pretty unique things there—and kind of kicked off, definitely, what's going on now.

"Things were going to be a certain way."

~ ~ ~ ~ ~

The setup was so strange: six players redshirting in one season, sort of like the junior varsity team, while the varsity lurched to one of the toughest years in school history.

"The turning point," Dan Fitzgerald, the head coach then, calls it.

After arriving in 1978 as athletic director and basketball coach, then relinquishing the bench for four seasons, Fitzgerald was seeing his first real downturn as a coach. Despite a couple of all-league players in Doug Spradley and Jim McPhee, the Zags would finish fifth in the WCC in 1988, sixth in 1989, and eighth in 1990.

But Fitzgerald had hired Dan Monson as an assistant coach in the spring of 1988, and they had put together some recruits who showed promise. As they prepared for the 1989–1990 season, Fitzgerald surprised Monson one day.

"We're gonna redshirt all of 'em," Fitzgerald said.

"What?"

"I'm the AD," he said. "And I ain't firing me."

And so they redshirted six of them. Three were invited walk-ons who would later get scholarships. Truth be told, there was a reason for each one to sit out.

Eric Brady, a 6'7" forward, had come from two years at Washington and had to sit out, per NCAA rules. The rest weren't really ready. Matt Stanford was a deceivingly athletic 6'5", 180-pound forward from Seattle who needed the weight room. Geoff Goss was a 6', 150-pound guard out of Boise who was so wild with the ball that Fitzgerald swore he needed to find a helmet.

Marty Wall was a complete project from Novato, California, a 6'10" player who, according to Brady, "could bench-press the bar" when he arrived at Gonzaga. Scott Spink of Bellingham, Washington, was 6'6", and like his brother Mark, who followed him to GU, spare and lacking physical maturity. Jarrod Davis was a thin 6'6" off-guard from Spokane and, subsequently,

Tacoma Community College, who possibly could have helped but wanted to redshirt.

Combined with 6'9" Jeff Brown, who would do his redshirt year the following season after leaving Washington, they changed the face of Gonzaga basketball.

Something happened almost the moment they arrived together on campus in 1989.

"The only way I can describe it is, it was strange," says Goss. "It was almost like we knew each other from somewhere else, because we all hit it off so well."

Brady was the leader, quiet and understated. Two years older than four of the others, he seemed to command respect.

"He had a tremendous amount of character and weight, relative to how much he talked," said Ken Anderson, Gonzaga's faculty athletic representative who was a volunteer assistant coach in 1991–1992. "It's hard to think of a better guy we've had in this program than Eric Brady."

Brady was the first in a growing pipeline of transfers from Washington. The state player of the year at powerhouse Mercer Island High in 1987, he had a lot of college choices, visiting Arizona, California, Texas, Northwestern, and Washington. Arizona signed another forward, and none of the other distant possibilities wowed him, so he chose the Huskies and coach Andy Russo.

It wasn't long before he would question his decision. Eager to prove himself fit in preseason conditioning, he was told to slow down in drills by some veteran players.

"If you wonder why the UW wasn't successful back then . . ." he says, leaving the sentence unfinished. "How much do you put on Russo? Well, he was the coach who catered to those guys."

Against his instinct, he decided to stay at Washington a second year. In midseason, after a blowout loss to Duke, he informed Russo that he planned to transfer, indicating he would be content to stay on the team and practice for the rest of the year. But during a victory by a wide margin soon thereafter, walk-ons got in the game, and with seconds remaining, Russo waved Brady in.

"No," refused Brady, believing he was being made an example of. He didn't win a letter that year, and two months later, Russo was fired.

The weekend Brady flew to visit Gonzaga, sitting across the aisle on the airplane was Joe Cravens, a Washington assistant coach who was headed to Spokane to see Jeff Brown, a UW signee. A few days before that, Monson had seen Brown, whom he had recruited tirelessly, and needled him.

"We've got your boy Eric Brady over here on a visit this weekend," Monson said.

"Really?" Brown said. "What's he doing?"

"We're teaching him to host," Monson replied, "so he can be your host next year when you come back here."

It would work out almost exactly like that. But for a year, it was only the six of the redshirts, seemingly inseparable except when they went to class. They were together, sometimes, even then.

They practiced together, coached by Mark Few, who was a graduate assistant in his first year at Gonzaga. They would be off by themselves, five guys and a substitute, and it was clear something good was in the making.

"Mark had a great time," says Goss. "We were always winning, just like he is now.

"The first scrimmage I remember, we ended up beating the varsity by, like, 40. Jarrod Davis had something like 52 points."

Says Stanford, "Probably three-quarters of the way through the season, they finally beat us in a scrimmage. They were high-fiving each other, the whole deal. I remember looking around, thinking, 'This is interesting. I think we've got something here.'"

They didn't go to road games that year, so they would gather to catch the games on the radio and wonder how they might affect the game differently. They would have their own practices while the team was away. They would go to parties together.

Pretty soon, they would win together.

~ ~ ~ ~ ~

Who would have guessed that one of the cornerstones of Gonzaga basketball would be laid at a Pete's Pizza joint in Spokane? That's a bit of oversimplification, but that's where Jeff Brown decided to meet Lynn Nance, the new basketball coach at the University of Washington, in the spring of 1989.

Brown, one of the last recruits of Russo at Washington, was at a high school baseball game in March when a couple of TV cameras circled around him, wanting to know about his thoughts in the wake of Russo's firing. Brown had a sense of foreboding. It would be confirmed shortly.

He was wearing walking shorts at Pete's.

"You can't jump very high, can you?" Nance said.

"He made some comment that my calves were not high enough on my legs to be a very good jumper," Brown says. "I had never heard that."

Nance was a truly different character, an austere man who seemed to sense a dark shadow coming around every corner. His resume included stints both in the FBI and on the NCAA investigative force, which might explain his manipulative side.

A graduate of Washington, he had just come from St. Mary's in the WCC, where a top 25 season made him an obvious choice for the Huskies—one that would nevertheless prove disastrous.

But Brown was an 18-year-old high school kid intent on making good at Washington, no matter that Nance threw the fear of God into him about reporting in shape.

"I was just freaking out," Brown says.

That fall, the fun would begin. Some days, they ran sets of 16 200-yard sprints at intervals, players throwing up at the finish.

Those might have been the good times. One day, a coach told the players to show up with two bricks apiece, so, as Brown recalls, "We cruised through the construction sites at the UW." Tuesdays and Thursdays, they would run a mile and a half, packing a brick on each side as hands cramped and the load banged against hips.

"Certainly by Christmas, I knew I was out of there," Brown recalls. "I didn't exactly enjoy my teammates. I had several close friends on the team, but that was probably the least of my decisions. I wasn't playing, I wasn't enjoying basketball anymore, and it was clear [Nance] didn't think I could play."

Washington had seemed so much the right place. "I got swept up in the I-want-to-go-to-the-Pac-10 thing," Brown says.

Even as Nance took over for Russo, there was reason to think Brown could play there. More than most players, he was suited for structure, skilled but not particularly athletic. That seemed to fit Nance, who liked the game played in the sixties.

"Everyone I talked to thought my skills were a good fit for what he had done at St. Mary's," Brown said. "Turned out that was furthest from the truth."

During that trying year at Washington, Brown got a call from Jarrod Davis, a high school teammate at Spokane's Mead who was two years his senior.

"Jeff, you need to get over here," Davis said. "There's good stuff happening."

Brown mentioned that he was considering Montana, which had been his number two choice out of high school.

"You're nuts," Davis said.

The Zags had played it smart when they lost Brown to Washington, ending the courtship on a positive note rather than trashing him. So one day Brown called Monson and said he had been released from his letter of intent at Washington. He recalls that Monson, trying to assemble his first full recruiting class as Fitzgerald's assistant, "had been to, like, 50 of my summer-league games."

"I'll be there this afternoon," said Monson. He jumped in his car, drove across the state, and hunted Brown down in his dormitory. Brown told Monson to cool it, he was coming to Gonzaga, he just wasn't ready to announce it yet. He had learned a lesson.

"Growing up in Spokane," Brown says, "I made an erroneous assumption. I thought I knew what GU was all about."

Davis told anybody who would listen that Brown would be a three-time All–West Coast Conference player at Gonzaga. But everybody, including Few, was mortified when they watched Brown in pickup games.

Says Goss, "A lot of guys were like, 'Why the hell did they bring this joker over here?'"

"He was horrid," Davis said. "The guys are looking at me like, 'We don't want this guy.'"

Davis had his stock response: "Trust me. You think he has 7 points and 4 boards, and he has 25 and 12."

~ ~ ~ ~ ~

Stanford remembers the 1989–1990 Zags as being beyond awful.

"I was glad I wasn't a part of it," he says. "You couldn't have a worse team, I don't think, than they had at that time."

It had to be very hard for Jim McPhee, a swingman who had a pair of 42-point games that year against the run-it-up Loyola Marymount teams of Paul Westhead.

"He was a great guy, incredibly talented and the hardest-working guy I've been around," Stanford says. "He was good, and he would have been good anywhere."

As for how he sold the concept of talented freshmen redshirting to a group of players who were losing 20 games, Fitzgerald says, "There wasn't a lot of selling. There was a lot of telling."

Somehow that team dug down and won its final two games on the road at San Francisco and St. Mary's. Its final game was a 121–84 loss to Loyola in the WCC tournament, just before the Lions' Hank Gathers dropped dead of a heart attack.

After the USF victory, Dons coach Jim Brovelli shook Fitzgerald's hand.

"These kids have been kind of a sacrificial lamb," Fitzgerald said.

It was a sacrifice apparently worth it. With the six redshirts newly eligible in 1990–1991, Gonzaga would edge back to .500 at 14–14, and it hasn't seen anything but winning seasons since.

Moreover, a culture was put in place. The bar was set higher, self-expectation rose, and there was a revised standard of what was acceptable.

"Those [coaches] really changed the attitude," said Davis. "'Hey, you guys can be a lot more than what this program has been.'

"We kind of started the whole concept of Fitz giving us keys to the gym. We just had guys who wanted it a lot more, who hated losing. Guys like Jeff Brown and Geoff Goss are as competitive as they come."

Even John Stockton could see it, in one of his annual returns to the campus in late summer before Utah's NBA training camp. Stockton was, and is, considered the gold standard for competitiveness at Gonzaga, so programmed to win that he could cause a scene when he lost to his older brother Steve at Trivial Pursuit. On this visit he joined the team in scrimmages and decided that he wouldn't mind taking the lesser Zags as teammates and then willing them to victory.

"I think it just showed that at the end of the day, we want to win as much as you do," Davis said. "I think it helped John respect us."

Having graduated from Few's milder ways as freshmen, the redshirts suddenly found themselves in the cauldron of Fitzgerald's countenance. He was unmerciful.

"'You're the worst that's ever played here!'" Stanford remembers hearing. "And that's coming off the court in the Martin Centre. Every booster could hear it. He was such a throwback."

In retrospect, Stanford wonders whether he would have picked Gonzaga had he known more about the program. Not only was he unaware of Fitzgerald's driving style, he was a baseline-to-baseline player who had to adjust to a rigid system.

"[Fitzgerald] would have liked to control every pass and shot on the court," said Stanford. "He was that specific about what he wanted."

As hard as it was for Stanford, it was worse for at least two of the others, Goss and Davis. As a point guard, Goss was supposed to be Fitzgerald on the floor. It didn't always look like that.

Asked about his role, Goss says, "Try not to kill people. Try not to throw passes off their faces."

Monson remembers what Goss' high school coach in Boise said about him: "He's a great athlete, but he has no idea how to play."

Fitzgerald would tell Goss he was the "worst point guard in the history of Gonzaga." Jauntily, Goss now tells Fitzgerald he's "the worst coach I ever played for."

"The Ritalin kid," Stanford said of Goss.

Brady remembers how some observers would always say of a point guard, "If only he were a step quicker." Says Brady, "With Geoff, the comment was, 'If only he'd slow down a step.'"

As a shooter, Davis was inevitably destined to face Fitzgerald's wrath. He remembers a game against Southwest Texas State in a December 1990 tournament at Montana, in which he struggled mightily in the first half.

Says Davis, "He spent the whole half two inches from me, screaming. At the end, he says, 'You have two minutes to figure it out, or you'll never play here again!' I took it to heart. I think I had 26 in the second half. He was a scary guy."

It became a running joke—in private—among players. Who would set the record for the quickest hook from Fitzgerald? It happened to Jamie Dudley, a point guard who shared time with Goss.

"He subbed in for Goss on a dead ball, and Dudley fouled a guy on the inbounds pass, so not a single second expired," said Stanford. "Fitz subbed for him. From that point on, you couldn't beat that record. It was comical. Of course, you didn't really laugh."

Referring to Fitzgerald, Davis says, "He was a phenomenal practice coach. But he was a nightmare to play for."

But Gonzaga was supremely prepared. Stanford remembers knowing where his opponent was supposed to line up, sometimes before he did.

"I'd tell my guy where he needed to be," he says. "It was like, 'Hey, you're not in the right place. Go set a back screen for that guy to pop out.' They'd go, 'How do you know that?'"

By 1991–1992, Brown was eligible as a third-year sophomore, and the rest of the redshirted six-pack were two years removed from their apprenticeship. They were mortared together. Several of them had nicknames: Brown became "Dough," for a less-than-ripped physique. Brady, the leader, was "Cap." Goss was "Gerbil." Stanford, who morphed himself in the weight room, was the "Body."

Brown was an astonishing force, considering his limited experience; he averaged 20.4 points in WCC play, had 6.7 rebounds, and shot a blistering .655 against 14 league opponents.

Davis, his old high school mate, proved not only a prophet about Brown but a skilled shooting guard, averaging just under 17 points a game, second on the team. He wasn't your prototype junior college recruit.

"He came into my office as a senior," Fitzgerald says. "I said, 'You're not a Division I player.' His father goes ballistic. I said, 'There's 300 schools. You're right and all 300 of us are wrong.'"

Davis, who would become a Rhodes Scholar candidate, was almost ready to attend Notre Dame and forget basketball. But he opted to sustain his game in junior college, and it was a prudent move; he would top the 1,000-point mark in two years at Gonzaga and break the top 10 list in three-point shots.

That team won 20 games for the first time at Gonzaga since 1948. Stanford, now filled out to 205 pounds, was third-leading scorer, and Goss was number four. Spink, who would become a solid defender and the team's leading rebounder two years hence, played significant minutes. Wall was still a deep reserve at that point, contributing later.

Brady, capping his college career, was the sixth-leading scorer at 5.2 points, taking only 97 shots as a senior. But nobody minimizes his role; indeed, he started every game.

"You look at one guy that kind of kept us squirrels together, and it was him," Stanford says. "He was kind of the elder statesman of that crew. He did more behind the scenes than people will ever know."

That team made a breakthrough of sorts at the WCC tournament. Until that year, Gonzaga hadn't so much as won a game in that event, going 0–5 since its inception in 1987. But it beat San Diego and Santa Clara and then lost a 73–70 decision to a Doug Christie–led Pepperdine team for the championship.

There had been talk that the near-miss could land them in the National Invitation Tournament against Washington State, an easy regional matchup. In fact, after the Pepperdine loss, they didn't go on spring break, staying on campus to practice. Then Fitzgerald led them into the Bulldog room in the Martin Centre to tell them they were done. Even at 20 wins, Gonzaga wasn't enough of a name to interest the NIT.

"We still vividly remember looking at the seniors, knowing their career was done," Brown says. "Knowing how painful that was."

At the season-ending banquet, Brady reflected on a career that began so inauspiciously at Washington but ended satisfyingly across the state.

"I remember thinking, 'This is really just the start of something here,'" Brady said. "I had no idea how big it would get."

With virtually everybody except Brady and Davis back the next year, the Zags might have had a better team, even as they fell back to 19 victories. But they played through a broken hand to a key player, Felix McGowan.

"We knew we had a good team," says Goss. "Trying to get over that initial hump was frustrating."

Finally, in 1994, they did. Fitzgerald had always said, "You can't win the league here. It's the worst job in the league." But they did. They stormed to a 6–0 start in West Coast Conference play, put a thunderous 121–85 whipping on Loyola Marymount, and finished 12–2 in conference, 22–8 overall. The victory total tied for second-most in school history.

Again, Brown led with 21 points a game. The nucleus of fifth-year players was buttressed by John Rillie, an Australian with an uncanny shooting touch, who hit 46 percent on threes and was second-leading scorer.

They did leave one piece of unfinished business that was a bitter pill to accept. Needing to win the league tournament to gain Gonzaga's first NCAA berth, the Zags lost to San Diego in the semifinals for the second time in nine days.

There was a consolation prize. This time, Gonzaga was selected by the NIT, marking the school's first postseason tournament as a Division I entity. They traveled to Stanford, which, among other things, meant Brown had come full circle.

"Coming out of high school, my number one choice was Stanford," he said. "Coach [Mike] Montgomery sat me down and said, 'Jeff, I think you have the offensive skills to play, but I don't think you can play defense at the Pac-10 level.' Which is fine. I respect him."

Montgomery was at least half right. Brown went off for 27 points on 9-of-13 shooting against a team that included Pac-10 freshman of the year Brevin Knight, and Gonzaga won, 80–76. Goss had 16 points, and his opposite number, Knight, went scoreless.

"Very fulfilling," Brown said.

Within a week, the careers of five fifth-year seniors were done, put down by a 66–64 loss at Kansas State.

If they left a legacy beyond 61 victories in three years, it is this: in camaraderie and competitiveness, it may not be possible to extract any more from a college experience. They were a model of sorts for what was to come half a dozen years later.

They worked hard, studied hard, played hard. Brown was a first-team academic All-American his final two years. Davis made it his final year. Brady was a two-time district all-academic pick.

When Goss applied to Gonzaga Law School, one of the admissions officers called Ken Anderson, the faculty rep who had been his undergraduate adviser. The officer had concerns about Goss's academic credentials for graduate work.

Anderson knew Goss as well as anybody, knew that he had done a great job athletically, a good job academically, and had had a wonderful social life.

Said Anderson, "The important question you ask Geoff Goss is, 'Do you want to graduate from law school?' If you believe him, he'll kick ass." And he did.

Hardly a day goes by without an e-mail buzzing from one of the classmates to another. They get together to golf, to ski, to see one another get married.

And often, to zing one-liners at each other. Their wit is not something to step in front of lightly. It's an extension of things that happened regularly during their Gonzaga years.

One day, in their off-campus house, Stanford and Goss were watching a major league playoff game with Dudley when Goss waxed skeptical about whether one team could rebound from a 6–1 deficit in the eighth inning.

"If they come back and win this," Goss said, "I'll strip naked, run and touch the library, and come back."

Sure enough, in the bottom of the ninth, it happened, and as Stanford and Dudley raised enough commotion to be evicted, Goss took off across campus wearing only his shoes, fulfilling his promise.

Another time, they boasted to part-time assistant coach Jerry Krause that they would win a certain number of games. They won, and when Krause's bill came due, he had to shed everything but his boxers and jump off the bridge over the Spokane River adjoining campus.

"At the end of the day," Davis says, "I don't remember Pepperdine or Loyola or my 39 against Portland. My six or seven best friends came from that experience."

In 1994, when they were basking in the WCC championship, Brown's mother was telling Dan Monson what a great experience it had been.

"If he'd done this right out of high school," Monson said, "we could have had even more fun."

"I'm so glad he went to Washington first," she insisted, shaking her head.

"Why is that?"

"Because he's so appreciative of the situation now, and I don't know if he would have been if he hadn't been somewhere else."

Among these Zags, the exit poll is pretty much unanimous. Stanford talks to players who attended other schools and says he usually hears that maybe they have one remaining friend, if that, from their team.

"No one's had the experience I had at GU," he says. "I haven't talked to a single guy."

Brown, who had once spent part of college lugging bricks, speaks in almost identical terms.

"I don't see how anybody could have had a better college experience than I did," he said. "I don't see how it could have been possible."

You could say they've landed on their feet. Today, Brown is regional manager for a San Diego computer software company. Wall is vice president of sales for Widmer Brewing Company in Portland. Goss is an attorney in Boise, Idaho. Spink is an engineer in Spokane. Stanford has a construction company in Seattle. Brady is an accountant in Spokane. Davis, who also got a law degree, does mergers and acquisitions for Jeld-wen, a multinational company in Klamath Falls, Oregon.

Musing on his last college team that fell short of the NCAAs, Stanford says, "That was a team that should have been in the tournament. We were pretty damn good. We would have given somebody a run in the first round, maybe won.

"Maybe the run would have started then."

Maybe it did anyway.

7

The Padre

When Gonzaga took the floor to play Wyoming in the first round of the NCAA tournament in 2002, the Zags wore jerseys with an embroidered patch above the breast. It said simply, "Fr. Tony."

What a small, modest circle of commemoration. What a life that inspired it. The great majority of fans at the Pit in Albuquerque and those tuned in on television couldn't have known the reach of this man, couldn't have comprehended how many couples he married and how many of their children he baptized and how many friends he made in his 73 years and how many people his words and his presence delivered from the edge.

He officiated so many of those life experiences, somebody once gave him a business card repeating his own bit of whimsy about his lifestyle: "Have chalice, will travel."

Quite simply, Father Tony Lehmann was the best of Gonzaga—even better than its basketball team—for, oh, as many years as he recalled names effortlessly and remembered to call people on their birthdays and lit up alumni functions just by showing up.

There is a high-octane feeling around Gonzaga, a sense that life holds wondrous things for everyone willing to work a little at finding them. "If one person embodies that whole feeling and spirit," says former Gonzaga coach Jay Hillock, "it would be Father Tony."

Before Gonzaga had a basketball program to play goodwill ambassador, it had Father Tony. He seemed to be everywhere at once, but he couldn't have been, because as part of his amorphous role as alumni chaplain, he spent two decades at the end of the basketball bench—no hood ornament, but a living, breathing example of all that's good in life.

His death March 8, in the days the basketball team was preparing for the NCAA tournament, cut deep. Cory Violette said Father Tony's life's course was a model worthy of duplication. "He was an amazing human being," Violette said. "He had a knack of seeing the positive in anything."

Sometimes, Violette said, players will hear "good game" from fans or parents, and it will infuriate them if they lost or played poorly. But Father Tony would say it, and somehow it would resonate with them.

"He was just a fixture," said former player Jarrod Davis, "like the Bulldog logo."

In the months when leukemia was draining life from Father Tony's body and he was unable to take his accustomed seat on the bench, the Zags always placed a spray of flowers on that chair. Before the game, Zach Gourde, the veteran forward, would dip before the chair and pause to remember some of the wisdom the Padre had imparted back in happier days when they always marked the introductions with a handshake and a hug.

Asked about his best moments with Father Tony, Gourde said, "Just him being in the locker room. Unless you win it all, you always go home a loser. After all those games, talking about what we meant to the school, to the community, what we meant to him and his friends . . . those moments helped make everybody feel better about the entire process."

"He loved the Zags," said a surviving sister, Pat.

They loved him, too.

~ ~ ~ ~ ~

Anthony Joseph Lehmann was born September 10, 1928, in Pinckneyville, Illinois. He grew up in Murphysboro, in downstate Illinois, about 90 minutes southeast of St. Louis.

His father was manager of the Midwest Dairy. His mother died giving birth to Tony's younger sister Barbara, and his Aunt Birdie helped raise seven children.

From the outset, Tony had a full life. Nicknamed "Curly" for a full head of hair he would lose in his twilight years, he got good grades, was excellent in sports—captaining the high school football team—and had a wicked sense of humor. A friend since childhood, Mary Endres of Creve Coeur, Missouri, remembers him being one of a group of miscreants who put her up to setting back a clock at St. Andrew's Grade School so recess would be prolonged. The nuns went across the street to the convent, and it seemed like an unusually long lunch hour, and it was. Sister Blanche was not amused.

"Yes sir," Endres says, "they slapped my jaws good."

Tony and his contemporaries were in their early teens during the height of World War II. In 1943, Murphysboro decided to try to raise funds to donate a Jeep to the American war campaign.

"Father Tony and all the buddies got together," says Endres. "They said, 'Let's do something different.' Behind everybody's back, they put on a drag-queen show—about eight or nine guys with wigs, big bazooms, bracelets, and high heels and gypsy skirts. It was unbeknownst to the school principal."

The revue was such a hit that they put it on again and raised enough money for the Jeep.

It was hard to say with whom he was more popular, boys or girls.

"He had as many girlfriends as he could handle," said another childhood friend, Dr. Bob Mills, a chiropractor still living in Murphysboro. "He had a continual smile going."

Occasionally, at the White City Arena in Herrin, 22 miles away, they would pull in big-name bands of the day—Stan Kenton, Count Basie.

"Tony had access to his father's car, a big Packard with a huge trunk on it," Mills says. "We'd put in two No. 2 washtubs of iced beer, and they'd let us in the side door and give us two booths to set these tubs on. We were some of their favorite people. I was only 17, and I know we went at least two years before that."

In 1946, Tony was graduated from Murphysboro Township High School. He received an athletic scholarship to the University of Illinois but grew disinterested there and told his father he wanted to drop out.

"He was a little bit astounded," said Father Tony, bedridden at the Gonzaga Jesuit House infirmary just six weeks before his death.

Without a military exemption, he went into the army for two and a half years. That took him to Korea, where he was a member of the occupation forces. It was also where, Mills swears, the army realized Tony Lehmann was different.

"My brother and I ended up in Japan," Mills says. "Every letter I would get, he would have a change in rank, clear up to master sergeant. This was done in a two-year enlistment. There's never been anybody to do that but Curly Lehmann."

One day, Tony was a private, then a private first class. Then a corporal and a buck sergeant and then, hash marks and stripes on his lapel.

"They were trying to keep him in the service," Mills says. "He impressed people that much. They broke the rules to get him to go to OCS [officer candidate school] as an officer. Those are supposed to come with years of service, plus experience."

Out of the service, Lehmann was uncertain about his future. He decided to attend Little Rock College in Arkansas on the GI Bill. By the early fifties, the Korean War broke out, but as a reserve, he wasn't called back. However, three of his friends from home were killed in the conflict, and neighbors would tell him, "You did it wisely," referring to his timing entering the military. He felt uneasy with that.

In a twist of serendipity fully in keeping with Father Tony's humor, he would tell you his life then turned at the top of a commode. In his college residence hall, there was a pile of magazines on one of those, and he saw a story about some Carthusian monks, a 900-year-old religious order of Roman Catholics who had established their first foundation in America in rural Vermont.

"And I was driven to it," he said. "I had been born Catholic and had lived in a culture of Catholicism. But it was talking about a group of monks that spent their best energy reminding the Lord about men and women rather than reminding men and women about the Lord. I just knew in the end I wasn't going to be at ease in my spirit unless I went to see what that was all about."

After graduation from Little Rock College in 1952, he painted a house to raise money for a Greyhound bus trip from southern Illinois to Brattleboro, Vermont. A rickety truck took him out to a rural outpost, where the priests had huts in a maple forest.

"They told me at the beginning," Father Tony said, "if you're truly interested to see more about this, and it's not just a lark, then you have to go to Europe."

He bit. At home, his decision was met with every reaction from skepticism to shock. For one, Tony had been engaged to a high school sweetheart.

"We always had the big Apple Festival in Murphysboro," said Mary Endres. "After the big parade, my mother was weeping. We said, 'Mother, what's wrong?' She said, 'You'll find out sometime.' Later on, we learned Father Tony had the calling."

"Curly," Mills admonished him, "you can go in any direction you want. And you're going to sit on top of a mountain and raise grapes."

He gathered up his belongings and was gone, leaving those behind to sort it out. His sister Pat had a daughter who was baptized just before he left. When he saw her again, she was 17 years old.

~ ~ ~ ~ ~

First, he went to Monastere De La Valsainte near Fribourg, Switzerland. At 31, in 1959, he was ordained a priest, at which point he moved to Italy and served in monasteries in Calabria and Pisa for another 10 years.

His sequestered years always were the most incongruous thing about a gregarious, fun-loving man.

"It's kind of like asking a man why you love your wife," he said. "Is she the most beautiful? The best cook? The best companion? Is she the best in bed? She may not be any of those.

"He loves her because he loves her. That's the only thing I could come up with to justify why I was attracted to this and was determined to see it through. I wanted to go because I wanted to go."

He was hooked almost immediately. "Within a week," he said, "I could see that, yeah, there is a possibility that this lifestyle, taken seriously, could actually be enjoyed and beneficial for the circle of relationships I had."

For all but two hours a week, Father Tony was part of a culture of solitude. During those two hours the 13 residents of the hermitage—representing 12 apostles and Jesus—would hike the surrounding mountains.

Three times a day, the monks would come together to chant the prayers and psalms St. Benedict had set down a millennium before them. They farmed a garden and an orchard and raised cattle and were totally self-sufficient.

A cooked meal was served once a day in midmorning, some to be saved for sustenance later in the day. The meal was delivered through a hole in the cottage, and the hooded monks never had eye contact, save for their weekly getaways into the mountains.

Much of the time was spent splitting logs the brothers felled in the forest.

"You had to be your own housekeeper and woodcutter," Father Tony said. "You had to be an Abe Lincoln. You had to reduce logs to stove size. I kept warmer those years sawing that wood than I did burning it."

One of Father Tony's idiosyncrasies in his Gonzaga years was a slightly loopy ability to stand on one leg and contort himself so that he could pick up a dollar bill on the floor with his mouth. Greg Jones of Spokane, a longtime friend who once toured the monastery grounds—now a museum—with Father Tony, believes some of that strength derived from his days as a wood-cutting monk.

"He showed us one of the workrooms," Jones says. "There was a radial-arm saw, all run off a treadle. You literally would be standing on one leg after the other, spinning the saw and cutting boards hour after hour. After a few months of that, you got quite a bit of strength."

When Jones and his wife, Anne Claire, accompanied Father Tony on a trip back to Italy in 1985, they were all on a shoestring budget and stayed in one room. The Padre, as he was known, would get up, do a few exercises, and then stand on his head for about 15 minutes. It was good for his circulation, he explained.

"He said it was his routine for years and years in the monastery life," said Jones. "You could really get an idea of how physical an existence it was."

~ ~ ~ ~ ~

Gonzaga runs a study-abroad program for those with junior standing, and on a trip to Florence in 1969 to renew his passport, Lehmann went by the campus. Then 40, he was asked by the head of the program, the late Rev. Clement Regimbal, S.J., if he could fill in and say Mass for the Anglo-American contingent for the summer months. Father Tony was subsequently allowed a leave of absence by his Carthusian superiors.

Perhaps those months made him realize he had a lot of bonding to do. He enjoyed the interregnum so much that he stayed until 1972, serving as chaplain and treasurer in Florence. Then he entered the novitiate in Sheridan, Oregon, in order to become a Jesuit, and his direct association with Gonzaga's Spokane campus began in 1974, when he became coordinator of Campus Ministry for two years. He would return to Florence for a six-year stint as dean of students there until 1982.

It was in Florence that Lehmann launched friendships with scores of future Gonzaga alumni, kids who were then footloose, adventuresome, and often out of control.

"Tony called himself the dean of students and troubleshooter," said Jones, whose wife spent a year in Florence.

Dean of students, troubleshooter. Ombudsman, father confessor, partner in crime, housemother. He filled all those roles and more.

"He was so familiar with the culture there, as far as being fluent with the language," Jones says. "He didn't just know how to speak it, he knew the idioms, he knew the phrases. There were students who got in trouble, students who fell in love. There were a lot of students who needed Tony's guidance."

One of those was Gary Ittig, now a trial lawyer in San Francisco. Ittig was among three Gonzaga students busted in early 1972 by the Italian cops for possession of hashish. They were sentenced to two years in jail.

"It was still a penal code written by Mussolini," says Ittig, only half jokingly. "You could have illegal aspirin and get two years, or 20 pounds of heroin and get two years."

Father Tony visited the three each week in jail, where at least once, his mischievous spirit and the hedonistic bent of the Gonzagans in Florence was in evidence.

"One time he brought oranges in," said Ittig. "The fellows had stuck vodka in the pulp of the orange with a syringe."

Ittig and his cronies received a presidential pardon after nine months, but it had to be approved at every level of a labyrinthine government. It was Father Tony and an associate who worked hardest to see that each level signed off.

"Imagine bureaucracy here," Ittig says, "and multiply it a hundred times. He certainly was the one on top of it, coordinating and cajoling."

In that matter, as in how he always dealt with religion, Father Tony was nonjudgmental, something that will always stay with Ittig.

"He just bridged that gap," he says. "That was during the Vietnam War, so there was a lot of alienation between older people and college students. He hadn't been out of the monastery life for three years, but he almost came out as one of us."

From Florence, the legend of Father Tony Lehmann grew. He returned to Gonzaga in 1982 as assistant alumni director—a position in which, recalls GU alumni director Marty Pujolar, he was completely miscast.

"That was on an organizational chart," Pujolar says. "Father Tony was supposed to be under me. The reality was, Father Tony worked at whatever Father Tony wanted to do. He was perhaps the best people person I have ever met and perhaps the worst administrator/employee I'd ever met.

"That's actually how his job eventually got to be alumni chaplain. I changed his title in an attempt to actually get someone in the office who would help with the work."

The Padre seemed to know everybody. He remembered their names, even after not seeing them for years. He was like a cross between the Pied Piper, Robin Hood, and Gandhi, calling friends on their birthdays, honoring survivors with a call on the anniversary of the deceased's death, reaching out to the troubled with a helping hand. Greg and Anne Claire Jones were with him one time, walking the streets of Monterosso al Mare on the Italian coast, when a couple of kids emerged from the shadows, cavorting and squealing, "Padre Antonio! Padre Antonio!"

If he met a Gonzaga student, he was likely to be at his or her marriage in a few years. He married dozens of Zag basketball players, baptized their kids, presided over funerals. Whenever somebody connected with Gonzaga had a seminal moment in life, he seemed to be there.

"You could never get where you're going on time, no matter where you were," said Greg Jones. "It happened in Butte, Montana; Spokane; Seattle; San Francisco; Phoenix. Everywhere we went with Tony, someone would recognize him and start talking. It was like walking down the street with Walter Cronkite."

Dan Fitzgerald, the longtime Gonzaga coach, put Lehmann on the bench in the early eighties, and together they marched through the joys and travails of basketball and life, his team and its chaplain.

"He was so good, so naive," said Fitzgerald. "He was at his best when things were bad."

Fitzgerald was hard on his players. He could scream with the best of them. Invariably, the player he had picked on most could be seen in the airport the next day with Father Tony next to him.

If he had a bad bone in his body, it never betrayed him. The team was at Marquette in 1985, Hillock's last year, when the hometown fans got nasty toward the Marquette coach, Rick Majerus, as Gonzaga wedged out a 60–54 victory for the title in the Milwaukee Classic. Lehmann had spent time with Majerus on the trip and was affronted by the booing. He talked to Fitzgerald about it and trudged back to the arena to tell a Marquette administrator the fans were making a mistake to boo Majerus.

At Christmastime, it could be hard for Gonzaga players, especially the young ones. They were finishing finals, perhaps headed soon for a tournament, probably going to be without their families for the holidays.

"He'd always be down at practice," says Fitzgerald. "Guys would light up. You'd think the 22-year-old college guys would mimic the naive priest. Never."

Those around him most know that he wasn't a front-runner, a priest merely for appearance sake at a Jesuit school. He was at his best when things got bad.

One night Fitzgerald heard a knock on his office door. Standing there was a female GU athlete who said she was at the end of her rope with a $500-a-week cocaine problem. Fitzgerald feared she might be suicidal. Such was the sway of the Padre that he was the first one Fitzgerald called to get her help.

He knew little about basketball, but knowledge wouldn't have affected his role anyway. In sports, as in life, he was nonjudgmental.

"He didn't have an out-of-bounds play," Fitzgerald says. "I never, ever heard him say, 'Why didn't you? . . .'"

Too ill to spend another night on the bench in early 2002, Father Tony reflected on the place he held inside him for the Zag basketball team. He admitted it was considerable.

"I realize I'm more involved in it emotionally than I pretend to be," he said.

During the John Stockton years, the Zags lost a buzzer-beater at St. Mary's.

"Well, that nagged at me," he said. "We went to a bar near St. Mary's and got rid of our anger there. I've always slept well, but I tossed and turned that night, thinking, 'If only this had happened, if only we had fouled him.' All the possibilities.

"You're letting something get to you that in the big picture doesn't have the importance you're giving it."

That was his priestly side speaking. Until then, he would tell his friends at those alumni functions, "Three billion Chinese didn't even know we played." It was a glib way of telling people to keep the proper perspective, when deep down, he couldn't either.

He decided to come clean. Some of the losses cut as deeply into him as they did the most avid Gonzaga fan.

"It does have importance," he said. "So ever since then, I threw in the towel at trying to just be a purist about the game and life. Somewhere in reflecting, my involvement in basketball helped a lot to have a realistic perspective, including hurting when you do hurt and telling others when you do.

"I'm kind of wedded to that now. Once I discovered that, I wasn't going to fight it anymore. I like this game, and I'm not gonna deny that I do, most of all because of the association with the men and women who are playing ball."

If he was a saint, he was also a character. Everybody, seemingly, has a Father Tony story.

Tim Barnard, a Gonzaga trustee from Bozeman, Montana, recalled attending the marriage of a friend in California years ago. After a night of long celebration on wedding's eve, several of them returned to their hotel and, in the wee hours, spontaneously took off their clothes and jumped in the swimming pool.

"I'll get my bathing suit," said Lehmann.

"No, Padre," somebody said. "You're jumping in."

And he did. In the meantime, the noise had prompted somebody's call to the cops. In the confusion, Father Tony scraped his forehead badly on the side of the pool. The next day at the wedding, as he dismissed mothers' and grandmothers' condolences for the ugly abrasion, his friends could only snicker in the background.

Barnard had grown to know Lehmann from the Gonzaga-in-Florence program, and soon after, Lehmann stayed at his home in New Jersey. Barnard worked for a time as a laborer on job sites for his father, a gruff, cigar-smoking contractor.

This was the heyday of the movie *The Godfather*. At one site, Barnard's father introduced the Padre only as "Tony, from Italy," drawing some raised eyebrows.

Rumors began spreading. Tony was a hit man from Sicily and the most powerful guy in Jersey.

"Wrong on all three counts," Barnard said in his eulogy to Father Tony. "No. 1, he's not a hit man, he's a priest. No. 2, he's not from Sicily, he's from Florence. And No. 3, he's not the most powerful guy in Jersey, he's the most powerful guy I've met in my life."

Larry Goulet of Everett, Washington, who worked in the GU Campus Ministry with Lehmann, was attending a Gonzaga-in-Florence reunion in San Francisco with his wife, Rose, when Father Tony emerged from his room wearing a white linen sports jacket given to him by the widow of a school trustee. Except one sleeve of the jacket was three inches shorter than the other.

"Tony, you can't wear that!" Rose exclaimed.

"I'll just put one arm through your arm," replied Father Tony, "and we'll get through the evening together."

To the Padre, substance was more important than form, which, truth be told, rankled some Jesuits. Once, holding his chalice while performing an outdoor baptism, he encountered a man who balked.

"I can't," he said. "I'm not Catholic."

"Oh heck," said Father Tony, "God never checks I.D."

His home baptisms used to nettle Sister Mary Therese at St. Aloysius Church on the Gonzaga campus. The good Sister believed that baptisms should be performed in front of the parish congregation at Mass, and she would exact a promise from the Padre not to do it again, after which he would conveniently have a memory lapse.

Knowing that friction, one child's parents expressed concern over the site of a baptism.

"Let me handle Sister Mary Therese," Father Tony said, waving them off. "I've learned it's much easier to ask forgiveness than permission."

At the sight of a sunrise or a sunset or to toast an occasion, he would whip out a flask of his signature Chartreuse. As he explained it, "Monk's medicine" was a liqueur made by the Carthusians from a recipe of 140 herbs passed down from the Middle Ages, when it was first concocted for returning Crusaders.

"Don't do too much," he would say, "just a little."

In his final weeks at the infirmary on the Gonzaga campus, he was visited by a group that included Gary Ittig, his old friend from Florence. They sneaked in a bottle of Chartreuse.

"Pour me a little water," Father Tony said.

Ittig did.

"Put a little of that Chartreuse in," he said.

Ittig did.

"Put a little more in."

He drank and sat bolt upright. "I'm cured!"

Recalling the Padre's touch months after his death, Ittig said, "You've got cynical lawyers here, who don't believe anything in humanity. But they believed him. He would never ask anybody for a dime, but I'm sure because of him, money flowed."

Father Tony never said good-bye to anybody. His trademark phrase in parting was, "To be continued." Every postcard or letter he sent ended with his personal way of saying "so long."

His ability to match faces to names even months or years after an introduction was truly astonishing. Asked about it once by Greg Jones, Father Tony explained that when he met people, he would look them square in the eye and at least twice in the ensuing minute, repeat their name.

"When you were in his company," said his childhood friend, Bob Mills, "there was nothing in the world but him and you."

The presence of Ronny Turiaf on the Gonzaga basketball team, a major breakthrough to the pool of players from Europe, is partly the work of Father Tony. Turiaf's mother speaks mostly French, and when she visited the GU campus, she fell in love with the Padre, who could communicate fluently in her language.

Similarly, at some remote level, the continuation of Mark Few's tenure on the Gonzaga campus might have something to do with Father Tony. Few would visit him in his final weeks and come away shaking his head at the pearls of philosophy he heard. Whether those echoes had some effect on his perspective in a personal debate over a career move—small school to large—can't be measured. But the profound resonance of those meetings was visible on Few's face.

Lehmann shared with Ittig once that he would zoom forward with his mind's eye and decide what he'd like to have on his tombstone. Then he would reverse the process and refocus on what steps he needed to take in his life to make it happen.

~ ~ ~ ~ ~

The Padre was always off to some distant spot—he traveled to 22 countries—and in December 2001, he flew to a remote area of Alaska, in a place where they still carry water. He was with native people there, saying Mass.

Right after Christmas, he planned to fly to New York and catch the Zags' game at Monmouth, and then he'd join old friends like Barnard and Bill Carlin, a Cleveland attorney, for the St. Joseph's game in Philadelphia, and they'd tear into those three-pound lobsters at Bookbinder's.

But he arrived in New York terribly ill and was taken to Lenox Hill Hospital. Carlin knew it was bad when Father Tony asked if Carlin could reposition him in bed.

He was diagnosed with leukemia. Meanwhile, Carlin got two calls from Dr. Dana Shani of Lenox Hill.

"This is one of the most beautiful people I've ever known," she said. "I actually bonded with him. I don't do that."

Word of the Padre's illness was spreading over the expanse of humanity he had touched. That brought the second call.

"Could you please do something to help me free up my line?" Shani asked Carlin. "My phone has been tied up two days now. We're getting calls from around the country. From around the world."

He would return early in January to Spokane, where the Jesuit House infirmary experienced similar clogging. Everybody, it seemed, needed to see him.

"Father Tony," said Pujolar, "had a thousand best friends."

That thousand, and a couple of thousand more, were in the Martin Centre on March 18, 2002, to pay last respects. After a two-hour service, Father Tony's body was taken to a private gathering at Mount St. Michael's outside Spokane, where his Jesuit brothers said prayers.

It was cold—nasty cold. The wind whipped snow at the procession. A cross was lifted from the top of the coffin and given to Father Tony's sister, and it was still silhouetted in snow as the Padre was lowered to rest.

"It seemed to glow," said Carlin, a pallbearer. "It was transcendent."

8

The Zag Way

All right, listen up, all you NCAA-tournament wanna-bes, all you hundreds of struggling basketball programs at every level of college. Here is the formula. This is the recipe that's harder to get hold of than Colonel Sanders', the one that will get your team on SportsCenter *and make it the one nobody wants to play in the postseason.*

You start with . . . well . . . uh . . . forget it.

The truth is, there is so much investment by players and coaches in Gonzaga basketball, so much practice and patience and time required, that it would be a leap to assume this system can be easily duplicated.

Gonzaga coaches are frequently asked about their method of running offense, or the workouts a certain player might run, and they can sometimes oblige the curious with a piece of a large jigsaw puzzle.

But, beginning with the fact that incoming players often redshirt before they ever put on a uniform, this is a program steeped in the idea that it's probably going to take a while—which is not a popular marketing strategy in college basketball. Just as good Kentucky bourbon needs to age, any program that would seek to imitate Gonzaga ought to start with an understanding athletic director.

Gonzaga does things differently, often seeming to run in the opposite direction of most college programs.

In college basketball today, there is an ever-greater emphasis on procuring talent. Never has the pressure been so intense to get the blue-chip athlete. Recruiting lists have proliferated; the Amateur Athletic Union (AAU) summer-basketball scene is a cesspool. A coach's ability to recruit is seen as an asset or liability unto itself, apart from his acumen at developing players once he has them.

A generation ago, when Gonzaga coach Mark Few was in high school, Oregon State had the number one team in the country 50 miles up the road from his home. The center at OSU, Steve Johnson, was a 6'10" player from San Bernardino, California, just east of Los Angeles, who somehow slipped under the radar screens of both UCLA and USC.

Today, that would never happen. Johnson would be spending summers on an AAU team and have all the recruiting attention he wanted. That's precisely the situation with David Pendergraft, the high school junior from tiny Brewster in central Washington, already committed to Gonzaga.

Realistically, Gonzaga, for all its growing reputation, isn't going to get very many prodigious, ready-made talents, although it's getting closer. So the Zags first have to project which players have the greatest upside.

They start with the premise that you're going to have to love the game to succeed there, because you're going to play it a lot.

"We want the kid who shoots before school, takes his ball to school with him, sleeps with his ball," says assistant coach Leon Rice.

Richie Frahm, the guard who was part of two deep NCAA tournament runs, was like that. Rice was leaving his office at 10:00 P.M. one Friday night when into the GU gym came Frahm with his girlfriend. He ran through a brisk shooting workout; she rebounded.

"It'd bring a tear to your eye, watching him work out," says Few. "Sweat would just be dripping off him, not beading. He'd have a set routine, flying around the floor."

If a Gonzaga player is in the gym, it's probably to do more than take idle jumpers. They have a familiar 300-shot workout that's supposed to be done at game speed.

"Most kids, if you don't tell them to do that," says Few, "they'll go down to the gym and screw around."

The tradition of having access to the gym began with John Stockton in the early eighties. It was passed from one basketball junkie to another, eventually to Matt Santangelo to Frahm to Dan Dickau.

It isn't always easy to know just how committed to the game a player might be. The Zags have tried to minimize that pothole by recruiting mostly in the Northwest, giving them more chances to pick the brain of a recruit's coach, counselor, or parents.

Once that passion for the game is in place, it's not so hard for players to pull off another staple of the Gonzaga way: staying around for the summer. The Zags regularly spend those months with each other, lifting weights, pounding the basketball, filing away rough edges.

Willingness to do that, however, magnifies a need for an attribute deeply embedded in the entire enterprise: the players must get along well. Indeed, the Zags have a high saccharine rating. It's something that goes back to a close assessment of recruits, especially on their visits to campus.

"We've probably had three or four guys that our players have vetoed over the years since I've been here," says Few. "'This ain't gonna work. You should have seen him last night.'"

Maybe the recruit was too cocky. Maybe he mistreated women he met. Maybe he got out of control at a party.

Zach Gourde, the GU big man, has been around recruits who were quiet—not normally a problem. "But not a shy, nervous quiet," he says. "More like a standoffish, I-don't-really-want-to-commit-or-get-to-know-anybody-here-because-I-don't-really-want-to-like-this-place quiet. I got the feeling they were afraid to connect because they might actually find something they liked."

Most of the visit screening has to do with determining whether the recruit is team-oriented or whether he's a product of the me-first genre that often makes a volatile sport even more unpredictable.

"Will he fit into the whole team thing?" Few asks rhetorically. "Rather than doing a normal kiss-his-hind-end weekend in recruiting, we'll find out where he stands by kind of calling him out and seeing if he'll blend in."

The Zags have no football program, so there's no Saturday afternoon spent among 80,000 people gauging the university's support of athletics. The focus is mainly on the basketball program, for better or worse.

This, says Few, is the pitch: "You come here, you'll have a bunch of guys who really care about you, and you're going to be part of something greater than yourself.

"Our staff is going to be at your service. We're here to make you as good as you can be. You're not here to serve us; we're here to serve you. We're going to try to take you from here and put you there."

Most schools have some similar means by which players can filter out recruits they term undesirable. But the more gifted the prospect, the more difficult it is for coaches to turn down a potential behavioral problem.

"Thank God for unanswered prayers," says Few, smiling.

At the same time, if the players on the roster aren't of one accord, there may be mixed signals on whether to accept the recruit. Thus, there is the need for cohesiveness.

"Sometimes," says Few, "you don't want to listen because a kid might be so talented."

The reason the temptation to recruit a potentially problematic player exists is that Few buys into the idea that collective good will overcome the marginal seed he may sign into the program.

"Our kids aren't perfect, but they're pretty darn dialed in," he said. "If you have one or two kids that are a little wild, that's fine, because the majority are always going to bring them back to where we are. Now if you get six of them, you've got problems, and that's what you have in a lot of these programs, I think."

Peer pressure is thus powerful within the program. A player from a decade ago, Matt Stanford, remembers it translating to matters like academics. Those whose grade point average fell below a 2.5 were required to attend study hall.

"It wasn't cool to be in study hall," Stanford says. "It was, 'What are you doing in study hall?'"

There are no-nos, big and small, often policed by players, not coaches. One is sitting in the back of classrooms; another is wearing headphones in class. When Cory Violette observed a young teammate doing that, he discussed it with Rice, who turned the matter back to Violette to handle.

Jerry Krause, the Gonzaga director of men's basketball operations, has observed coach-player interaction in his roles as head coach at Eastern Washington and professor of physical education at West Point. He sees that traditional barriers between coaches and players have been broken down at Gonzaga.

"Players seem to be more empowered," he said. "They're important. When you're empowered, you do more yourself."

In a game in December of 2000 at Wisconsin–Green Bay, Few approached the locker room at halftime, ready to excoriate his team for a lousy first half that would turn into a 72–61 loss.

"I hear Mark Spink just crucifying them," says Few, referring to one of his senior leaders. "As I walked in, he continued to do it. It was not just words; it was calling some people to the carpet. That's what it's all about. If you have that, you have people buying into the system."

~ ~ ~ ~ ~

The first thing a Gonzaga freshman basketball player does when he gets on campus is track-and-field.

Freshmen are paired with seniors, and they compete against teammates in a two-man decathlon. It includes a mile run in a required six minutes (with a penalty of morning conditioning for the laggards); a 40-yard dash; a mile relay, each member running two legs alternately; three weight-room exercises, including bench press, military press, and pulldown; a jump reach; a side-to-side box jump; free throws; and a two-on-two game of hoops.

If they're not too exhausted, the teammates bond.

The next discovery for many freshmen is to find out they're redshirting, sitting out the season to develop physically, learn the system, and make a transition into the classroom. Gourde did it, and Matt Santangelo before him, and a whole line of players before them.

"I got that from Fitz," said Few, referring to former Gonzaga coach Dan Fitzgerald.

It isn't for everybody. Increasingly, Gonzaga finds itself on the final lists of more gifted players, who usually prefer to play early if they can. And while the Zags can cite many players whose steady development began with a year sitting out, redshirted guard Josh Reisman points out that it's not necessarily an effective opening to a recruiting pitch to say, "Hey, come here. You're going to redshirt."

But for those players in it for the long haul, the ones realistic enough to know they probably aren't going to be millionaires at 22, it's a sensible preamble to their careers.

"You're going to be a better player at 22 than you are at 18," Few says. "Maybe you'll play 8 minutes as a freshman, but if you look at the potential at the back end, that could be a 32- or 33-minute [a game] year."

Among recent Gonzaga standouts who didn't redshirt are guard Richie Frahm; Casey Calvary, who, as a raw talent with tremendous upside, would have been a great candidate; and Violette, who played 12 minutes a game as a freshman but took a quantum leap forward by his sophomore season.

"I was very competitive," said Frahm, who played professionally in the Philippines and is trying to restoke a shot at the NBA. "I would have had a hard time sitting on the sideline. At the time, I didn't regret it. But as you look at your professional career, I wish I would have redshirted. It's easier said than done."

The close bonds forged at Gonzaga, both in basketball and on campus, bring two dynamics to the redshirt phenomenon. First, a player figures to be more receptive to sitting out, and prolonging his college career, if he is surrounded by people he enjoys.

On the other hand, as Gourde points out, "It's hard at the end of your fourth year, when the guys you came in with are gone and all your friends on campus outside the basketball team are getting ready to graduate.

"All my friends are moving to different phases of their lives, and I'm still running around playing college basketball." Having said that, Gourde acknowledges, "There's something to be said for not going out into the world for another year."

Guard Ryan Floyd, a key piece of the Zags' 1999 and 2000 runs, redshirted almost out of necessity. He came from tiny Sprague-Harrington High in eastern Washington, where there were 50 students and a graduating class of 11.

"I can't think of one person that's come in here that it didn't benefit," he says of redshirting. "I see no negative in it."

Reisman, part of a state-championship team at Mount Vernon, Washington, in 2001, sees the value in being able to spend a freshman year adjusting to school.

"It definitely helped me academically," he said. "I struggled the first semester in school. Instead of averaging 16 credits, I can average 13."

Fundamentally, the concept of redshirting is part of the bigger Gonzaga theme.

"The mantra has been development, development, development," says Krause. "The elite programs always get the best players in the country. If you're not always going to get the best players, you'd better develop them more."

~ ~ ~ ~ ~

If you're wedded to the old coaching bromide that defense wins championships, you might not expect this response on that front from the Gonzaga coaches: horsefeathers.

True, the Zags pay more than lip service to defense. They were seventh in the nation in 2002 on opponent field goals, allowing only 38.5 percent a game.

"You can certainly play containment-type defense," Few says. "Team defense has always been our philosophy, that you're going to have to score over a hand. We've been really solid defensively the last couple of years."

Still, when a Gonzaga coach scouts a prospect, he's going to be less focused on whether the player moves his feet and plays defense than he is on some other things the Zags consider more important.

Can he shoot? Can he score?

"As long as they're keeping score, and the object is get more points than they do, . . ." Few says, not needing to finish his thought.

If shooting percentages are an indication, today's basketball has become less precise and more athletic. It's ever more ballistic and fast-paced but not more exact.

NCAA statistics show a long downward trend in field-goal shooting, recently broken every three or four years by a slight uptick. In 1981–1982, the national field-goal percentage was 47.9. By 1991–1992, it had dropped to 45.7, and five years after that, it had dropped another two percent to 43.7. It was 43.8 in 2001–2002.

John Wooden, the legendary UCLA coach, coined the phrase, "Be quick, but don't hurry." The best way for a team to become quick is to recruit athleticism, and that's the approach of many college coaches.

This is the thinking: the athletic player is better able to move his feet and play defense, better equipped to jump, and more apt to separate himself on offense from the less athletic player.

Gonzaga is not likely to consistently attract a stable of superior athletes. Instead, its philosophy on the floor has to do with this observation by Few: "I don't think you can take a nonscorer and teach him to be a scorer."

Ergo, not very far into any recruiting assessment, Gonzaga coaches want to know whether a player can shoot.

"One thing we put a premium on is skill," says Few. "Shooting the basketball is very important to us."

Gonzaga's best moments in NCAA tournaments have been when it was flowing on offense and scoring. It has never won an NCAA game scoring in the sixties. All four times it did, it lost.

Its tournament trademark has been offense—at least until the uncharacteristic 2002 meltdown against Wyoming. Before that, the Zags had shot a creditable 45.5 percent in their 10 recent NCAA games and hit 42.2 percent of three-point shots. They had scored 86 against Virginia and 82 against Stanford and St. John's.

Few's basketball philosophy has always had an offensive lean to it, dating back to his high school days in Creswell, Oregon. Even today, he puts defensive strategy in the hands of his top assistant, Bill Grier.

Gonzaga's recruitment of Aaron Brooks, a point guard from Franklin High in Seattle, is instructive. As the Zags looked for a point guard for the future, they scouted Brooks closely. He was a junior in 2002, quick, a shade under 6', and considered ahead of the curve as a defensive stopper.

He was also from a solid family and represented a possible inroad into the Seattle inner city, a lode that has been tough for the Zags to mine. He might have seemed a must-have prospect for them, but as the summer of 2002 approached, they had reservations. They weren't convinced he could shoot.

Along with shooting and scoring ability, Gonzaga looks for the hard-to-define attribute of "feel" for the game—a sense of timing, flow, and anticipation. It's important in their motion offense that players have something innate that allows them to make the crisp pass and find the open man.

"Zach [Gourde] was kind of a lumbering ox in high school, and you could see where some guys just weren't interested in that," says Few. "But again, you put a premium on being smart, understanding the game of basketball—and he could score. He's always been able to score. He had great hands, and if you're a big kid with great hands, there's always a spot for you."

Ditto Rich Fox, the Colorado transfer newly eligible in 2002–2003. "He's big, slow, whatever," says Few. "But he can score. He'll catch everything, and he'll pass out of there."

~ ~ ~ ~ ~

During a lengthy apprenticeship under Fitzgerald that began in 1988, Few looked at the offense and wondered: is there a better way? Fitzgerald was an exponent of the "flex" that has been widely associated with Gonzaga, a highly structured system in which the five players circulate to the same five spots on the floor interchangeably. It was successful, but Few thought it somewhat stifling, especially combined with Fitzgerald's penchant for stern oversight of any lapses in execution.

"All the way back from high school," Few says, "I knew the best teams were the ones that played with a lot of freedom on offense, that played up-tempo and weren't looking over at the bench. Our early teams with Fitz were always looking over at the bench."

Few thus developed an offensive style based on "motion" offense, retaining the flex when he wants to rein it in somewhat but giving players a high degree of freedom. It is at once complicated and spontaneous.

"I call it real cerebral," says Krause. "It isn't for every player."

Motion offense has been associated with coaches like Clair Bee, the icon from New York; Hank Iba, better known for his defensive wizardry at Oklahoma State; and, more recently, Bob Knight. It's a system based on screening away from the ball and requiring offensive players to "read" what defenders are doing, creating options for cutter and screener.

Few has developed at least 55 offensive sets tied into the motion offense, so as to direct the ball to a specific spot—to a hot shooter or a preferable matchup. He calls them "entries."

"It's a great way to score," he says. "Instead of just coming down and running motion, we get a huge percentage of our points off our entries."

Basketball savants like Pete Newell had a warning about motion offense: it could easily become too perimeter-oriented, as teams relied heavily on the screener popping out for a shot. Gonzaga has had success in curbing that by posting a big man while the requisite cuts of motion offense, toward and away from the basket, are taking place.

Few is the brains behind the offense, with Rice providing an extra layer of evaluation. Says Krause, "Mark and Leon are really very good. For young coaches, they're exceptional at innovation in motion offense."

Grier, guaranteed in writing to replace Few if Few leaves and he stays at Gonzaga, handles the defense. The Zags play primarily man-to-man but throw some zone at opponents in a system that Krause says "has improved over time. Before, under Fitz, there wasn't a real defined philosophy. He was kind of groping around a lot of different places. I thought Bill brought a real simplicity and consistency."

~ ~ ~ ~ ~

In keeping with the goal of development, Gonzaga does something else that sets it apart from some other programs. It uses part of its NCAA-allotted 20 hours a week in-season for individual workouts.

Says Krause, "Coaches generally say, develop the team during the regular season, but you develop individuals during the off-season. I think we've carried it a step further."

Gonzaga players get 45 minutes of individual work twice a week during the season. It's in small groups that can number no more than four—per NCAA rule—but it's pointed at skill development.

"It might be in the morning, before practice, or after practice," Krause says. "Usually it's by position—perimeter or post players. It isn't like you're spending appreciably more time, but I think you're sending a message that individual development is important, that you've got to take responsibility for yourself, too."

Those sessions are important especially to Gonzaga's many-faceted offensive system. "You really need to get good fundamentally," Krause says, "in footwork, passing, and catching."

Before Gonzaga ever saw an NCAA tournament, Fitzgerald remembers Dan Monson, his chief assistant, leaping off the bench in a game and screaming, "Goddamnit, that's not us!" He was immediately understood.

"Us" at Gonzaga is a tightly controlled way of doing things, but it's control by consensus, not by autocracy. Gonzaga has found a means to success from acclamation within.

It has always been bothersome to the Zags that they are pictured as something other than very good basketball players, as if they were a phenomenon that materialized from ethereal vapors.

"It used to drive me crazy when we were winning 20 games," said former player Jeff Brown. "At times, we were viewed as a well-coached, hard-nosed, scrappy team. However, we weren't viewed as having good players."

After endless references to Cinderella through 1999 and 2000, those tired analogies have mostly died off. They've expired in the wake of tedious redshirt years put in at Gonzaga, and individual workouts, and summers sacrificed for the team good.

Or maybe they disappeared when those T-shirts sprung up on campus: "Cinderella, My Ass."

9

The Zag Effect

About a 10-minute walk southeast of the Gonzaga campus is the West Coast River Inn, and it is here that the effect of Zag basketball is felt keenly. On the surface, it's your basic clean motel, hosting conferences and businesspersons coming through Spokane. But its guest list also includes some 80 Gonzaga students, who have bigger rooms than those in the dormitories, their own bathroom, and use of a pool.

"I hate to admit this," says Philip Ballinger, Gonzaga's dean of admission. "They can even get room service."

The students represent a spillover in the Gonzaga enrollment for the school year 2001–2002. Over the years, university officials had come to anticipate a "yield" of 33 to 35 percent on its admissions, meaning the number that actually choose to enroll once the school admits them. All of a sudden, the yield jumped to slightly above 40 percent. Although the school was expecting slightly fewer than 900 entering freshmen, some 979 jumped aboard, stunning Gonzaga officials and sending them scurrying to make a deal with the River Inn.

"This year," Ballinger says, "there is a cap number. Up to now, we've had a pot without a lid."

Gonzaga had a couple of strong years of enrollment in the early nineties, but the numbers flattened in the midnineties, hovering slightly above the 500 mark annually. As late as 1998, freshman enrollees totaled only 569.

Then something happened. In 1999, five months after the Zags went to the NCAA Elite Eight, enrollment jumped to 701. It would be a risky conclusion that basketball created the bump, yet students have until May 1 to declare their intentions, and there was a five-week gap between Gonzaga's near-miss against Connecticut in the regional final and the deadline for declaration.

The trend continued. By the time the incoming students of 2000 were attending classes, Gonzaga had won five games in the NCAA tournaments of 1999–2000. Enrollment had climbed to 796 in 2000, and it shot to the record 979 by 2001.

Skeptics say too much of the boom is ascribed to whether five guys can direct a ball through a steel hoop. The demographics pointed to an enrollment rise anyway; Ballinger cites a mini–baby boom, particularly in the Northwest but also across the country, which augurs a high number of upper teens being college-ready until perhaps 2010.

But those in the know at Gonzaga realize there's something else at work.

"I don't know of that many students who decided to come to Gonzaga University because we had a winning basketball team," says Ballinger. "I think I've had one student tell me that out of hundreds and hundreds.

"But I'm sure basketball opens a window. That's part of what's going on. I can't prove it, but I'm pretty sure about it. The Flutie Effect, huh?"

That's the name that was given to a phenomenon in the eighties at Boston College, when Heisman Trophy–winner Doug Flutie seemed to boost the profile not only of the football team but of the school, particularly after a memorable last-second "Hail Mary" pass to beat Miami.

While there is no empirical way of pinpointing whether students are picking Gonzaga because of basketball success, it's a virtual certainty that basketball is introducing the name to candidates who might not have known it otherwise.

"I'm thinking of basketball, but sort of indirectly," Ballinger says. "Somebody who might not even be a basketball fan . . . a kid might not care about basketball one way or another, but they care about fun and they care about excitement and they hear their classmates talk about GU in this neat sort of way.

"Maybe they get something from us, or they're at a fair and they pass our table. All of a sudden, there's something there that allows them to take the next step that wasn't there before. Buzz, I guess it is."

Ballinger has a suspicion that the buzz may even be attracting top-notch faculty.

"All of a sudden, it has a little bit of cachet, a little bit of burn to it, and they say, 'Oh, at least I'll look at it,'" he says. "And then they start to look at it, and they say, 'It sounds possibly pretty neat.' So I'm thinking it's going to help us across the board."

Ballinger's is not an isolated opinion. One floor above him in the Administration Building, whose offices are fronted by handsome, wood-carved double doors, sits Father Robert Spitzer, the president of the university. A Honolulu native, he has had a long association with the school, beginning with an undergraduate degree in 1974.

Spitzer, 50, is nothing if not bullish on the effect of basketball at Gonzaga, a rise that has paralleled his own tenure beginning in the summer of 1998.

"I think it's had four major effects, certainly," he says. But when he's finished with those observations, he comes up with a fifth one.

The first involves enrollment. Spitzer has seen two facets of that phenomenon: the same increase in yield that Ballinger noted, plus a greater geographic diversity than the school knew before. "We get applications from quite a way's away," Spitzer says. "We're getting a lot from the Midwest now that we never got, quite a few from Texas. We even have some from the East Coast."

The second is name familiarity. "Gonzaga is a household name," Spitzer says. "Reputationally, we have moved from a regional university to a national university. We're known everywhere. I say 'Gonzaga' in New York City or Florida and people know who we are and what we are. No one ever has to say 'Who's Gonzaga?' anymore, or 'Where's that?'"

In concert with the expansion of reputation, there has developed, Spitzer believes, a sense that Gonzaga stands for more than winning basketball games. He likes the fact that when the Zags have appeared on the NCAA interview dais, they have presented themselves well. "It's that Gonzaga is a good school for character," he maintains, referring to the public perception. "Gonzaga is great for education, because those kids are speaking in complete, complex sentences. They look like they're really good kids to be around. Or, Gonzaga is a great school for . . . you name it."

The third effect has to do with fund-raising. Spitzer has witnessed an increase in both the school's athletic fund-raising and the general university coffers. The Zags announced last April a $119-million capital campaign, a drive surely fueled in part by the momentum of the basketball team. "It's an intangible that's darn near impossible to measure," Spitzer says, "but anyone with instinct knows that it's there, and it's helping. I'm on the fund-raising trail a lot, and I know this is really helping."

Fourth is campus spirit. No one can quantify what it means or to what degree it has been boosted by basketball, but clearly it's there. "Spirit on campus is generally high and has always been high," Spitzer says. "But this has added an extra level. It's been wonderful to be around."

Before Spitzer can complete his thought, he comes up with a fifth benefit. Fund-raisers talk about endowments, and you could think about this aspect as endowment: the mere fact the basketball program is growing by dint of its own momentum.

"No one in my position likes to lose anyone like Dan Dickau," Spitzer says. "That guy is wonderful on all levels—from the level of athletic performance, his character, his values, just who he is as a human being. On the other hand, I also have to say, he has contributed to the future, because he has attracted people like himself right back to the program."

In addition, it's possible that Gonzaga's success has rippled out to affect admissions at other schools in the league. At least that's the belief of Dick Davey, the longtime coach at Santa Clara.

"What they make you realize is, it is possible to carry the thing beyond just getting into the tournament," Davey said. "All that helps admissions at all the small schools.

"I would venture a guess that every school has improved because of their success. Maybe in a minor way, but it's not a league anymore that doesn't have identity. It has identity now."

~ ~ ~ ~ ~

In athletic director Mike Roth's office in the Martin Centre sits the by-product of Gonzaga basketball that most excites those around the program. Actually, it's only a mock-up resting on the floor against a wall, but there's apparently no stopping it now.

It's the Kennel: the Sequel. As of last spring, the Zags were attempting to raise 80 percent of an estimated $23 million needed to launch work on a new arena that would go up at the site of August/A.R.T. Stadium, where the Gonzaga baseball team now plays. That field would be relocated to a site near the law school.

"It'll be a great situation," says Mark Few. "It'll be just like an extended Kennel. Instead of having one side over there [for students], we'll have them on three sides."

That probably will not excite Gonzaga opponents, who are 12–140 in the Kennel over the past 12 seasons. But it certainly has Roth, as well as those who crunch numbers for the athletic department, titillated.

During the high times of Gonzaga hoops, the Zags haven't been able to capitalize fully on their success because, at 4,000 capacity, the Kennel is so small.

"They're just not generating money off our games here," Few says. "There are not enough seats to generate money, where this could have been, and should have been, quite a revenue-producing cycle."

These are the numbers: in the Kennel, the Zags had only about 1,500 seats sold as the result of season tickets, held by about 425 patrons who had to donate a minimum of $150 to get a single seat. Roth thinks that in a new, improved 6,000-seat Kennel, the allotment of season-ticket sales could double to 3,000, bringing with it a significant increase in revenue from so-called seat licenses.

Gonzaga hasn't offered ticket sales on a per-game basis for four years. Roth says there is no formalized waiting list for season tickets, but he adds, "If we wanted to put out a press release that Gonzaga is taking reservations for season tickets, that list [of committed seats] would exceed 3,000 in a heartbeat, if not more. The interest in the program is somewhat mind-boggling."

Given that, is a 6,000-seat arena large enough? Roth says it is. Gonzaga arrived at that size with the help of a Midwestern consulting firm that spent time with officials of the Spokane Arena and did a feasibility study on the habits of the Spokane population.

Such an arena would be the largest on-campus facility in the West Coast Conference, topping the 5,300-seat gym at San Francisco and the 5,000-seat capacities of Santa Clara, Portland, and San Diego.

"We don't want to sacrifice the atmosphere," said Roth. "We just want to get more people into it. Ultimately, the goal would be to never turn anyone away, or only turn one person away. We feel very confident that 6,000 is the right number that will allow us to expand our season-ticket base."

As the Zags were in the homestretch of their 80 percent fund-raising requirement last spring, the debate du jour was whether to include suites in the building as well. Suites would be an obvious way to tap the cash cow of basketball, but would they ruin sight lines? Would they diminish the atmosphere now created by the Kennel Club? And perhaps most crucial to the Jesuits in charge, would they be counter to the image of a small, liberal-arts college that prides itself on academics?

"There are some people who think suites don't do anything to affect the reputation, to affect the community spirit," said Spitzer. "Suites are just suites. They're just up there. There are others who think it pushes you one step further toward looking like a pro team or something."

Few, who always thinks big, shrugs at the suite dialogue.

"I think you should have them," he says. "I don't see how that would take away, if they're up higher, keeping students down low. I don't see how it's going to affect the ambience at all."

~ ~ ~ ~ ~

While the Kennel's limited capacity has kept Gonzaga's financial intake at less-than-optimum levels, the same can't be said for the West Coast Conference office, which has been—and will be—cashing checks thanks to the Zags for a few more years.

A few years ago the NCAA attempted to eliminate the so-called "$250,000 free throw"—in which tournament victories, sometimes hinging on just one free throw, resulted in a flat payout to the winning team (for its conference) for advancing to the next round. Now it dishes out the booty from its multibillion-dollar deal with CBS on the basis of an ongoing, six-year window. For instance, the year after Gonzaga made its surprise run to the Elite Eight in 1999, the West Coast Conference began a six-year cycle in which it received each year a "unit" payment of $94,000 per victory. For the 1999–2000 season, in other words, it took in $282,000 for three additional games from Gonzaga's 1999 labors in the NCAA tournament, on top of the unit of $94,000 that the Zags—or the WCC automatic representative—would earn. But that $94,000 has been going up because of increases in CBS's rights fees, to the neighborhood of $130,000 per unit.

The league will realize payments from those extra three units all the way until the 2004–2005 season—plus an extra two units earned by the Zags on top of their automatic-berth unit for their Sweet 16 appearances in each of the years 2000 and 2001.

If that sounds complicated, this shouldn't be: Mike Gilleran, the WCC commissioner, calculates that by the end of the 2006–2007 cycle of six-year periods—finishing the last of the Zags' three straight Sweet 16 appearances—Gonzaga will have banked $5,434,757 extra for the league on top of what its first-round games would have netted.

For the Atlantic Coast Conference or the Big Ten, that's loose change—money that's almost come to be expected from a Duke or an Illinois. For instance, while the Zags won seven NCAA tournament games from 1999–2001, Pac-10 teams combined to win seventeen, worth about $13 million for their league.

In the West Coast Conference, that $5 million–plus is a windfall. The participating school gets a little kickback from the league via this formula: $20,000 for one NCAA game, $40,000 for two, $80,000 for three, and $100,000 for four. But the rest goes to the WCC office, where it is used to defray a wide range of expenses, like payment for basketball officials, lease of computers, office needs, and tabs for putting on other league championships.

"It isn't a question of us needing a certain number of units per year to stay in business," Gilleran says. "But the reality is, it's always nice, whether it's your personal or your business life, to have more money coming in than less.

"The broader benefit, the more important benefit for everybody in the country that doesn't play Division IA football, is that it sends a message: it can be done. Success can be achieved, and it can be accomplished without compromising academic standards."

While Gonzaga and, to a lesser extent, Pepperdine, have buffed up the national profile of the West Coast Conference, in terms of television the WCC is still a 19-inch black-and-white compared to the HDTV big screens of the ACC, Big Ten, and Southeastern Conferences.

"We've been looking for ways to enhance our television," says Gilleran. "It's been very difficult to get through."

Any occasional sliver of an opening in ESPN's Big Monday programming, however, has been filled by conferences like the Mountain West. One reason is the WCC presidents have been loath to approve any measure that would result in more missed class time.

"If you're not a football conference, basically you're paying to get on television," Gilleran says. "We were able to get a deal with ESPN in which they guarantee us a couple of appearances. It doesn't sound like much, but it's two more than most leagues have."

~ ~ ~ ~ ~

To the rest of the coaches in the WCC, Gonzaga has become both boon and bane. Yes, they like the "drafting" effect, that some recruits might have a passing knowledge of their league due in part to the Zags' success, and yes, they appreciate even a slight betterment of their TV exposure. As San Diego's ninth-year coach Brad Holland puts it, "I've seen things get better in the conference, and Gonzaga has certainly helped to that end, with an ESPN contract for the first time. That's not going to get done without Gonzaga."

That's the good news. The bad is that even as university presidents are wont to keep perspective on athletics versus academics, they are more inclined to wonder why it's happening at Gonzaga and not at their own school.

"Oh yeah," Davey says. "To a certain extent, administrators at other schools say, 'If they can do it, why can't we?'"

Holland says Gonzaga has changed his recruiting, or at least put a blue-and-red tint on it.

"You know how the PGA players talk about, 'Hey, if I'm going to beat Tiger, I need to train hard, hit the ball farther'?" he says. "I do that with our program. If we're going to beat Gonzaga, we're going to have to get better, because they're the standard."

So when Holland looks at a high school forward, he wonders whether he can bang with Cory Violette. When Holland assesses a big guard, he evaluates whether he can play with Blake Stepp.

"I don't know whether it's put pressure on us," says Holland. "But it's challenged the rest of us. I feel our program has really improved. But Gonzaga's program has gone to the moon. While we've gotten better, they've gone national."

~ ~ ~ ~ ~

Back in 1992, Gonzaga assistant coach Bill Grier had a suggestion for the head coach, Dan Fitzgerald. Grier was aware of a successful basketball camp for high school teams at the University of Nevada and wanted to try such an overnight camp at Gonzaga.

"He said, 'Try it,'" Grier recalls. "'I don't think it's gonna fly.'"

It flew.

Today, Gonzaga's summer basketball camps are easily the most popular in the Northwest, as the Zags have taken advantage of their own emergence and the descent of other programs in the region.

Some 200 teams were due onto the Gonzaga campus in the summer of 2002, split into three weekly sessions. During one week of the 2001 camp, 82 teams were on hand—kids being coached, coaches soaking in training methods, and relationships being established.

The camp scene, like that of college basketball in general, is ever changing. In the seventies and early eighties, former Washington State coach George Raveling put a major emphasis on it, and the Cougars had a huge following extending into Canada. But the lean times of recent years crimped that trend, and for the summer of 2002, WSU offered just day camps for individuals, and only on four days.

Washington had some momentum with its camps in the late 1990s, but that was blunted by two forces: a complete renovation of its arena, Hec Edmundson Pavilion, which caused the camps to be farmed to local high schools; and the competitive bottoming out of the program.

Meanwhile, the popularity of the Gonzaga camps has exploded. The Zags offer all sorts of options, from team camps and individual camps to a parent-child camp. Not only is it a financial bonanza, it's also one of the most common means nowadays for colleges to get an early footing with prospective recruits, who can get a flavor for the coaches, players, and campus. Gonzaga players like Blake Stepp and Sean Mallon got an early bead on the place—and, in turn, Gonzaga coaches on them—at camp.

You can't be anywhere near the Martin Centre in the summertime without hearing the bounce of a basketball. Gonzaga has six indoor gym floors and puts up 12 portable baskets on the adjoining tennis courts. Still, that's not enough to accommodate 82 teams, so the school has been renting out some of the local high school gyms to handle the crush.

"The camp was rolling pretty good before we got into the last four years," said Grier. "But the last four years helped."

By tradition, the least-tenured assistant coach on the staff is a key organizer of the camps. In 2002 that was Tommy Lloyd, a 28-year-old Washingtonian with a perpetual smile and a thick file of not only camp registrations but also applications of coaches who want to work it.

"I get requests to work our camp from all across the country, even Europe," Lloyd says. "We get them from Croatia, Germany, France. Three years ago, we didn't get any requests. We were scrapping and clawing to get workers locally."

The high school and junior-college coaches who accompany their teams or work the camp get a glimpse into the Gonzaga system. There are a lot of Division I coaches who would love one as well.

Those coaches want to know about the motion offense. They want to know about the flex. They want to know about the improved rebounding.

Cal-Irvine coaches spent a day with Mark Few to discuss motion. Marquette wanted Dan Dickau's complete workout schedule.

"We get coaches that take over programs," said assistant coach Leon Rice. "They call and want the whole blueprint."

After Gonzaga mangled Fresno State, 49–32, on the boards during a victory in December of 2001, the coaches were having a beer in the hotel bar when a man with a familiar face walked in. It was Jerry Tarkanian, wanting to pick Rice's brain on what the Zags had done to upgrade their rebounding.

On some fronts, Gonzaga is reluctant to be too forthcoming, like the restaurant chef who won't reveal his recipe for beef *bourguignonne*. Fundamentals, no problem. Nuances, house secrets, forget it.

"I like to be a little guarded in what we give out," Rice said.

Then there was Texas. Gonzaga had a 12-rebound edge in a victory over the Longhorns in the 2001 Great Alaska Shootout, and the Longhorns wanted to fly in a couple of coaches to spend a day learning the basis of Gonzaga's board work.

Few said he'd do it, with a hitch. Texas would have to agree to play a home-and-home series with his team.

So far, no response to that one.

~ ~ ~ ~ ~

More evidence of Zagmania is hits on the school's athletics website, GoZags.com. In November of 1999, just after the Elite Eight run, there were 67,911 hits. A year later in the same month, the number was 133,946. After three straight runs to the Sweet 16, the count in November of 2001 was a bustling 336,821, or an increase of 151 percent over November of 2000. January's comparison was even more stark. For January 2000, 2001, and 2002, the increases went from 102,930 to 139,639 to 376,496, the last jump representing a 170 percent increase.

The only month that showed a decrease? March 2002, when Gonzaga bowed out of the NCAA tournament nine days earlier than it had the previous year.

~ ~ ~ ~ ~

As sharply as visits to the website have risen, nothing symbolizes Gonzaga's rise quite like sales of merchandise.

True story: last spring, a routine campus tour for prospective enrollees began with this introduction:

"Hi, I'm Ashley from Portland," said a high school girl. "And I just want to get some Gonzaga gear."

Ashley is not alone. Figures from the Official College Sports Network (OCSN), formerly FansOnly, show Gonzaga ninth in gross revenues behind Oklahoma, Maryland, Miami, Notre Dame, Illinois, Purdue, Michigan State, and Tennessee. Of those eight, only Tennessee and Illinois have had a "store" with OCSN for less time than Gonzaga. Mike Carlton, OCSN marketing manager, says Gonzaga's monthly average of gross revenues is higher than any Pac-10 school on its network.

Numbers from Collegiate Licensing Company (CLC) of Atlanta also show Gonzaga doing well at the cash register. CLC is the intermediary between licensees, or manufacturers, and retailers. Licenses are granted through CLC, which represents about 200 universities, conferences, bowl games, and the NCAA.

In the third quarter of 1999, after the Elite Eight appearance, there were only two licensees producing Gonzaga products. That number had shot up to 58 by the second quarter of 2000, and for the same quarter of 2001, to 100.

All of this means not only a sharp uptick in revenue, but also national exposure. It's possible now to walk into an airport in Philadelphia and buy Gonzaga apparel.

The change in royalty dollars is dramatic. For the fourth quarter of 2001, those numbers skyrocketed by 323 percent over the same period of 2000, according to CLC.

Gonzaga assistant athletic director Mike Hogan says nationwide sales of Zag gear could top $4 million in 2002.

According to ESPN.com, Gonzaga was 107th in 2000 in sales of caps produced by Zephyr. But in 2001, the Zags had leaped to number 16, past Arizona, Kentucky, Ohio State, Michigan State, and Tennessee.

"Two things happened," says Hogan, referring to the overall growth. "Number one, we started winning games, and, number two, we changed our logo. Our new bulldog is much more aggressive."

The redesign of the logo took it from a benign Bulldog to more of a menacing mutt with sharper teeth and fierce intentions.

"They had this butt-ugly bulldog in some kind of childish sailor's hat," designer Todd Wood told ESPN.com. "So I gave the bulldog some edge and changed the color from royal blue and red to navy blue and red. It's perfect, because we're kind of America's team now."

At home, merchandise sales are also off the charts. Hogan says the Gonzaga bookstore did $200,000 in clothing three years ago and $1.2 million in the 2001–2002 school year.

~ ~ ~ ~ ~

Caps are one thing. Connecting is another.

In Spokane, it's hard to find a discouraging word about Gonzaga's outreach to charities and schools. The demand for appearances is intense.

"It's over a hundred requests annually," Few said in the spring of 2002. "This time of year, you could do something every day."

The Zags have worked with the local mission and the Shriners. They fulfill simple requests for school readings or brief talks.

Forward Zach Gourde, one of the most requested players, helped promote a University Elementary School read-a-thon, along with a Gonzaga soccer player and rower. At an assembly, Gourde talked to the kids about goal setting and pursuing dreams. The athletes then went into separate classrooms to read. Finally, Gourde presented a basketball signed by his teammates to be used for a PTA auction.

"They were really personable young people, and we appreciated their support," said principal Phyllis Betts. "To those kids, they might as well be movie stars."

Bart Orth, a business and marketing teacher at Lakeside High School, also lined up Gourde for a similar presentation.

"It doesn't even matter what he's saying so much," says Orth. "In our community, the Zags are kind of minilegends.

"We don't have a lot in the college arena for students to look up to. With the success Gonzaga has had, it just elevates it to such a huge platform."

Every year, basketball players and coaches join other members of the Gonzaga athletic department in pouring concrete and pounding nails for Habitat for Humanity, the international organization that partners with low-income families to build houses sold to those families with the aid of interest-free loans.

The Zags also have a tradition of helping the Spokane-based Children's Miracle Network, an organization that raises money for kids' amenities such as play equipment, televisions, and VCRs in hospitals and care-related entities in the Northwest.

Former guard Matt Santangelo was an early force in that relationship, which has continued with autographed balls going for $1,000 at auction and appearances by coaches and players at a telephone fund-raiser.

"They're just great," says Angie Lorenz of Children's Miracle Network. "They just get how important it is."

10

21st-Century Pioneering

Last spring on his way out of Spokane, the place where he became an icon, Dan Dickau passed Erroll Knight, who aspires to succeed him. It was good that they met and conversed and talked about the stuff basketball players talk about, because many common threads bind their dreams.

So much alike, yet so different. Dickau grew up in a modest-sized town in southwestern Washington, indulging a basketball jones almost since he could toddle. He had two parents around him and a good life in high school with a lot of close buddies, and from the moment he lit it up at a national Nike camp one summer, it was apparent he was going to be a star point guard in college.

He chose Washington, which showed the earliest interest.

Four years later, along came Erroll Knight, who was from inner-city Seattle. He was raised by his mother, and he was a Johnny-come-lately to basketball, not playing on an organized level until he reached ninth grade. But he shot up six inches just before his sophomore year, and when it became clear he could be a standout off-guard in college, he attracted scholarship offers from Syracuse and Oregon and Gonzaga as well as steady attention from Kansas.

He chose Washington, which showed the earliest interest.

Then the forces that have made Gonzaga the vortex of college basketball in the state of Washington swept Knight up, and in the spring of 2002, he asked for a release from his scholarship. He soon found himself telling the Zag coaches what he was seeking for a new start: a place where he could concentrate on school and immerse himself in basketball.

"It was like the same two quotes," said Gonzaga coach Mark Few. "You would have thought it was Dan Dickau."

~ ~ ~ ~ ~

They say Dan Dickau knocked 'em out at Gonzaga on the night of the sports banquet last spring, just as he did Pepperdine in the finals of the West Coast Conference tournament. "It was a great talk," said Few. "Best I've heard in my time here."

"Vintage Dan," says his father, Randy, who indicated his son didn't plan much. "Earlier in the afternoon, I'd asked him: 'Dan, the seniors usually say something. Do you have anything written down?'"

Not yet, the younger Dickau said. He thought he'd take a nap and then jot some notes down.

"I'm sure that's what he did," Randy Dickau said. "He doesn't sweat over anything."

Dickau got up and zigged between serious and funny. He recalled how Casey Calvary had beseeched the underclassmen a year ago: "Don't screw this up." And Dickau repeated that.

He applauded Few's decision to spurn Washington's advances and stay at Gonzaga, bringing down the house. "Coach," he said, "I have to tell you, you made the right decision. I've been there, and it's a dead-end job."

He wanted to thank people, not just do the perfunctory, general-interest thanks but name people who had been pivotal to his development. And so he did. He told them why he'd had a great experience at Gonzaga.

And his audience, if it hadn't already wondered what the Zags were going to do without Dan Dickau, Gonzaga's only first-team All-American, wondered it now.

Few is asked what Dickau meant to the Gonzaga program. He says, "Kind of . . . everything."

Shortly after that banquet, Dickau left for Chicago, where he would set up a base camp for National Basketball Association clubs wanting to work him out before the NBA draft. Then he would try to do something that, at least initially, escaped all the other good Gonzaga players of his era. He would attempt to stick in the NBA, with the Atlanta Hawks.

It was the Holy Grail for all of the good ones, and it eluded them. Richie Frahm had an ankle injury that derailed his attempt, and he played in the Philippines before paralleling Dickau's quest last spring with some NBA workouts. Casey Calvary played in Japan. Quentin Hall, the definitive Bulldog, could absolutely lock down people like Quincy Lewis and Khalid El-Amin in the 1999 NCAA tournament, but he ended up in the Netherlands. Matt Santangelo's 2002 home was in Poland, not his hometown of Portland.

Unless one of them broke through, then, it would be left to Dickau to assume the mantle. Gonzaga has had a lot of guys who could play the game, but not since 1984, when John Stockton was a rookie with the Utah Jazz, has any GU player forged a real career in the NBA.

Referring to the prospect of a bigger Gonzaga representation in the league, Few says, "It's not going to hurt. The program can stand on its own accomplishments. But it helps. Kids have NBA stars in their eyes, obviously. Certainly if he does make it, it's going to do even more for us."

Surely Earth will continue to rotate on its axis if Dickau or another recent Zag doesn't make the NBA, but the lack of NBA alumni has become an oddity that begs recompense. There aren't many more illustrious alumni than Stockton to which a college program can point, but he is 40 now, and no matter how finely conditioned he keeps himself and how deathly competitive he continues to be, not every 18-year-old prospect can relate to somebody a generation older whose shorts stop at his thighs, not his knees.

Of his immediate predecessors, Dickau says, "I think those guys are eventually going to get to the NBA. It's just a matter of, maybe I take a straighter route than those guys did."

Dickau would know straight from circuitous.

At Prairie High School in Vancouver, Washington, Dickau was recruited by Washington, Pepperdine, and Portland. Randy and Judy Dickau accompanied him on his Pepperdine trip, and there was a moment when he sounded as if he might choose the Waves.

"This is not Dan," thought his father.

Fortuitously, perhaps, fog shielded the view to the nearby Pacific on their visit to Malibu. Looking back, Dickau's dad wonders if it wasn't a heaven-sent sign, "almost like the Lord said, 'No, you're not to see this.'"

If the Almighty was pointing Dickau toward his dream school, He was slow to get it right. Dickau initially chose Washington.

At the time, it seemed logical; he wanted to play against the best, and the best point guards—Kidd, Payton, Stoudamire, Bibby—come from the Pac-10.

Gonzaga had showed some interest, but Dickau told the coach, Dan Monson, he didn't like cold weather ("So I went to Seattle," Dickau would say, "and had to deal with the rain every day"). He also was skeptical about the West Coast Conference, and besides, he knew the Zags had a young point guard in Santangelo.

"That's one of the crazy things," Dickau can say now. "All these high school kids make decisions, and I would say hardly any of these guys are making decisions based on the right thing. I'd have to say a lot of these guys aren't happy with where they're at—they just decide to play through it."

On the surface, he had a successful freshman year at Washington. Averaging about nine minutes a game, he showed glimpses of his dazzling shooting ability, hitting 16 of 30 three-point attempts and 79 percent of his free throws.

Things weren't perfect, but he was a freshman, and he played 17 minutes in a taut NCAA victory over Xavier. Anyway, he wasn't sure how it was supposed to be. But his sophomore year began in disappointment, with a foot problem that kept him out of some fall conditioning, and 13 games into the season, he broke his foot. Also fractured, as it turned out, was his career at Washington.

He lived way over on Ninth Avenue, blocks west of Edmundson Pavilion, a tedious drive through relentless traffic on Seattle's Northwest 45th Street. "Some days, I didn't have access to my car, because my sister needed it," Dickau says. "So I'd have to walk to campus. You wake up, see the rain, and say, 'Aw, I think I'm just going to stick in my apartment.' That's nothing the university or the basketball program can control. Still, it has a big effect on things, especially for somebody who likes to spend time in the gym."

He didn't feel any particular bond with many of his teammates, nor did he believe he was improving much. His sophomore shooting percentages declined by all measures. He would talk occasionally to his old southwestern Washington buddies at Gonzaga, Frahm and Zach Gourde, and college basketball seemed so different for them.

"I knew he was capable of more than what he was getting over there," says Frahm. "I know he was frustrated. He's not one to tell you he was frustrated, but he was venting a lot."

Early in December of his sophomore season, the Huskies took a trip to Boise State and Gonzaga. They blew a big lead against BSU and lost 69–61. UW coach Bob Bender went off on his team in the locker room. Later, Randy and Judy Dickau met their son at the hotel.

"We've got to talk," Dickau told his father. "I'm just not having any fun."

"I've never seen him so down," said the senior Dickau, who nevertheless encouraged his son to stay the course.

Three nights later, at the Spokane Arena, Gonzaga's soon-to-be Elite Eight team faced a Washington club that would play in the NCAA tournament. The Zags took a big second-half lead and won 82–71.

Dickau had five points and no assists in 26 minutes. Few put an arm on his shoulder afterward and, in the ultimate irony, said, "Just keep working hard and something good is going to happen."

"We got killed," Dickau says. "They absolutely took it to us. Whatever we tried to do offensively, they had a counter to it. After we lost that game, I was thinking to myself, this team is gonna be pretty good."

He was talking about Gonzaga.

Well before Washington's season ended with a bizarre one-point loss to Miami of Ohio—when Wally Szczerbiak had 43 of his team's 60 points, an NCAA-record percentage of contribution—Dickau knew he had to get out.

"Something my dad said stuck in my mind," Dickau told *Sports Illustrated* last February. "He said, 'I don't care if you transfer, but if you stay, have a nice career.'"

Dan Dickau has always been relatively mild about the reasons for his transfer. His father, on the other hand, is bitingly candid.

"I want to be careful I don't hurt anybody with what I say," he says. "I can't say enough about the difference in coaches, not only the head coach but the assistant coaches.

"The coaches at Gonzaga were head and shoulders better. They were more passionate, more determined, they would work forever. The kids love to play, and they leverage that love with the coaches' willingness to work. All of a sudden, two plus two equals seven."

At Gonzaga, Dickau would have greater freedom in the offense, particularly after a redshirt year. Some of that could have resulted from maturity.

"Maybe that's what he didn't have at Washington," Randy Dickau says. "At Washington, Dan's job was to bring the ball past halfcourt, pass the ball to the wing to Donald Watts or Deon Luton, and it would never come back."

The Dickaus were clueless about how to put a transfer in motion. Randy Dickau got advice from the father of Michael Johnson, Dan's UW teammate, and called Dan Monson, then the Gonzaga coach.

"I realize you didn't recruit Dan very heavily . . ." Randy Dickau began.

"Let me interrupt you," Monson said. "Truth be known, we didn't think we had a chance at him."

"You probably know where this is headed."

As fate would have it, the other school Dickau seriously considered was St. Louis. The coach was Lorenzo Romar, who had made an impression on him at Pepperdine.

"Honestly, I think you'd like it here at St. Louis," Romar told Dickau. "It'd be a good place for you and I'd love to have you here. But to tell the truth, I think Gonzaga is the perfect place for you. If for some reason it's not where you want to go, then call me and we'll bring you back here on a visit."

Dickau appreciated Romar's class. And now it is Romar, Washington's new coach, who must find a way to stanch the stream of Huskies checking out of Seattle for Spokane.

With Romar's blessing, Dickau was Gonzaga-bound. Suddenly, it didn't matter that Spokane winters are cold.

"When I chose to transfer, I said, 'This is my basketball career I was worrying about, not the weather,'" Dickau says.

If things weren't immediately better for Dickau, they would still improve at Gonzaga, even through a redshirt season. "You could tell he wished he was on the floor," said his father, "but on a daily basis, he was learning more and having more fun."

It was like a new life. He took No. 21, in deference to his idol, John Stockton, whose No. 12 is unofficially retired. He grew out his hair, a complete makeover from his close-cropped Washington days, and became a college-hoops heartthrob.

A precursor of his best days at Gonzaga came in the early season of 2000–2001 at Arizona, when he had 20 points and seven assists before he broke an index finger. He returned in January to some dazzling numbers in West Coast Conference play, including a 31-point second half at Santa Clara when he scored 20 straight Gonzaga points in a loss.

He had an astonishing shooting touch that perfectly complemented Few's requirement for a point guard that can score. He could launch a shot so soft that sometimes it seemed to defy the demands of physics; twice in an NCAA victory over Virginia, his three-pointers met rim but somehow went in.

As a senior, Dickau had at least two games that won't be forgotten. At Loyola, he had 34 points—all in the first half. He was 11 of 15 from the floor and 9 of 12 on threes and took a single shot in the second half, which missed.

His description: "The ball was rolling off my hand, like practice. It just happened to be a game."

Then there was the Pepperdine game in the WCC tournament, when the Zags were mucking along in the second half, trailing by a few points and looking vulnerable to losing the league's automatic bid to the NCAA. Then, in one crackling stretch of seven and a half minutes, the Zags outscored Pepperdine 32–10. Dickau had 19 of his 29 points in a five-minute compression of that burst, keyed by a trip to the free throw line after a Pepperdine technical foul.

"I was just looking for one opening to get me going in the second half," said Dickau. "Then the technical foul. Sometimes that's all you need, is just to see the ball go through the hoop."

Someday, on some NBA floor, Dan Dickau might get that hot again. Certainly, there are liabilities to his game, which he heard about last spring in preparation for the draft: his defense needs work. At 6', he might have trouble getting off that shot against bigger, quicker defenders, needing screens to do it. Without a bruising NBA body, he will get roughed up going to the basket.

"There are plenty of guys in that league that can't play defense," Dickau insists. "But I'd bet money there are not that many guys that can shoot the ball as well as I can."

After a workout at Detroit last spring, he confided to his parents that Joe Dumars, the Pistons' general manager, told him he thought Dickau would be in the league a long time.

That would not only fulfill a personal dream. It would crack a long-standing trend as difficult for Gonzaga to break as John Stockton's will.

~ ~ ~ ~ ~

By day, Che Dawson is an attorney specializing in immigration law for a Seattle law firm, working on the 29th floor of the Washington Mutual Building.

In his other job, he is the boys basketball coach at Chief Sealth High School in south Seattle, where 6'7" Erroll Knight generated enough athletic plays to gain scholarship offers from several big schools.

Over coffee, Dawson is recounting Knight's moves. There was the game against Ballard at the end of his junior season, when Sealth needed to win to advance to the regional playoffs.

"I recall Erroll catching the ball at the top of the key late in the game," says Dawson. "The lane opened up. He kind of turned and looked; his eyes got big. He took one dribble into the key and went up with this spectacular, one-handed tomahawk dunk."

"I crossed the guy over," Knight says knowingly, an hour later in his apartment near the Washington campus. "I think I took off between the dotted line and free throw line. The guy jumped. Bodies collided and I dunked over him."

Sealth won that game. It lost the one the next year against Tahoma, a game that remains in Dawson's memory. A couple of Knight's more physical teammates fouled out and he had to move down on the block. He had 25 points and 18 rebounds.

"I was like an animal," Knight says, smiling at the recollection. "A madman."

Knight is not usually given to idle hyperbole. Polite and deferential, he has been told more than once that he needs to be more aggressive. "One of my challenges," says Dawson, "was to get some of that tiger out of him."

People who have seen Knight on the floor supply enough superlatives for him. *The Sporting News* ranked him number 71 on its national list of 100 top high school players, and he was rated similarly by several other services.

"Erroll Knight is maybe as good an athlete as has ever worn a Washington uniform," Bender said when Knight signed with the UW. "Can he have the same impact as Richard Jefferson at Arizona? I think that's a good example."

When the Zags inched past Florida to get to the 1999 Elite Eight, Richie Frahm had 17 points, five rebounds, and four assists; that night, he said, "I don't think too many people slept."

At one time Matt Santangelo thought he might get to play for Stanford; his 22 points, six assists, and six rebounds against the Cardinals helped the Zags advance to the 1999 West Regional in Phoenix.

Cory Violette was an instrumental member of the Zags 2001–2002 league championship team. A tenacious rebounder, Violette averaged 8.3 rebounds during the season, more than any Bulldog since Paul Cathey in 1978.

Dan Dickau, Gonzaga's first player to win AP first-team All-America honors, drove opponents crazy both with moves to the basket and deadly shooting beyond the three-point arc. He was the catalyst in a scintillating seven-and-a-half-minute, 32–10 run against Pepperdine in the 2002 WCC tournament final.

Assistant coach Leon Rice is a sounding board for Mark Few on offensive strategy.

Mark Few's right-hand man, assistant coach Bill Grier, is the heir apparent and a defensive specialist.

AP/Wide World Photos

No matter what coach Mark Few and Dan Dickau tried against Wyoming in the 2002 NCAA tournament, it wasn't enough to make up for the Zags' 26.8-percent shooting; they lost the first-round game to the Cowboys.

Always full, always noisy, the Kennel has served as Gonzaga's student section for over a decade.

Father Tony Lehmann provided inspiration, perspective, and humor for the Gonzaga basketball team for years. He died in March of 2002 and was remembered with this memorial during the Zags' opening round NCAA tournament game against Wyoming.

Knight's time at Washington was half as long as Dickau's. Choosing the Huskies over Syracuse, Oregon, Kansas, and Gonzaga, he became part of a fractious, undisciplined outfit that resulted in Bender losing his job.

Ironically, the beginning of the end came early in December, when a 6–2 Washington team, playing at home in front of a capacity crowd, went limp against a Gonzaga zone and lost by 20.

Neither Knight nor Dawson can seem to pinpoint what went south for the talented freshman at Washington. Knight says his dissatisfaction was roughly half with the academic side and half with basketball, despite the fact that he played significant minutes, averaged 7.1 points, and shot 43 percent from three-point range. When the combination of the two began dragging him down, he felt less and less motivated to try to deal with the downturn.

"If I had to express it in as simple a way as possible," Dawson says, "Erroll is the type of young man, and player, who excels when things around him are positive, and doesn't necessarily excel when things around him are negative."

Said Knight, "I need to get away where I can focus on basketball and school a little more. At Gonzaga, all they do is play basketball and do schoolwork."

How receptive was Gonzaga to Knight? If NCAA rules had allowed the Zags to send a stretch limo across the state, there would have been a uniformed driver knocking on his door.

"The sky's the limit," Few says.

It is hard to say which may be more important to Gonzaga: getting Knight for his abundant physical skills or for what he could symbolize in the bigger picture.

Much, obviously, will depend on Knight's willingness to plunge into academics and Gonzaga's basketball system, and the rate at which he absorbs both. Few envisions a 2003–2004 Gonzaga team with Knight, Blake Stepp, Ronny Turiaf, Cory Violette, Rich Fox, and Sean Mallon and says, "It'll easily be the most talented group we've ever put out there."

And what of Gonzaga's recruiting on the west side of the state? Knight represents a rarity for the Zags: an African American from Seattle's inner city.

"Seattle is still the one place where they just don't really understand Spokane or something," says Few, naming prominent Zag players like Quentin Hall, Winston Brooks, and Alex Hernandez who have come from inner-city backgrounds. "Seattle is one of the last bastions. It's kind of strange.

"This sends a loud, clear message that it's all right—especially if we develop him."

Knight hails from a culture of urban basketball in Seattle that has become rife with politics, peer pressure, and some of the scurrilous dealings so common to other major population bases.

Once Knight became a recognized future force as a high school sophomore, he also became a target. Dawson says it wasn't the notorious excesses of AAU summer-league basketball that tried to get their hooks into Knight; it was others who tried to avail themselves of lax rules for high school transfers.

Knight played for the AAU Friends of Hoop team, and Dawson was one of its coaches for a couple of years.

"I trusted the coaches in that program," Dawson says. "Now the non-AAU people who wanted to advise Erroll on what to do when he started to show some promise as a basketball player, that was another issue. Some would confront me directly about what I was or was not doing that I should be doing with Erroll—and certainly a lot of that was going on behind the scenes."

As Dawson explains it, there is virtual "open enrollment" in Seattle high schools. Technically, a would-be transfer must show that he isn't switching only for athletic reasons, and he cannot be recruited, but the rules are relatively easy to get around.

"That scenario is causing different forces to be pulling at kids," Dawson says.

That was precisely what was going on with Knight. Sealth's recent records, which had not been among the best in the city, made him vulnerable.

"People were definitely trying to get him to transfer to other high schools," said Dawson. "But he and I always had a good enough relationship where we communicated about those things."

Dawson tells a story. He had a chance to take another high-profile coaching job in Seattle after Knight's sophomore year. He was concerned that if he left, Knight might bolt for another top program.

"If I told you right now, for your junior and senior year we weren't going to win another game," Dawson postulated to Knight, "would you stay at Sealth?"

"I'd stay," Knight said. "Because we're doing things the right way."

And so they formed a bond, inviolate to outside disruptions.

"I stayed loyal to my coach, and he stayed loyal," Knight says. "Coach Dawson molded me. We worked day in and day out, in the gym, lifting weights, working on footwork, agility drills. He really did a good job sticking with me."

But it is the unusual player who can repel those advances as well as shrug off the suggestions of an entourage of extended family members and friends who become barnacles around a promising player.

"There's a lot of things that are distractions," Knight says. "Just the city alone, that's a distraction. There's a lot of things you can do—downtown, you have all these clubs, you have girls. I saw myself starting to do some of these things I didn't normally like doing."

That is a key reason why he decided to try to rededicate himself at Gonzaga, a school that has had about as much luck recruiting in Seattle as it might in scouring the Cabrini-Green projects of Chicago.

Jason Kerr, the coach at Franklin High in Seattle, weighs in with an opinion about why it's hard for Gonzaga to recruit in Seattle. He believes the phenomenon has less to do with an aversion in the inner city for Gonzaga than with facts of life about urban hoops.

"They've been successful because of the amount of buy-in they get with 16 kids strong," he says, speaking of Gonzaga. "'We're going to come in, work our system, teach our fundamentals, and get our individual growth as well as our team growth.'

"You're in a day and age now where kids want to come in and start. We've got kids in our own damn community leaving to start school, talking about how in two years they're going to the NBA, and there ain't a chance in hell of them making it in the NBA. But that's what's going through their head."

Not only that, says Kerr, the style of play in the city sometimes doesn't match what is found at Gonzaga.

"They've looked for a special, unique kind of player," he says. "The first thing that comes to mind is the kid with the ability to shoot the basketball. Traditionally, you don't find that many shooters in the inner city.

"A lot of our kids in this area are caught up in the hoopla of what's going on at the NBA level. They're hung up on doing the [glitz and glamour] routine and what the crossover is. Because they have speed, it's about getting to the rim. You get a lot of going-to-the-basket stuff."

Within an hour after Knight informed Romar he was definitely leaving Washington, Gonzaga coach Bill Grier was on the phone to Dawson. "I've still got to find out what his sources are," said Dawson, smiling.

Knight asked Dawson to check into Kansas, which told Dawson its scholarship allotment was full. But Knight always had Gonzaga at the top of his transfer list, and on his visit there, he made it a done deal.

"I think," said Dawson, "he was looking for a situation where he could hop on a train that's already moving."

Dawson concedes Knight's choice of Gonzaga may represent a possible inroad for the Zags in Seattle. But he cautions that there may be only so many Knights.

"In some ways, them having Erroll is a breakthrough on that perception," he said. "Whatever the average perception of an inner-city kid . . . 'He's black and he only wants to be around black people . . . he's more interested in glitz and glamour than substance' . . . Erroll is a pretty typical teenager with regard to being interested in some superficial things like clothes and uniform.

"But there's a lot more depth there than just the perception of a typical inner-city kid."

~ ~ ~ ~ ~

And so they talked in Spokane—one player about to go out the door and the other coming in.

Dan Dickau and Erroll Knight discussed things about Gonzaga and Washington, about how your absence from class isn't noticed at a big school and how it is at a small one. They talked about how the four- or five-hour drive creates a separation from your home, how you don't just jump in the car on Saturday morning on a whim as Dickau used to do at Washington and drive half that long and be home for the weekend.

"He seemed to me a guy with a load of potential who's going to be a great player once the Gonzaga coaches help him with his game," Dickau said, adding, "Maybe he was a kid similar to me, that didn't fully check out all his options."

They were two players pointed at the same goal who had been to a lot of the same places. As Gonzaga watches them, it envisions barriers falling.

11

Stocking the Cupboard

From Wenatchee, in central Washington, you wind north along State Highway 97. The mighty Columbia River has created a deep cut dwarfed by twin promontories as the road bends its way toward Canada. On a February Saturday, those slopes are brown, spotted by forlorn patches of snow.

This is a section of the nation's fruit basket. For mile upon mile, there are orchards—neat rows of apple, cherry, and pear trees—interrupted only by the occasional packing plant or farmhouse protected by a stand of poplar trees.

Forty miles up from Wenatchee, the highway crosses the Columbia and traces it from the west side. The horizon flattens a bit. In another 25 minutes or so, you hit the town of Pateros, and six miles later, you're in Brewster.

It's not much. There is a single, blinking red light a block off the highway toward the river. There are three gas stations; a couple of motels, banks, and auto-parts stores; a barber shop; and maybe three or four restaurants. Brewster has a movie theater, but it plays only three days a week. If you want to go bowling, you drive 30 minutes up to Omak.

"Brown double-wide," Mike Pendergraft had said, and indeed, his home is easy to spot down Seventh Street.

Outside the door, the first thing you notice is a pair of shoes, size 15s. They belong to David Pendergraft, who is 16 years old and a sophomore at Brewster High School. He is one of the hottest college basketball prospects on the West Coast.

Recruiters, however, are not taxing themselves with long airplane and car trips to north-central Washington. Three full basketball seasons before he would earn a diploma at Brewster, Pendergraft committed to accept a scholarship at Gonzaga, one of the earliest such pledges in the nation's history.

There are those who believe Pendergraft is among the best two or three sophomores in the West. "Just a baller," says somebody at Gonzaga who has seen him. "He might be kind of a poor man's Mike Dunleavy."

Such is the sway of Gonzaga's recruiting in the Northwest that the Zags are now attracting players who have scarcely outgrown their learner's permit.

David's parents, Mike and Lori, grew up in the Okanogan Valley to the north. They lived in Omak before moving to Brewster in David's eighth-grade year. The Pendergrafts say the move was strictly related to basketball opportunities.

"He had been playing AAU ball with these kids for many years," says Lori Pendergraft, referring to her son's Brewster High teammates. "They really have a solid AAU program here, whereas in a couple of other communities, it's a little more sporadic."

Their eighth-grade son had no school team in Omak, either.

"We believe in sports programs, to keep them off drugs and alcohol," says Lori. "To keep them involved, and we keep involved in their life through that."

Because Brewster is not exactly on the regular itinerary of college recruiters, Pendergraft was widely unknown until a spring Youth Education Through Sports tournament in 2001 at Hec Edmundson Pavilion on the University of Washington campus. There, he was noticed for his shooting, quick jumping ability, feel for the game, and facility for finding the open man.

In Seattle, he also developed a friendship with Sean Mallon, a 6'9" junior from Ferris High in Spokane. Only days later, Mallon would announce his intention to enroll at Gonzaga in the fall of 2002.

It turned out that not only did the Zags have Mark Few, Bill Grier, and Leon Rice recruiting for them, they had Mallon as well.

"We're pretty good buddies," said Pendergraft, sitting on a couch in his family's comfortable living room.

Mallon extended an invitation: why not join him later in the summer and drop over to the Gonzaga campus to play some hoops?

Pendergraft accepted. Late in summer, he and his father drove the two and a half hours to Spokane, and he found himself on a basketball floor with people like Zach Gourde and Cory Violette.

"What year are you?" Colorado transfer Rich Fox asked Pendergraft.

"A sophomore," Pendergraft answered.

Fox figured he meant a sophomore in college.

"Half the guys, you watch on TV and cheer for: 'Man, I want to do that some-day,'" said Pendergraft. "The next summer, you're standing next to them. It was like, 'Whoa.'"

Pendergraft had no intention of making a college decision so early. There were other things to think about: driving an automobile, hunting and fishing around Brewster, beating Omak and Pateros.

But summer melted into autumn, and he went back to Gonzaga. And again and again, four times total for three-day stays. Pretty soon, he was one of the guys, even if he was two and a half years from high school graduation.

At Gonzaga, the younger Pendergraft saw competitiveness and he saw camaraderie.

"They go and have team dinners, just because they're all friends. They play Nintendo together in the three-dorm apartment. They get along on the court and off it. I saw that right away. That's one of the things I like most about it."

Gonzaga had already popped the question: Pendergraft was offered a scholar-ship. Mike and David were taken aback. Lori, who had stayed home on the weekend forays to Spokane, was the skeptical mother, disbelieving this could all be happening.

"These guys would come home and try to convince me," she said. "I'm like, 'Right, sure, they're just telling you what you want to hear.' You know moms."

Then came the weekend of November 18, 2001. The Zags had their official home opener against Montana, and Lori joined the men in the family to get to the bottom of things in Spokane.

"Everything they had told these guys, I heard the same story," she said. "I went in there expecting something else. I know he's a talented young man, but I kept waiting for them to say, well, we're interested in him if he grows, or learns to dribble better with his left hand, or learns a couple of more moves. But none of those things happened at Gonzaga."

The clincher was what the Pendergrafts heard about a college degree and any potential injury to their son. Lori was concerned that if David didn't graduate in four years, he wouldn't remain on scholarship, but the coaches assured her otherwise. And they believe they have an "insurance policy," in Mike's words, that if David gets hurt before he enrolls, Gonzaga will still honor the agreement.

"It was almost that we were dumb if we don't take it," Mike said.

By this time, Pendergraft was getting a considerable rush from elsewhere. Surely those schools were unsuspecting of Pendergraft's deep involvement with Gonzaga. They would check up on Pendergraft through Brewster's athletic director, Brooks Smith.

"Stanford was calling my school to say, 'You keep your grades up, and you'll be at Stanford in two years,'" said David, who has a 4.0 grade average. "My AD would come in, 'Oh, this is what Stanford had to say this time.'"

A lot of high-profile schools were corresponding: Duke, North Carolina, Indiana, Virginia. And closer to home: Wyoming, Brigham Young, Air Force. This was all so new to the Pendergrafts that as the school year began, they wondered: were they crazy not to let the process develop? Should anybody turn his back on a possible chance to go to Duke on a basketball scholarship?

"We brought up Duke," said Mike Pendergraft. "He was absolutely sure."

The Pendergrafts had traveled the country as David played AAU basketball. They had been to Florida, Tennessee, and Minnesota as part of his summer junkets, so they weren't exactly bumpkins who would be persuaded by the lure of nearness. Besides, David wondered, whom might a school like Duke recruit "over" him?

"I didn't really want to go to Duke," David said. "The location of GU is awesome. I'd love to stay close to home. I love Washington; I love Spokane. It's Spokane's pro basketball."

Not that the Pendergrafts don't have skeptics.

"We've had a lot of people express that it wasn't a good decision," Lori said. "They felt they wanted Davey to take advantage of all those recruiting opportunities. But really, it just wasn't important to him."

"Funny how people come out of the woodwork," said Mike. "Coaches, people . . . they just don't know. A lot of people think, 'Well, they're just lying to you. They can tell you anything they want. You didn't sign anything; it doesn't mean anything.'"

That night the focal point of the town is the high school gym, where the Brewster boys and girls are hosting Oroville, a same-sized burg five miles from the Canadian border.

Brewster, a Class AA school—4A is largest in Washington—has a considerable basketball history. It pieced together a state-record 82-game winning streak back in the seventies, and proudly displayed from the gym's rafters are eight state-championship banners, five earned by the boys.

But there is evidence of an odd phenomenon the Pendergrafts had talked about. It's mostly a mature crowd watching the Bears, as if the younger generation isn't fully aware of the tradition in the town. And while the crowd is ample, there are seats to be had. Often, it's not like that when the Brewster teams travel. They're the Yankees of their league. One opponent's administration told the school not to bring a rooter bus because there wouldn't be seats enough in the gym.

Aside from his height, David Pendergraft's most distinguishing feature is his thick, flaming, wavy red hair. Combine that with a slender—but hardly skinny—build and his upraised shoulders as he runs downcourt, and you have a vision of what Bill Walton must have looked like three decades ago in high school.

Against a scrappy Oroville team, Pendergraft does not dominate. He struggles for much of the first half and, indeed, sits for a spell of nearly four minutes. He gets beat on the baseline for a layup, and you wonder about that. And then you remember that he has two full years to iron out such lapses.

He shows bursts. He hits an open man for a score; he tracks down a loose ball 35 feet from the basket and gallops in to jam it; he gets position underneath over a shorter opponent and sticks the rebound back in. He's fundamentally good. You sense that Gonzaga knew what it was doing, and probably, the Pendergrafts did, too.

"Everything is taken care of," Mike Pendergraft had said back at the family home. He smiled and added, "Except they said he'd have to buy his own CDs."

~ ~ ~ ~ ~

Sometimes it seems Gonzaga doesn't recruit as much as its growing reputation recruits for it. Of course, it doesn't hurt when the prospect lives 15 minutes from campus.

Sean Mallon is a local kid, a relatively rare high-profile prospect from Spokane. He scored 1,669 points in his four-year career at Ferris High School, more than any player in the history of the Greater Spokane League. Mallon, who was due to enter Gonzaga in the fall of 2002, began impressing people as a sophomore.

But he didn't take any visits. The campus froufrou, the notion of being glad-handed in some sunny clime amid halter tops and shorts, doesn't seem to hold automatic appeal for a lot of Gonzaga recruits.

"I knew I wanted to do it," says the bespectacled Mallon, sitting in a Spokane motel lobby with an Atlanta Braves cap turned backward. "I didn't want to lead anybody on or give false impressions. I pretty much had my mind made up."

Not that he wouldn't have had choices. He attended the Utah basketball camp of coach Rick Majerus and didn't fail to catch eyes there.

"He's a great prospect," said Majerus. "He could end up being one of the best forwards to play at Gonzaga. He's a great shooter. I thought he was Keith Van Horn on the come."

Bob Gibbons, longtime talent evaluator for *All Star Sports Report* in Lenoir, North Carolina, saw Mallon play at the USA Basketball festival in Colorado Springs in 2001 and was impressed enough to rate him in the top 60 of U.S. high school seniors in 2002.

"He's a hard-nosed kid, very intelligent, the kind of kid Mark Few loves to bring in," Gibbons said. "They know how to go backdoor, pick and roll, set screens well. He had the best fundamentals of any of the big men I saw this year."

Mallon had the good fortune—or the bad karma—to play on three teams in his four seasons that lost in the Washington 4A championship game. He was well known to Gonzaga coaches by the time he spent part of the summer between his sophomore and junior years working out against former Zag Casey Calvary. When he began his junior season at Ferris, Mallon already had an offer from Gonzaga.

First, Mallon had a visit with the Zag coaches. A week later, that group expanded to include Mallon's parents, Gary and Cam, plus the late Ferris coach, Wayne Gilman.

"When we walked out of there, I felt Sean was going to go there," said Cam. "They were very, very good explaining what they were about, what the program was about. Their impressions of Sean as a person and as a player were right on. And they were very articulate as far as explaining how he'd fit in. I just thought it was such a good fit. I didn't say anything because I didn't want to influence him. Kids don't necessarily do what their moms want."

Cam Mallon's comments were strikingly similar to those of Lori Pendergraft. Gonzaga often has the luxury of recruiting not only in two-parent households but in homes with strong parental influence.

"When you get to the point where you're going to turn your son over to another environment . . ." she said, trailing off. "I couldn't imagine feeling more comfortable with anybody, as far as trusting them to make good decisions and help Sean and care about him as a person as well as a player. All those 'mom' kinds of things."

She steals a glance at her son. "Sorry, Sean. That's really what I thought."

Gary Mallon helped coach some of Sean's youth teams. He admits to thinking it wouldn't have been imprudent to wait longer to commit to Gonzaga.

"But certainly I thought the fit was perfect," he said. "How rare is that in your hometown? You get a team like Gonzaga and an opportunity like that."

Sean Mallon has excellent grades and good college-board scores. There were programs that his dad wouldn't approve of.

"There's an emphasis at Gonzaga on both academics and character," Gary Mallon said. "To me, that was really huge. When it became apparent Sean was going to be a recruit, I told him I would never tell him where he could go to school, but I would tell him where he couldn't go to school."

At the end of his junior season, Mallon played in the same tournament in Seattle that included David Pendergraft. He strolled the Washington campus with then–UW coach Bob Bender. A few days later, Stanford would be in to talk to Mallon. He told his parents he needed to talk to them.

"In a rare exchange of ideas," Gary Mallon says, kidding his son for his taciturn nature, "he spent about the next two and a half or three hours explaining why he chose Gonzaga. It caught me off guard. I did not really realize the depth of thought he had given to this decision. I tried to ask as many pointed questions as I could, and he had responses for everything I asked."

Said his son, "I just kind of liked the guys they had down there. At the same time, I knew they had a great team. I figured I'd get the best of both worlds."

That simple. And it made for a pretty simple recruitment.

~ ~ ~ ~ ~

For a medium-sized city, Spokane hasn't exactly been a fountain of basketball talent. But the Zags like to think it's getting better, partly because of Adam Morrison.

Almost precisely a year after Mallon made his commitment to Gonzaga, Morrison followed him, announcing before the end of his junior year that he would attend Gonzaga in the fall of 2003.

He is a 6'5", 185-pound swing player from nearby Mead High School who didn't catch many eyes as a sophomore but actually nipped Mallon for the Greater Spokane League scoring title as a junior, averaging 25.3 points a game. Morrison is considered to have only average foot speed but is an uncanny shooter and scorer, having strafed Rogers High for 38 points in one game before totaling 49 in two games in the 2002 state 4A tournament.

Morrison is a coach's kid. His dad, John, was a junior-college coach at NAIA Dakota Wesleyan who got out of the game in 1993. Adam was a ball boy for his father and did the same for Gonzaga as a fifth- and sixth-grader.

The family got to know former Gonzaga coach Dan Fitzgerald, and Adam was attending Fitzgerald's camp as an eighth-grader when he had a life-changing experience. "I think I made one shot the whole three days," Adam said. "I was sicker than a dog. I didn't want to play. I couldn't do anything."

There was handwriting on the wall. John Morrison's grandfather was a diabetic, and so was Adam's grandmother on his mom's side. Sure enough, in a Spokane hospital room, he was told he had the disease.

He took it well. The second time a nurse arrived to administer insulin, he stopped her.

"Since I'm going to be doing this the rest of my life," he said, "you might as well show me how to do it."

He wears an insulin pump, allowing him to dial up the right dosage. He unhooks it during games but checks his blood sugar during timeouts.

"He's done an excellent job handling that," said his father. "It's not a concern at the next level. There are all kinds of pros playing with it. He's got it down to a pretty good science now."

Nevertheless, the subject was discussed when Few and assistant coach Leon Rice sat the Morrisons down in early April 2002. Morrison likely will redshirt his freshman year as he monitors whether the pace of college basketball calls for an adjustment in his insulin intake.

Morrison had competed against Gonzaga's players for a few days when the coaches offered him a scholarship. He gave the decision all of 30 minutes, called

Few back, and accepted, thus joining an ever-growing legion of future Zags to cast their lot without ever taking a visit to another campus.

"I just said, 'Sign me up,'" Morrison said. "GU's a top 10 program in town. You can't get any better than Gonzaga. I didn't see a reason to wait and put it off."

Nor did Gonzaga. Morrison was showing some of the same offense against the Zags that he displayed as a high school junior.

He has always been a shooter. He accompanied his father to camps even when he was only five years old. His parents have video of him at two, shooting at a toddler's undersized basket. Along the way, he soaked in knowledge of the game from his father.

"He knows more than most other dads," Adam said. "Obviously, it has helped. Some kids, they don't have somebody that knows the game, so they've got to learn it themselves."

Adam Morrison didn't have to do that. But he had to do something the others didn't: learn about how to balance his body chemistry with basketball.

~ ~ ~ ~ ~

"Blake was a little different dude," his father says.

So is Dean Stepp. A longtime high school basketball coach in Oregon, he had seen some of the faux glitter of the college recruiting process. He calls it the "baloney" of the game. So he devised a different sort of process for his son Blake, who became coveted across the western United States for his ability to shoot the ball. The reins were going to be in the family's hands, not the other way around.

Stepp, who was to enter his junior season with the Zags in 2002–2003, never took an official visit to any school. At times, it seems possible that Gonzaga may have almost an entire roster of players who chose the place without setting foot on another campus.

"We do it a little differently," Stepp says. "I'm a basketball coach. I've been around this game for many years. We decided to do only unofficial visits."

In other words, no parties for Blake Stepp, no thick porterhouse steaks at Morton's of Chicago, no locker-room jerseys with his name stitched on the back. Just quiet, unheralded visits on his own.

"They didn't even pay for a Coke," said Dean Stepp. "The visits were short and sweet. You go talk to the players, talk to the coach, see the campus. There's not a lot of baloney going on."

At his father's advice, Blake discounted some high-profile schools at the outset—Duke, Kansas, Indiana, Purdue.

"You don't want to go to a place," said his father, "where they get five All-Americans every year."

Stepp winnowed his choices to four Northwest schools—Gonzaga, Washington, Oregon, and Oregon State—plus Stanford. He and his dad did it on their own terms, seeing the Oregon schools in half a day, doing overnights for the rest. But it was strictly business.

Gonzaga had a couple of hole cards. First, the Stepp family has a summer place on nearby Lake Coeur d'Alene, so there was a familiarity with the Spokane area. Second, the Zags availed themselves of the sag in the Washington State program.

For years, the Cougars had huge attendance figures at their summer camps, dating to an emphasis on them by their coach in the seventies and early eighties, George Raveling. Blake was a WSU camper for years, but then the program waned through the midnineties under Kevin Eastman, while Gonzaga's camp gathered momentum.

Before Stepp's junior year, he and his father opted for the Gonzaga camp, and a relationship was born.

"It's the most popular basketball camp in the western United States," said the senior Stepp. "It's not even close."

Soon, Blake Stepp would be signing with Gonzaga, marking a breakthrough in the program's recruiting. Different dude, different decision.

~ ~ ~ ~ ~

When Gonzaga's Rice interviewed for the job at Montana in the spring of 2002, he was asked which pool of recruits he would base his program on—high school, junior college, transfers, or foreign players. He replied that he thought it was prudent to draw from each available resource.

Gonzaga mined Australia successfully in the midnineties and took the quintessential Zag, Quentin Hall, from the Bahamas. But its quest for Ronny Turiaf was perhaps the most ambitious undertaking for a foreign player in its history.

Turiaf, whose first name is pronounced Rō-ny, grew up on the island of Martinique, a French possession with a population of 240,000 southeast of Puerto Rico. He hardly had a basketball in his hands until he was 14, instead doting on soccer, handball, and tennis.

"I loved soccer," he said, kicking off his sandals in the Gonzaga basketball offices and flexing his feet. "That's my game."

Turiaf is wonderfully expressive, both physically and facially. He'll dance into the night at parties around campus.

"If I know they've got some music—and of course, girls—I love that," he says whimsically.

Initially, he hated basketball. He was about 6'6" in his middle teens, and the game required so much coordination.

"My dad said, 'Start playing basketball. You're so big,'" said Turiaf.

At 14, he left Martinique to join the French national developmental team. He became a quick jumper, grew to 6'9", and began to pique the interest of U.S. colleges, many of them big-time programs in the Big East, Atlantic Coast, and Southeastern Conferences. He had interest from Connecticut, Miami, Duke, North Carolina, Wake Forest, Georgia, and LSU. Several of them were there one day when Turiaf turned in a modest performance, "like 15 points and eight rebounds," he says. "They said, 'Oh, he's not really that good.'"

Shortly thereafter, Turiaf says he went lights-out, with 30 points and all sorts of other numbers. "Now they say, 'We're sorry,'" he says. He waved them away.

About this time, Gonzaga got an assist from former Olympic pole-vaulter Kory Tarpenning, an old college crony of Mark Few at Oregon. Tarpenning, who now lives in Monte Carlo, had competed for Insep, the same athletic club for whom Turiaf was playing. Tarpenning was able to tell Turiaf that Gonzaga could be trusted.

"For whatever reason," Few says, "some of those Big East schools just kind of dropped off."

Gonzaga assistant Bill Grier watched Turiaf play in France and eventually coaxed a visit from him. Turiaf took a West Coast Conference tour that included Pepperdine and St. Mary's.

He says he was tempted by Pepperdine but he knew better. "It was cool, too cool," he says. "Too many attractions outside of school. I know myself. I know me. Just like in my country, I would not go to school."

When Turiaf visited Gonzaga, he was pleasantly surprised at the weather: "Ooh, not that cold."

It was June.

"Tommy Lloyd [Gonzaga assistant coach] told me, 'Yeah, the winters are kind of like Paris,'" Turiaf says. "But I didn't know it snowed for like four or five months." Momentarily, he seems deeply aggrieved. "I'm pretty mad at Tommy. Pretty mad."

The weather is only one of the transitions for Turiaf. He hasn't seen a lot of his family since he was 14, owing to his time in France with the nationals.

"I love my family," he says. "I love to spend time with them. It's really tough for me when I think about it."

His family helps to pull him through the lonely times.

"We have such a great Kennel Club," he says. "Great 'pooblic.' I like to get them crazy when I dunk the ball. Get them crazy, pull my shirt."

They seem to like him doing that, too.

~ ~ ~ ~ ~

Rich Fox grew up in Denver and chose the University of Colorado because there was a sense of comfort in being close to home. Unfortunately, he was way too comfortable in his two seasons there.

At 6'11" and 270 pounds, he became eligible for Gonzaga in the 2002–2003 season. His look back at Colorado is as much mea culpa as it is indictment of anything the Buffaloes did wrong.

On one hand, there were a lot of transitions he couldn't make from high school to a big college campus—large classes, an absence of professor-student relationships, no sense of responsibility.

On the other hand, Fox admits he did nothing to foster accountability.

"There, if you didn't go to class, it was no big deal," he says. "If I wasn't in class, the teacher had no idea. I stayed up late; I did the wrong things. I didn't prioritize. I didn't work as hard as I probably should have. At the same time, I didn't feel I was wanted. I didn't feel they really cared about me."

He waded through a freshman season with some worthy numbers—6.5 points and 6.6 rebounds a game. He had a phenomenal first start against California, with 23 points, 12 rebounds, seven assists, and three blocks in an easy victory, and he gave Gonzaga something to remember him by with 15 points and 11 rebounds in a Colorado win over the Zags in the Rainbow Classic.

Fox spent his sophomore year growing gradually more unhappy. He had a broken hand early in the season, came back, and saw his playing time diminish. He finished with 6.3 points and 4.6 rebounds a game and a certainty that he had to get out.

"They had confidence in other guys," he says. "They didn't have any confidence in me. I didn't have any confidence in myself."

He told himself he would know his future by the reaction of the coaches if he were to tell them he didn't want to come back.

"How are they going to react?" he asked himself before a meeting with Ricardo Patton, the head coach. "Are they even going to care?"

"I went in there, and Patton didn't care if I was leaving," he said. "He didn't feel I'm a good player, and I feel I'm a good player."

Fox got his release from Colorado with the help of assistant coach David Moe, who knew the Gonzaga coaches and told them he was interested. Fox had watched the Zags on TV and had a sense the place would be good for him.

He awaited their call. It didn't come, so he called Few. They set up a visit, and five hours into it, Fox said he was coming. Gonzaga had struck again.

Surely, players soured on their first experience at another four-year school often arrive at their second stop wiser, more accountable, and more apt to work at the relationship. The Zags have reaped those benefits. Reciprocating, they can offer transfers from bigger schools some of the things they might have missed in major-conference programs: more personal attention in class and on the court and a cozier environment for their "last chance."

It worked that way for Eric Brady and Jeff Brown and Dan Dickau. Now it's Rich Fox's turn.

First chance or last, a lot of recruits are finding Gonzaga appealing. Most are even old enough to drive there themselves.

12

Zags: What Next?

For a whiff of worthwhile perspective on the Great Debate—Gonzaga versus the rest of the West Coast Conference—consider what the controversy was when the Zags entered the league in 1979–1980.

"They absolutely did not want us," said Dan Fitzgerald, the former coach who ushered in that era of Gonzaga basketball. "It was, 'Hey, why are we taking them? What the hell do they bring to the table?'"

Relative to a league whose members were cozily situated near one another in California, Gonzaga might as well have been in the upper Northwest Territories. Spokane was an outpost to the WCC's southern members, and the Zags hadn't won much of anything since a couple of Big Sky cochampionships back in the sixties.

"Then the bastards made us play downtown," said Fitzgerald.

Indeed, they did. Gonzaga's Kennedy Pavilion was judged not good enough, and the league required GU to play its inaugural season in the WCC in the Spokane Coliseum. In fact, Fitzgerald remembers a Sunday when the Zags loaded all their gear into vans for the short jaunt downtown, one of the ball racks broke, and suddenly, there were basketballs bouncing willy-nilly in the snow.

157

How different it is today. Gonzaga has dominated the conference in the past five seasons, going 59–11 and winning four straight WCC tournaments. With the Zags having buffed their image nationally to an unprecedented level in 2002, the operative question has changed dramatically: how much is the WCC dragging down Gonzaga?

How much would a boulder bring down a hang glider?

It's worth stating, up front, that Gonzaga's basketball ascendancy probably isn't going to last forever. The Zags aren't always going to beat the so-called power conference teams more than they lose to them. They won't always be as appealing an entry to the Great Alaska Shootout or the Maui Classic. There will be years when they would yearn just to be in the NCAA tournament.

But maybe not soon.

The Zags clearly have it rolling, while the rest of the WCC, except for Pepperdine, just as clearly does not.

Why does it matter? It's important on several fronts. First, Gonzaga wouldn't be seeded No. 6 in the 2002 NCAA tournament with a 29–3 record if the WCC were stronger. Gonzaga would play a weaker opponent than Mountain West regular-season champion Wyoming in the first round and probably beat that team. That would help not only Gonzaga but the WCC, which reaps roughly a million dollars over a six-year period from every victory its conference members achieve.

It has further-reaching effects. The best programs, knowing they will be downgraded nationally for the company they keep in the WCC, must schedule harder outside the conference, a headache unto itself and an exercise that can be nigh impossible if a school is trying to satisfy its fan base and avoid selling itself to the highest bidder.

Dr. Ken Anderson, the Gonzaga faculty athletic representative, has a fair perspective on the competitive landscape in the WCC. He grew up around Los Angeles, attended junior college there, and then played at GU while earning his undergraduate degree. He has recently served as president of the conference's executive committee.

In his office at Gonzaga's Jepson Center, where he teaches management, Anderson is asked if he recalls when the league represented a less competitive dichotomy—a couple of good teams at the top, one or two in the middle, and the rest residing in the poorhouse of college basketball.

"I don't," he says. "The gap certainly isn't closing."

Certainly there has been excellence before in the WCC, going back to San Francisco's consecutive national championships in the midfifties with Bill Russell and K. C. Jones. Two decades later, USF assembled strong teams again, and Pepperdine has been the most consistent force in the league, going to nine NCAA tournaments in the past 20 years.

Through most of the league's existence, however, there has been more competition for the top. The fact is, in recent times, the WCC has been a competitive wreck. The league simply isn't as good as it once was.

"Even when Pepperdine was running it under Jim Harrick and Tom Asbury," Anderson says, "I don't think it was quite as disjointed as it is now."

Fitzgerald quotes veteran colleague Dick Davey of Santa Clara, who recalled headier days for the WCC in the eighties. "There were 12 pros in the league," Davey said. "Right now, there's not 10 guys recruited by the Pac-10."

Just about everybody in the WCC has had a spasm of glory in recent years; save for San Diego, each program played in the NCAA tournament in the nineties. The problem has been sustaining it when you're not on television. The Pac-10 Conference is routinely pulling away the better players in the region, and the coach who succeeds is apt to move on.

Anderson remembers playing pickup games at Loyola Marymount in the late seventies and entertaining the same question about a school whose absence from the NCAA tournament (12 years) is second-longest in the WCC after San Diego.

"Why aren't they better?" Anderson says. "It's a great school, a relatively great location. It's like a different world on their campus. Outside of when Hank Gathers and Bo Kimble were there, why haven't they been able to have the success we've had?"

For Gonzaga, it's the ultimate paradox. Yes, it's great dominating the conference. But yes, it would help the Zags immensely if the bottom half of the WCC began acting like it belonged in the league.

These things are, of course, cyclical. To which a Zag supporter might say: long cycle.

How, then, to get the league to grow?

"It's a conversation we constantly have," said WCC commissioner Mike Gilleran. "Nobody sets out to be mediocre. We're all competitors. When we do lose, we don't enjoy it.

"Having said that, you're not going to transform an arena overnight into a place of 15,000 seats. We're not going to become Kentucky overnight."

It was a massive slap in the face when Gonzaga was seeded sixth in the 2002 NCAAs after it played a difficult preconference schedule. As much as it stung the Zags, the hidden haymaker was to the WCC, particularly when selection-committee chairman Lee Fowler put the blame on Gonzaga's strength of schedule.

Anderson found himself seated next to some of the Gonzaga coaches on their flight home following their first-round loss to Wyoming. They talked about how the league might be improved—akin to finding one's way out of a house with no windows and no doors.

Anderson threw out some mild possibilities. He says the Big West Conference used to require that each school satisfy a certain standard in its nonconference opponents' average Ratings Percentage Index (RPI) computer ranking, based on the previous year's numbers.

But that's a fix fraught with problems, starting with the disparity of a team's fortunes from year to year. Then there's the negative of removing scheduling options from any particular program—essentially requiring that it must go on the road if quality opponents won't "return" games.

Probably the biggest flaw, however, is the thinking that scheduling can substitute for competitiveness. Portland could have taken its No. 289 RPI ranking on the road to play six Atlantic Coast Conference and Big Ten teams last year, but it wouldn't have solved a lot to lose each one by 30 points.

Another proposal would allow WCC programs "grants" of, say, $2,000 to use in marketing themselves—specifically, to buy a game on television. But that seems fated to make a less-than-significant dent in the identity crisis, and it speaks to another conundrum in the cycle of the downtrodden. If you're a television syndicate or network, whom do you put on TV from the WCC, Gonzaga or St. Mary's? The answer is obvious. Indeed, last March in Albuquerque, Gonzaga coach Mark Few had informal discussions with CBS officials about a possible future game on the network—something that likely would benefit the Zags a lot more than it would the WCC.

It doesn't appear that Gonzaga is going away anytime soon; in fact, the talent level appears better than ever. Referring to the competition in the league, GU athletic director Mike Roth says, "There may have been a little bit [of thinking] among the other schools, 'Yes, Gonzaga has been winning, but they'll come back to us.' Those other schools are no longer saying, 'They're going to come back to us.' I think the reality is, they're thinking, 'Why can't we, at this other institution, get to where they're at?'"

Both Few and Roth are hopeful. Santa Clara, for instance, is well coached and had three NCAA teams in the midnineties. The two witnessed improvement under current Loyola coach Steve Aggers when he was at nearby Eastern Washington.

But, as Gilleran says, if the makeover is going to happen, it won't happen overnight.

Says Brad Holland, coach at San Diego, "I think they've got it rolling in such a way that, maybe they don't win the conference tournament every year for the next five years, but I think they've got their program to the point where they're always going to be knocking on the door to the NCAAs, and a conference title. They're not going to go away and be fourth or fifth for three or four years in a row.

"I'd love to know what they think."

They think exactly that.

~ ~ ~ ~ ~

In this corner, carrying with him the weight of 18 years as WCC commissioner, Mike Gilleran. In the other corner, with an 81–20 record in three years as a Division I coach—unprecedented in NCAA annals—Mark Few.

If coverage of West Coast Conference basketball weren't so far removed from the national consciousness, the Few/Gilleran relationship would be the stuff of promotions by Don King.

Few on Gilleran: "To bring about change in this league is just amazing. There are just so many people who are conservative, averse to change, even though it's for the betterment of the entire league. It's scary, and it starts with him.

"You need a strong leader to kind of sway people. That's what leaders do. They make people do what they didn't think they could do, or they might not have wanted to do. He's not like that. He knows the presidents, and they kind of basically OK his job. So as long as he doesn't ruffle anybody, he's going to stay on that job quite a while."

Gilleran on Few: "I have no problem with people taking a position that might be different from what the league is doing. The only thing I'd like us to do is keep our disagreements in the family, so to speak."

So it's a dysfunctional family.

At the core of Few's disdain for Gilleran is the measured pace at which change occurs in the West Coast Conference. And surely Few's outlook is somewhat colored by Gonzaga's contribution to the WCC—both in image and on the balance sheet—and the modest return the Zags seem to realize for their trouble.

Touchstone for the Few-versus-the-league-office debate is the WCC postseason tournament. Since its inception in 1987, the event has taken place four times in San Francisco, twice in Los Angeles, seven times in Santa Clara, once in Portland, and twice in San Diego. It has been to Spokane the same number of times it has been to New Delhi: none.

Debate and acrimony over the site of the tournament is ongoing, deep-seated, confounding, and never ending. Sighing, Ken Anderson says, "It really is, in my opinion, an intractable problem."

Wearily, Anderson has trudged into WCC meetings from Spokane and tried to articulate the angst of his coach, Few, and his athletic director, Roth, to the executive committee. He has returned, often more discouraged, and tried to explain the stance of the rest of the league to Few and Roth.

"The perfect solution would be a nice, 6,000-seat arena in Palm Springs," Anderson says. "If we had that, I'm pretty confident we'd be there. Every place we look at is too run down, too expensive, too big—and I don't think we're looking for a perfect solution."

Or, as Gilleran puts it, "This conversation probably started back in 1986. I don't think there's a formula or format that hasn't been considered."

In June of 2002, three months after a fusillade of criticism from Few at the league tournament, the WCC presidents settled on new format and siting procedures. It provides half the loaf Gonzaga had been seeking, easing the path to the tournament title for the teams that dominate the regular season, but keeping the event at campus sites, much to the Zags' chagrin.

All eight teams will continue to participate, even though Few says, "If you're seventh or eighth, you probably have no business being there."

There are two levels of protection for the better-seeded teams. In round-one games, seed Nos. 5 and 8 will meet, and seed Nos. 6 and 7. In the second round, seed No. 3 faces the winner of the 6-7 game and No. 4 meets the survivor of the 5-8 game. At that point, seed Nos. 1 and 2 still haven't played.

In the semifinals, seed No. 2 meets the winner of the game involving seed No. 3. Seed No. 1 faces the victor of the game involving seed No. 4. The two survivors meet in the championship.

This format means that the top two seeds—Pepperdine and Gonzaga in 2002—only have to risk themselves twice rather than three times. In the WCC, that means one less game against a team whose computer ranking is often in the 200s. Still, because of campus siting, it leaves open the possibility of a capable team outside the top two playing in the semifinals on its home court—something that makes Few crazy.

The presidents simultaneously approved a proposal that will rotate the tournament on a regional basis from San Diego in 2003 to the Bay Area in 2004–2005 to the Northwest in 2006–2007 and to southern California in 2008–2009. Bidding will determine which school hosts in those cycles. Gonzaga expects to prevail over Portland, hosting the tournament for the first time two decades after it was instituted.

"If we have a new building, I expect to have it," says Anderson. "If we don't have a new building, we have no chance."

Anderson says the overwhelming impetus for the format revision was a realization of just how much NCAA tournament money could be at stake.

"It's pretty clear the conference now understands the importance of generating revenue in that tournament," Anderson says. "We want to get our best team in, and we want to get that team in with the best seed possible."

"It's important to recognize regular-season success," said Gilleran. "This sort of marries together the two elements of rewarding regular-season merit and including all student-athletes."

Few is encouraged, but hardly satisfied. "I think it's a step in the right direction," he said. "Certainly it's better than what we were doing. However, it still needs to be put on a neutral floor or the winner's home court. The home-court advantage is so huge in college basketball. It's hard to feel great about this when that's still probably the biggest issue.

"At least it's a step."

In a perfect world, the WCC would find a neutral, warm-weather site that splits the difference geographically—say, somewhere in the Bay Area or Sacramento. But the world of the WCC is far from perfect.

Gilleran says the basic added cost of a neutral site over a campus venue—mostly in rental fees—would be $60,000 to $120,000. Since one of the primary aims of having a tournament is to make some money, another key consideration is whether going off-campus would forfeit a part of the gate receipts the league now enjoys.

Gilleran says the WCC netted about $18,000 from the 2001 tournament in San Diego, but preliminary numbers from 2002 bump that total to about $63,000. Some estimates put the total number of Gonzaga fans having traveled to USD's 5,000-seat Jenny Craig Pavilion as high as 2,000.

The mandate is clear from the WCC presidents: Don't lose money on the venture. So the executive committee has been scared off from locating the event at a neutral site in any of the 15 seasons it has taken place.

That has left the powers-that-be to consider how to make a campus site fair. As luck would have it, no host school has ever won the tournament, which, to some people, is a fine argument for preserving the status quo.

The latest resolution comes on the heels of an endless debate that has entertained every possible clannish, myopic argument—along with some visionary ones—over the years. To illustrate, only a year earlier, the league's executive committee, which consists of two representatives from each school, proposed a six-team format with the top-seeded team hosting the surviving four. First, the idea passed the committee in a split vote. Whoops, in came new information: some Bay Area hotels were said not to be able to guarantee rooms at reduced rates with the minimal five- or six-day advance notice that might result from a close league race. There were similar concerns about airfares.

To some, that news seemed preposterous. If the tournament were played at Santa Clara, for instance, would residential hotels out in the east Bay Area soak participating teams for $189 a night? After all, unless the women's tournament landed at the same site, the event would involve only three teams needing probably 25 to 30 rooms each.

"I didn't like the numbers either," says Roth. "But I'm not there. They said they talked to the hotels."

That fostered more discussion; the WCC is as fretful—some would say indecisive—as Ally McBeal. This is a league in which the subject of possible snowstorms in Spokane has arisen as a dark possibility during tournament talks.

Anderson cites another factor that has figured in the debate. He says the WCC "places a huge premium on the experience at the championship, whether it's basketball or other sports." Until the past couple of years, that meant competing teams stayed at the same hotel—such is the commitment to a collegial atmosphere at the tournament.

"Some institutions buy into the 'festival' atmosphere," says Anderson. "If I'm a basketball player [from Gonzaga], the last thing I want is to walk down the hall and see somebody from Pepperdine."

A league that should focus on producing revenue and positioning itself best for the NCAA tournament seems caught up in too many trifling concerns. For instance, somebody worried aloud about traffic if teams were stationed too far from the venue. Others seem wedded to a warm-weather site. "It's one thing after another," says Anderson. "We've been talking about site location forever."

In another split vote in 2001, the executive committee reversed itself, leading to the policy change of 2002. No doubt Few's outburst after a hard-fought semi-final victory over San Diego brought the issue to a head. "If USD wins here next year," he said bitterly that night, "I'll be happy."

San Diego Union-Tribune columnist Nick Canepa took Few to task, writing that he "was a few bricks shy of a load last night. . . . It's easy to see where Few is coming from, but he was out of line on this one. He made it sound as though his team is too good for all of this . . . Gonzaga, for heaven's sake, has been good for a few years. It has built a nice program up there and should be proud of what it's done . . . but this isn't Duke. Gonzaga didn't even win the WCC's regular-season title outright, tying with Pepperdine."

Only a couple of hours after Few went off, Gilleran hosted his own press gathering and fired back at Few, saying, "None of us is bigger than the group. I represent the group; I work for the group. So the day I start to think I've got the answer better than the collective wisdom of the group is the day I should leave."

Gonzaga's frustration is understandable. Not only has it been the league's cash cow in recent years, it also found itself in a lose-lose proposition in San Diego. If it had fallen to the Toreros, it probably would have been tagged with a No. 7 or 8 seed in the NCAA tournament. But winning against the No. 138–ranked RPI team didn't help its status either.

"Campus sites are fine if you take it to the [regular-season] winner," Few says. "Campus sites are a joke if you keep giving it to the fifth-place team."

He points out that the Zags, despite a 25–6 record in 1999, might not have been selected for the NCAA tournament without a championship-game victory over Santa Clara, the host team—meaning the Elite Eight run that ignited Gonzaga's national prominence would never have happened.

Gonzaga officials are on a campaign to locate the tournament at neutral sites. The 12,000-seat Spokane Arena would be a wonderful adjunct to their argument; unfortunately, the building already hosts a venerable institution in Washington, the state Class B tournament, during the weekend of the WCC. The Class B brings together the smallest schools in the state, and it's essentially an immovable object.

"The Spokane Arena is committed to the B tournament through 2006 right now," Roth says. "The B tournament sells out every year; it has tremendous history. For us to come in and say we want to supplant that, I don't think that's realistic."

Nor, he says, is the notion of pushing back the WCC tournament a couple of days.

"The only way to do that is to miss three days of class," he says. "I talked to our president, Father Spitzer, and he basically said, 'No way. Our student-athletes miss enough class as it is.'"

If for no other reason than as recognition for its value to the league, Gonzaga deserves to have hosted the tournament at least once. But with a capacity of only 4,000, the Kennel is not an attractive venue.

Roth has pushed hard for the San Diego Sports Arena. Few has proposed neutral sites in rotation, with one year in the Northwest, two years in the Bay Area, and another two in southern California.

"Have a plan and figure it out," he says. "They can't."

Roth waits for the day that the floor on Gonzaga's new 6,000-seat building is lacquered.

"The only reason people say we can't host is the building is too small," he says. "When we get our new building, that excuse goes out the window."

The vote to bring the tournament to the Northwest by 2006 means the league is thinking like Roth. Gonzaga's first hosting of the tournament would come two decades after it was inaugurated.

That will be a step for the Zags, as should the new tournament format in a league whose positioning for the NCAA is vital.

"Hey, we run the league with NCAA men's [tournament] money," Anderson says. "If we go back to having one team in and they're one-and-done, based on what I've looked at, in about four years we're hurting."

~ ~ ~ ~ ~

Does any of this really matter? To Gonzaga, it matters plenty. The second-rate profile of the league nationally is a millstone for the Zags, particularly when judgment day—Selection Sunday—arrives in March. The basketball committee has consistently looked askance at Gonzaga's portfolio. Indeed, the Zags' No. 12 seed in 2001 indicated clearly that without a league-tournament championship, Gonzaga would not have made the field.

That weighs most directly on Gonzaga's nonleague scheduling. The Zags have been loading up their November and December schedules admirably, both to try to better a growing program and to buff their credentials for the NCAA selectors in March.

As of the spring of 2002, the 2002–2003 schedule was representative of Gonzaga's burgeoning success. It included the Maui Classic—with Kentucky, Indiana, and Utah—and games against Georgia, Stanford, and St. Joseph's.

But a by-product of the Gonzaga success is that it finds itself in a scheduling no-man's-land.

"I can't believe what a nightmare that's been," says Jerry Krause, GU's director of basketball operations, who handles much of it. "I don't believe I was naive about it, but it's changed so much in the last 10 years, it's unbelievable."

As a program in a so-called midmajor conference, but one that aspires realistically to bigger things than most of its colleagues, Gonzaga dwells in a strange vortex of forces that conspire to make scheduling like solving a Rubik's Cube.

Schools from the so-called power conferences have a built-in head start; the strength of their leagues will ensure a quality schedule. They can thus supplement with nonleague "guarantee" games—in which they pay a lesser program to come in and sacrifice themselves for a victory for the host—or perhaps a sprinkling of home-and-home arrangements with schools at a commensurate level.

Those schools hold the cards.

In this game, Gonzaga holds almost none.

It has trouble getting games against "power-conference" schools. Those programs won't venture into the Kennel as part of a home-and-home deal, so Gonzaga offers to put it in the Spokane Arena. But those powers know the risks, and usually, they don't want to venture to a place where they're liable to lose. They also know they might drop such a game on their home floor, and although

Gonzaga has the respect of basketball savants nationwide, it still looks a lot better to Kentucky fans to lose a game to Illinois than to lose one to Gonzaga.

Gonzaga, naturally, doesn't want to sell its soul by playing a raft of "guarantee" games. There has to be some equity in the process.

Last spring, the Zags called Nebraska coach Barry Collier to inquire about a home-and-home series.

"We're filled next year," said the wary Collier. "Matter of fact, we're filled for the next millennium. You guys are too good."

Krause says the Zags get calls all the time from the midmajor programs, or higher, but not the power-conference schools. Butler, Ball State, Creighton, and Marquette are willing to do a home-and-home. But those have their dangers; the RPI of such prospective opponents may not be high enough to help Gonzaga, and most of those schools are so far distant that travel considerations weigh in.

The NCAA selection committee routinely rewards those programs willing to go on the road and play quality competition. That makes for mutually exclusive athletic-versus-academic forces, especially pertaining to a school like Gonzaga. If it can't realistically schedule tougher without spending significant days on the road, it inevitably is missing classes and running afoul of a mandate by its president and counter to the tide of sentiment in college athletics.

Gonzaga's 2001–2002 schedule was a fine example of damned-if-you-do-damned-if-you-don't happenstance. The Zags played Washington and Washington State, blowing out both. Those are sensible regional matchups, but both Pac-10 schools turned out to be bottom-feeders, doing nothing for the Zags' power rating.

Gonzaga scheduled St. Joseph's on the road and Fresno State in Los Angeles. St. Joe's was widely seen as a preseason top 10 team, and Fresno State's coach then, Jerry Tarkanian, believed he had a Final Four–quality team when the matchup was drawn up. Both teams flopped, and so did Gonzaga's effort to fortify its schedule.

Then there are the financial realities of being Gonzaga. Few wants two "guarantee" games of his own—teams he can pay to play at GU on a one-shot basis. But there is considerable demand for such fodder, and the 4,000-seat capacity in the Kennel means limited revenue available to pay off such visitors. In that bidding, Gonzaga can't offer money with the big boys, who may go up to $60,000 or $75,000 if their arena size can justify it.

As the Zags were finishing their 2002–2003 scheduling last spring, Krause had a cap of $35,000 he could offer for a guarantee game. People in the athletic department crunched numbers for three days to see whether they could possibly bump that to $40,000.

"Mike Roth [athletic director] has said that as soon as the new arena is done, you'll have this much money for guarantee games," Krause says.

Says Few, "Scheduling at somewhere like this is the hardest thing of the whole job, harder than recruiting. It's just a never-ending thing. There's more high jinks going on than there is in recruiting. The ADs are involved with sneaking out of deals and not keeping their word. Everybody wants all home games. It's just a big poker game."

A coach whom Krause knows told him how his old school, a power in the Big 12, often handles home-and-home arrangements. It signs up but always ensures that it gets the first home game of the deal. Then it buys its way out of the second game with, say, $25,000, provided for in a default clause. Contractually, it's fine. Ethically, it's dubious.

For Northwest schools, the scheduling game is tougher because of geography. There are only four Division I programs in Washington, and if philosophical or petty differences between them militate against a contract agreement, it often means a longer and more costly road trip.

Last spring, Few threw up his hands over a disagreement with the University of Idaho, only 90 miles away.

"We were scheduled to play them down there last year [2001–2002]," Few said. "They're struggling. They would have sold out. They didn't want to do it. I've never heard of a team giving up a home game. Luckily, the Fresno State thing opened up."

Few says Idaho coach Leonard Perry indicated the Vandals would come to Gonzaga two years in a row to atone for the bailout. Then, when that verbal agreement morphed into a home-and-home proposal, Few turned it over to Roth to work out with Idaho athletic director Mike Bohn.

An eight-year agreement was hatched, Few says. But Bohn then called back and pleaded financial problems and pulled out.

"It really just had to do with the fact we needed to schedule a little smaller to try to give us a chance to build it back up," said Bohn, who indicated a five-year agreement, with three games at Gonzaga, may still begin in 2003–2004.

"Financial considerations have hit our state since September 11. As our budget has been affected by cutbacks in state funding, we were forced to play a couple of guarantee games for financial reasons. We're going to go to another institution and receive a significant guarantee."

By June, Few likes to be wading into a trout stream and casting a fly. Increasingly, he's pounding phones in his office, trying to hook one last opponent.

~ ~ ~ ~ ~

For those who wonder whether Gonzaga has forever outgrown Loyola Marymount and St. Mary's, there's this tasty debate: could the Zags be better served in a different conference?

"We're looking into it," Few says. "I think leagues would want us for our basketball. To step up from here, you're probably looking at football leagues. It'll be interesting to see where basketball goes."

There are all sorts of pie-in-the-sky possibilities: Gonzaga in the Pac-10 or Conference USA for basketball? Gonzaga as part of a Western conference dominated by basketball programs? Gonzaga as part of a breakaway coalition of schools that feel frustrated by the constraints of the lower echelon of 326 Division I basketball programs?

For the foreseeable future, any of those seems unlikely.

"There's a question of Gonzaga basketball," says Mike Roth, "and there's a question of Gonzaga. For the most part, those are mutually inclusive. They work together and in very close harmony."

Institutionally, the WCC schools are compatible—mostly Catholic, half Jesuit. Any proposed split of Gonzaga to maximize its basketball possibilities would be seen by many as an intrusion of athletics over academics.

Roth concedes the Zags have discussed it, all the way to the office of president Father Robert Spitzer. But there are significant snags, prominent among them that the conferences usually ranked ahead of the West Coast have football programs. It would be something of a square peg in a round hole for the Zags to try to join a football conference just for basketball.

It happens. Notre Dame has been a member of the Big East in basketball and an independent in football. Army has been a basketball member of the Patriot League and a part of Conference USA in football.

But it would take a change in West Coast Conference membership rules to accommodate any such hybrid move by Gonzaga. One of the sports expressly required by the league is basketball.

"My guess is, they're not gonna let that happen," said Roth. "We lose that vote 7–0."

There are no obvious avenues for Gonzaga. The Pac-10, for instance, is football-dominated, and when it has had a chance to consider church-affiliated schools like Brigham Young as potential additions, it has turned thumbs down. Conference USA has interested the Zags from time to time, but it is fraught with downside, from the oily reputation of a few of its basketball coaches to the prospect of some hideous travel itineraries. Imagine a Gonzaga road trip for a conference game at East Carolina.

Says Roth, "There's really no other place for us right now."

~ ~ ~ ~ ~

Notwithstanding all the difficulties with scheduling and the WCC, these are good times at Gonzaga. To steal a line from three decades ago by the band The Who, the Zags can see for miles and miles, and they have to like the view. They're getting better players all the time—unprecedented players against the backdrop of their history of slow-developing works in progress.

The coaching lineage is established. Dan Monson begot Mark Few, who someday will give way to Bill Grier, per a written agreement in the spring of 2001.

"As long as I remain the assistant coach at Gonzaga, in the event Mark were to leave, I would step into the head-coaching position," Grier says. "It gives you a great sense of security, but at the same time, it makes you a little more hungry, because we better do a great job of recruiting. Not only do we want to keep it going now, we want to have a good base if he leaves.

"It keeps me pretty focused."

The administration is committed; the players and coaches are in place. So is there any fragility to the Gonzaga phenomenon?

It's an intriguing question. As grounded as the whole operation is, might it be only one poor coaching hire away from a return to harder times, one mistake from scissoring the successful line of coaches, one wrong move away from rendering Gonzaga questionable as a destination spot for recruits?

The likable Roth, himself a former assistant coach at Gonzaga, is the man with the keys to that vault.

"That's part of being successful," he says. "If we had a coaching change, could we become mediocre? Yeah, those things are all potentially there. It's our job to make sure we make the right decisions."

There's a larger issue, one that would have been unthinkable at Gonzaga as recently as five years ago: can the Zags have it both ways? Can they embody the concept of student-athlete while being a top 15 program? And will their public accept it if they suddenly go 15–12 again?

Can you be quaint and cold-blooded at the same time?

"I worry now that they're feeding the monster a little bit," says Dan Fitzgerald.

At a gym working out, Fitzgerald overheard this: "God, I can't believe they lost to Wyoming."

Ken Anderson was aware of people last winter making reservations for the West Regional at San Jose, rounds three and four of the tournament. The Sweet 16 was a foregone conclusion.

"I think eventually somebody will get fired, somebody will have a tough time," Fitzgerald said. "Or does the institution change because of your athletic program? I think it has to be cocurricular, not extracurricular.

"You can begin to believe your own bullshit. They've done a wonderful job of handling that."

For his part, Few seems undaunted by expectation. On the other hand, he's never had a .500 season.

"We've been dealing with expectations since the Elite Eight run," he says. "Whether it's fair or not, it really doesn't matter. They're out there. I'd rather have expectations than apathy. We, as a staff, and our players are going to have a lot of expectations on ourselves anyway."

Gonzaga can't yet recruit with Kansas and UCLA, but it is growing ever closer. The day could come when somebody fudges on issues of character or academics to accommodate that "monster."

"Do we have to recruit a different type of kid?" Anderson asks rhetorically. "Or do we *think* we have to recruit a different type of kid?"

Over in the administration building, Father Spitzer makes it clear he has mulled the athletics-versus-academics debate.

"We want to make sure our priorities are straight," he says. "No one has ever suggested we become a factory. I haven't had to put the kibosh on anything. Our AD and our coaches do just fine. I have never, ever felt the need to go, 'Uh, oh, something's getting out of control.'

"I don't think anybody's in the exoneration business here. I know. We're in the business of trying to make sure we have a program that really befits the reputation of this school."

Spitzer raises money for both academics and athletics. He tries to ensure that any budget increases for basketball have a commensurate bump in the classroom.

"If we ever get to the point where we say, 'Win at all costs' . . . God, it won't be under me," says Spitzer. "It's not in me. It's not in our vice president. It's not in our athletic director, and it's not in our coaches."

If any of the Zag brain trust is sensitive to the ills of college athletics, it is Krause, a veteran coach whose credentials include authoring 13 coaching books and a professorship in sports philosophy and physical education at West Point. It was there that he monitored a survey in the early nineties showing that ethical standards and moral values involving sports eroded among cadets in their four years there—and most among those in the high-level intercollegiate sports.

It is poisoning like that—among administrators, coaches, players—that Gonzaga must now avoid to fully consummate its basketball miracle.

"With all that success, there will be more and more temptation to cut corners," Krause says. "The monster must be fed. But these guys have done a marvelous job of not buying into the compromises."

Today, it is not easy to forecast what might take place to reverse the meteoric rise of Gonzaga basketball. But then, it isn't easy to explain exactly what caused it to spark in the first place.

"My counterpart at Santa Clara was asking the question," says Anderson. "Like somewhere in the basement of the ad building, there was this huge master plan for Gonzaga basketball.

"I don't think it's that simple. If I sat down for six months and had to develop a blueprint for Loyola to copy, I couldn't tell you."

13

Gonzaga Confidential

Wednesday, March 6, 2002

Winter has not yet deserted Spokane. An early-morning storm has dumped several inches of snow on the area.

The weather is in stark contrast to what the Zags left behind in San Diego, where they won a fourth straight West Coast Conference tournament by beating Pepperdine, 96–90. In fact, the team stayed behind most of Tuesday, changing its schedule to celebrate another title by the hotel pool. The Zags were supposed to fly out at 8:00 A.M.; they caught an evening flight instead.

"We just figured with everything that would be waiting for them back here . . ." says Jerry Krause, the director of basketball operations, trailing off.

What's waiting is anticipation and adulation. Mark Few calls it a relaxing time, and indeed, there is comfort in knowing the NCAA bid is in the bag and that the rest of the college basketball world is busily scouting opponents and playing back-to-back-to-back games.

There are demands nonetheless. The Zags are scouting College of Southern Idaho guard Ricky Clemons in a tournament at St. George, Utah. Because of the terrorism of September 11 and reduced flight schedules, that now means a flight to Seattle, a connection to Las Vegas, and then a drive north. At the same time, there's the state 4A boys tournament in Tacoma. Other than highly regarded 6'9"

Sean Mallon of Ferris High, it's unlikely Gonzaga would sign anybody from what it sees there, but there are always juniors and sophomores to ferret out.

Then there are the media requests. One wouldn't think the crush would be so great: the local newspaper, TV and radio stations, the media on the more populous west side of the state, maybe a call from CBS or ESPN.

Not so. It's an all-out blitz. In his office, sports information director Oliver Pierce is winnowing down an unwieldy list of media needs. He says he cleared his voice mailbox on Monday morning while in San Diego, and by 3:00 P.M. Tuesday, there were 50 new messages.

Pierce's office seems to reflect the glut of requests. It's the prototype publicist's office, with promotional posters and stacks of press releases, videotapes, CD-ROMs, and press guides, some perilously close to sliding off to oblivion.

A radio station in Birmingham, Alabama, wants an interview with a player or coach. A radio guy in Nashville, Tennessee, wants one. So does one in Providence, Rhode Island. All of those, and many others, will have to be turned down.

"'Fraid we're gonna have to say no," Pierce is saying. He hangs up and dials another number.

"Matt, based on the time you said in the voice mail, that's probably not going to work. Cory's probably in class."

"Sorry I couldn't accommodate you this year."

Somebody wants a few minutes with Dan Dickau. Failing that, he asks for Heather Nevenner, Dickau's comely fiancée who recently appeared in a photograph with him in *Sports Illustrated*.

"If you can get hold of her, go ahead. You go through the Portland Trail Blazers dance team."

Everybody, seemingly, has an angle in mind, certain it will tell the story of this team. Pierce gets a call from *The Men's Journal*, requesting to shadow one of the coaches through the NCAA tournament.

"I know how the coaches feel about that kind of stuff," Pierce says. "I didn't even ask them."

This is the standard for interview requests: local media get priority. Regional outlets come next, along with hometown media of players and the playing site where the Zags are headed.

"There just comes a point," Pierce says, "when you've got to say no."

~ ~ ~ ~ ~

Across the way in the Gonzaga athletic offices on the third floor of the Charlotte Y. Martin Centre, Jerry Krause is compiling report cards. The business of a college basketball team may seem all performance, a final score, and a subjective critique from the coach, but there's more.

"I picked it up from a junior high coach in Ohio, Paul Keller," Krause says, referring to his grading system. "He started charting Ohio State in the Jerry Lucas days."

The basis is points per possession. Before the three-point shot, success was measured by whether a team scored above or below 1.05 points per possession. Now the goal is 1.15.

Because of its scintillating second half against Pepperdine—"unbelievable," Krause calls it—Gonzaga was off the charts. The Zags rang up 1.33 points per possession after halftime, giving them a robust 1.23 number for the game, compared to a season average of 1.14. Pepperdine answered with two halves of 1.15, much higher than Gonzaga normally allows.

"Defensively, we're at .94," Krause says. "The goal is .95."

It was Dickau who fueled the searing second half with a jaw-dropping, seven-and-a-half-minute stretch in which he scored 19 points during a 32–10 Gonzaga run. Krause says he "saw Bill Bradley in Portland" (in a third-place game against Wichita State at the 1965 NCAA finals, Bradley threw in 58 points—hook shots from the baseline, jump shots, free throws—to lead Princeton to a blowout victory). He also saw Dickau's game on the road at Loyola Marymount this year, in which Dickau tied a conference record with nine three-pointers on 12 attempts amid 34 points. And this game against Pepperdine will find its proper place in Krause's memory bank.

"You're seeing something special," Krause says, six days before Dickau will be named to the Associated Press All-America first team. "You don't often see kids step up and take the bit like that. He's really got courage."

Turnovers are also monitored. The Zags attempt to hold them to 18 percent of their possessions.

But points per possession is simple math. The grading system goes much deeper, measuring defense and rebounding as well.

In the game that knocked the Zags from the NCAA tournament in 2001, they were bludgeoned on the backboards, 47–28, by a much more physical Michigan State team.

"That was one area we've never emphasized here," Krause says. "Leon Rice went back to all the NCAA games we'd lost, and in almost every one, we'd been completely wiped out on the boards."

Players can get stronger in the weight room—and they did, judging by the fact that as Krause spoke, Gonzaga led the nation in rebounding margin at 9.3—but how could they gauge rebounding effort in a game other than cold statistics?

The Zags devised a plan to put a number on it, seeking a 90 percent effort. Players are charted by whether they hustled to the open spaces on offensive rebounds rather than simply leaned over the defensive rebounder's back. Four players routinely go to the offensive boards, and the fifth, the "deep safety," must retreat to the center circle by the time of the rebound to get a favorable grade.

"When we started practice in the fall, guys were in the 60s and 70s," Krause says. "Now, at this point in the season, it's in the 80s and 90s."

So refined is the system that during any given timeout, instead of barking that they need to hit the boards, coaches will inform players exactly what the percentage might be at that point. The goal is to come up with 40 percent of offensive rebounds and 80 on defense. Gonzaga snagged 42 percent on offense against Pepperdine but succumbed to the Waves' athleticism and got only 65 percent of defensive rebounds.

On defense, the Zags have always been more about containment than deny-and-smother.

"We're probably not going to get the best athletes in the country," Krause says. "But one thing we picked up from Marquette that we always emphasize is trying to get your hand on the ball."

Like most teams, the Zags thus count deflections. They had only 30 against Pepperdine, lowest in their three games of the WCC tournament—again, a reflection of the Waves' quickness and ability to get shots off the dribble.

Finally, each player will get a letter grade for his performance. Against Pepperdine, Alex Hernandez and Ronny Turiaf turned in As. Stepp and Dickau had only B-pluses because of missed free throws.

Dickau finished with 29 points in a performance for the ages. Stepp had 24 points.

Tough graders.

~ ~ ~ ~ ~

In Few's office, a television is on, with a fuzzy picture of another tournament game—fuzzy because on several other, better TVs, the Zags are videotaping games just in case they include NCAA opponents.

"We're taping maybe 50 games down the stretch," Few says. An enterprise on the East Coast specializes in rushing game tapes to tournament qualifiers after the pairings are announced, but the national network of coaches also helps to provide information. "This time of year," Few says, "you bank on your buddies out there."

Dinner is Thai food at the home of Mark and Marcy Few in woodsy south Spokane. Few is driving a large GMC Yukon. "I learned you want to have a big dog out there," Mark Few says.

Several years ago on a Sunday morning, he and Marcy were headed to church, Marcy driving, when they stopped shortly out of the house to fasten seat belts. In that brief moment of inattention, their Honda Civic slid slightly to the left into the path of a large oncoming car. The seat belts didn't get engaged. Marcy was tossed against the steering wheel, bruised but otherwise unhurt. Mark was thrown to the windshield but then recoiled backward, opening a deep gash on his scalp and another on his left cheek.

"It was so weird, feeling warm," he says, "all this blood running down."

He turns the Yukon left up a sharp hill to their home. On this wintry night, there's no way you'd make it without four-wheel drive.

Marcy has gone out to pick up groceries with the couple's two-year-old son, A.J. But the television in the living room is on, tuned to the St. John's–Seton Hall game in the Big East tournament.

On the screen, ESPN commentator Jay Bilas is assessing the early tournament happenings. One of the bright minds on the tube today in college basketball, Bilas brings a sense of erudition to the game. He was in Spokane for the Pepperdine-Gonzaga game in mid-February, and Few recalls how, on "senior night," with parents in town and everyone in a celebratory mood after a 91–78 Zags victory, people wanted to chat Bilas up and have photographs taken with him. He obliged willingly and hung around until 2:00 A.M. despite an early-morning flight.

Now Marcy and A.J. have returned, and the moppet, who has his mom's dark Basque eyes, is delighted to see his father. Few gets down on the kitchen floor so they can play a game of catch with a motorized toy airplane amid A.J.'s happy squeals.

Later, Marcy whips up a blueberry cobbler and vanishes to put A.J. to bed. Twenty minutes later, he bursts from a bedroom into the living room, eyes bright, nowhere near sleep.

Maybe he's caught up in March Madness, too.

Thursday, March 7, 2002

"Sit. Sit! No, stay. Stay! No, down. Down!"

Inside the Kennel, the Zags' 4,000-seat arena at the Martin Centre, the center of attention is a real, live mascot, known to everybody around the athletic department only as "Q."

In 1999, Gonzaga, in its second NCAA appearance, got a gift from the Peak, an FM radio station in Spokane. He was a full-bred English bulldog, 16 weeks old, given to celebrate the school's nickname.

Mike Hogan, Gonzaga's young assistant athletic director for development, volunteered to be the dog's keeper. Most of the time, that means Q lives life at home, but on the third floor of the Martin Centre, he also is part of the landscape some days, roaming freely in and out of offices like the coaches, chomping on a rawhide bone in a hallway, lapping water from a dish inside Hogan's office.

When the school accepted the bulldog, there was the question of a name. People suggested "Mons," for Dan Monson, who coached that '99 team to the brink of the Final Four. But in honor of Quentin Hall, who had 62 steals and was a defensive stopper on that club, the pup was christened "Q."

"Quentin was the ultimate little bulldog," says Hogan.

Technically, Q's name is Spike Q. Gonzaga, but everybody knows him as Q. He has reached a level of canine celebrity few pooches know. He has been pictured on a poster for Spokane's annual three-on-three summer Hoopfest, and he is the object of many a television camera operator's lens.

"He's become fairly famous," Hogan says.

Today, Q, a brown-and-white 60-pounder, ascends to a new level of fame. CBS is in town to do interviews with Few, Dickau, and Zach Gourde; to shoot the campus—and to photograph Q as a prop for a segment on Gonzaga.

The lights in the Kennel are turned off. The only illumination is a spotlight on Q, which he is finding a bit nerve-racking. Hogan is trying to coach him through several positions, while Q casts a bemused look at the glare behind Hogan.

"He's not Lassie," Hogan says. "That's the first time he's ever been in a dark room being photographed."

But Q settles down to oblige the three technicians, sitting and finally lying down with one leg splayed behind him.

"I bet he gets more babes," says one of the camera operators.

Q doesn't deny it.

~ ~ ~ ~ ~

If you want to get Mark Few going, bring up the National Basketball Association. For a long time, the only Zag in the NBA has been John Stockton. There is scant obvious connection between the Gonzaga program and the NBA, this being a place where talents are frequently maximized and athleticism is not necessarily a primary component.

Few is on the phone talking to a friend about the NBA and scouting director Marty Blake. Some of Few's distaste for the league stems from its treatment last year of Casey Calvary, who wasn't invited to the 2001 NBA predraft camp in Chicago, the major proving ground.

"They said we'd been on national TV seven or eight times and they had a couple of junior-college kids come out that they hadn't seen," Few says. "They said they didn't know anything about them."

Calvary ended up starring for the Isuzu Giga Cats in the Japan professional league in 2001–2002. Few, meanwhile, crosses his fingers and says, "It's taboo to be a senior now."

Few believes that while the NBA professes concern about the rush of underclassmen and high school players who come out early, those players also provide the league with a certain comfort zone. His take: franchises realize the seniors come with the outside expectation that they will contribute early, thereby putting pressure on the club. But the younger prospects usually have a "future" label attached, giving teams a convenient out if the players don't develop.

~ ~ ~ ~ ~

This will be the Zags' first practice since the WCC championship game three days earlier. First, though, there's a midafternoon bustle outside the gym, as some 15 professionally dressed men and women are milling about.

They're with Festival 2002, a revival featuring Franklin Graham, son of evangelist Billy Graham. It happens to be a crusade that encircled Shaun Alexander, the Seattle Seahawks running back, who did some setup and staging for the cause when he was a student at Alabama. Alexander is in town representing the event at a breakfast and luncheon.

"He saw the Gonzaga U. road sign," says festival director Danny Little, "and said, 'Dan Dickau.'"

That led to an introduction of Alexander and Dickau, and here in a hallway outside the gym, the NFL player is hugging good-bye to a future member of the NBA.

Moments later, it's practice time. Few, in jeans and a blue plaid shirt, talks briefly to the team and then goes to the locker room to change into sweats. At the end of a warm-up period, Blake Stepp casts the last shot before the players gather around Few, hurling up a contorted half-hook from midcourt that rips through the net.

It's a purposeful workout, mostly spent on refining the Zags' endless offensive sets. Few is an inveterate offensive tinkerer who says he puts in about three new sets a week, depending on who might be shooting well or how an opponent defends the Zags.

"We probably call 50 or 60 sets, quick-hitters," Few says.

There are seemingly as many names for them as there are in some phone books. Depending on who's setting the on-ball screen, there's one for Cory Violette ("Boise") and one for Ronny Turiaf ("Paris").

"We give 'em names of their girlfriends," Few says. "We run out of names."

Few is clearly the man in charge, involved and instructive. But there is precious little yelling, just an abundance of coaching. The lingo is mostly coach-speak—the shuffle, the curl, the high pick.

"You big guys are starting to drag a little bit," Few admonishes. "I don't know why you're not getting down the floor."

There's a jauntiness to the workout, a give-and-take. Few is the conductor, but there's no me-versus-you sense to the session. Clearly, they're all in this together.

Few directs them into a quick scrimmage: Islands of the Caribbean (Turiaf and Alex Hernandez head up this unit) against Idaho-Washington-California. The IOC team wins, 20–12, which plunges the losers into some brief conditioning drills.

At one point, Turiaf and reserve forward Jay Sherrell, jousting in the key, lock gazes, butt heads, and give each other healthy shoves. But it doesn't materialize into anything of consequence.

This will not be a practice Few wants to bottle. Clearly, the Zags are sluggish, probably from the time off and the emotion spent on Pepperdine.

"We were a little down, I suppose, from the tournament," says Jerry Krause.

At the finish, Few tells a manager to put seven minutes on the clock. He starts the players through a few baseline-to-baseline sprints, gives them a short message, and then has them repeat the sprints. They end by going through a wind-sapping circuit of the six baskets in the gym, stopping two-by-two at each one to jump to the rim five times in rapid succession. Gourde, last in the procession, punctuates his circuit by grabbing the rim and chinning himself.

Practice must get better, and it will. Later, Few will say, "What the heck was that? We haven't done that all year."

Friday, March 8, 2002

At the bookstore on campus, it's a bull market on Gonzaga shirts. Two cashiers are working registers, yet the line to buy paraphernalia at times goes 10 deep during the noon hour.

"Half the shelves are empty," says a clerk. "We have to stock 'em every day."

Four days later, Dave Heinze, the store director, will put it in perspective: in a week's time, he figures they sold probably 5,000 shirts from one vendor, with tournament-oriented design. Including the ones with the generic Gonzaga logo, he guesses 10,000 were sold in a week, including website orders.

"People buy multiple items," he says. "People come with shopping lists. It's not that they wander in and say, 'I'm going to see if I can find something that catches my eye.'"

On the Saturday preceding NCAA selections, Heinze opened the store for four hours and did $14,000 worth of business. He says sales in December of 2001 were up 73 percent from the same month in 2000.

"Year after year, the intensity of interest just seems to build and build," he says.

~ ~ ~ ~ ~

In a hallway, grade point averages of all Gonzaga teams are on a bulletin board. The basketball team posted a 2.57 GPA—nothing spectacular—in the fall of 2001, following a spring semester in 2001 of 2.92.

This is midterm week, fortuitous in that after Monday night, there are no basketball games.

"It's relaxing," says Gourde. "We wait until Sunday and then we find out our fate. Right now, we try to get caught up in class.

"I've been missing a lot of class lately. Most of the professors are pretty understanding. They have a pretty good feeling of what we're going through."

He smiles impishly. "Some of them, I ran into down at the tournament, anyway."

~ ~ ~ ~ ~

This will be a light day of shooting and weightlifting for the Zags, the last day without practice before the NCAA tournament. There is thus a midafternoon gap in which Oliver Pierce has four of them ticketed for a studio radio appearance at "the Cat," 93.7 FM, with hosts Jay and Kevin.

Dickau seems reluctant. "I gotta get a good workout in today," he says.

But they're off at 2:30 for the south hills of Spokane, Dickau driving his white Jeep Cherokee, Ronny Turiaf, Cory Violette, and Kyle Bankhead with him.

The heat in the studio is turned up, but Turiaf—the Caribbean import—is wearing a parka with a ski cap pulled over his ears. Dickau has a red "And One" cap turned backward as the four sit in front of microphones.

Turiaf is asked how he likes the snow.

"I'm alive," he says laconically.

Kevin, the host, says his four-year-old son is a big Bankhead fan, spurning chances at autographs from Dickau or Violette, which draws yuks.

"What's wrong with that?" Bankhead deadpans.

Dickau is asked about his December 23 marriage proposal to Heather Nevenner. Debating how to pop the question with some élan, Dickau had Bankhead shoot a photograph of him holding an engagement ring and took it to Kinko's, where they made a puzzle from it. At home in Vancouver, Washington, Dickau had his sister light candles in a room. Dickau then instructed Nevenner to put the puzzle together, but he supplied the missing piece, the one with the ring.

"Thankfully," he says, "she said yes."

Now the hosts take a break and warn that they're coming back with a worst-disk-jockeys bit, miming radio jocks in sotto voce, asking stupid questions, and making inane observations.

"Dave Chipper and Tom Gay, Chipper and Gay, live in Green Bay," Jay intones.

"You, Kyle, you're from Walla Walla?"

"Yeah."

"A place so nice, they named it twice."

Before the group can depart, Turiaf commandeers the controls of a PlayStation game between Duke and Gonzaga. The Zags' uniform numbers in the game correspond to those of Gonzaga players.

As Dickau makes a turnover, Turiaf exclaims, "Don't be casual, Dahn Deekau!" A lob pass to Violette—nicknamed "Chisel"—is slammed home for two points, eliciting this from Turiaf: "Alley-oop—you, Cheesel!"

It's 23–14, Gonzaga leading Duke, when they leave. It was a good session. Nobody seems in much of a hurry to get back to the gym after all. In 48 hours, the Zags will find out where they're headed in the NCAA tournament. Life is good.

~ ~ ~ ~ ~

Back on the floor at 3:30, players are doing 300-shot workouts, after which they will hit the weight room. Perched on a bleacher seat is Mike Chrysler, 29-year-old strength coach at Gonzaga.

When you think college strength coach, you think Boyd Epley at Nebraska, surrounded by assistants, presiding over a weight room only slightly smaller than a hotel's grand ballroom. This is not Mike Chrysler.

He spends six to seven hours at week at Gonzaga, hardly making a big-time salary. "It's minimal," he says. "It helps out with my rent. The budget here is a little tight."

The Gonzaga program doesn't have a full-time strength coach. It's pretty much left up to each sport's coach to incorporate weight training into the regimen.

Basketball, Chrysler says, added his services only three years ago, when Matt Santangelo, Richie Frahm, Quentin Hall, Axel Dench, and Casey Calvary and company went to the NCAA Elite Eight and wanted more.

"Those guys were kind of hungry on their own to do something different to get back there the next year," says Chrysler. "Now it's a position here. The coaches have bought into it. The first time, it was, 'Who is this guy coming in working with our guys? Is he going to get 'em too big?' I've learned a lot. With Casey Calvary the first year, I got him up to 255 pounds, benching 400. I probably got him a little too big."

But Chrysler is clearly proud of his role and excited to contribute.

"I give these guys pretty much individualized attention," he says, "as opposed to having to be spread out. I don't like to brag about it, but it's almost pro quality. They get that in-your-face, one-on-one training."

The crucible for Gonzaga came in the Sweet 16 of the 2001 NCAA tournament, playing Big Ten bully Michigan State. The Spartans were the No. 1 team in the country all season with a thunderous rebounding advantage, and they abused the Zags on the boards, 47–28. Chrysler took what was said and written personally, and Gonzaga made a renewed effort in the weight room.

"The day after the tournament last year," Chrysler says, "we set a goal to become the strongest team in the country. I don't care whether this is quoted— we are the strongest team, pound for pound."

He could make the case. The Zags would enter the 2002 tournament with a rebounding margin of 9.3. That isn't Michigan State–2001 territory, but it's good enough to lead the nation entering the tournament. Players bought into the workouts and liked the results. As soon as the Zags would return from a road trip, Chrysler would know a call was coming: it would be Dickau, inquiring about the next weight workout so he could round up his teammates.

"That's not normal," says Chrysler, a former defensive end at Eastern Washington.

Nor is Chrysler's take on his part-time job.

"I don't care if they take my paychecks away," he says. "I'd come in and do this for nothing. It's the synergy between the guys. They're motivated; they're hungry.

"I'll never be a millionaire with that attitude, obviously."

Saturday, March 9, 2002

Mark Few is back from a recruiting trip to see College of Southern Idaho point guard Ricky Clemons, a 5'10", 170-pound scoring machine.

With Dickau graduating, the Zags are temporarily in the netherworld position of not knowing who will immediately inherit his spot. They would be comfortable with Blake Stepp switching from the number two guard to the point—he's excellent in transition and the kind of outside scoring threat Few loves—but his troublesome knee makes his 2002–2003 status questionable. Stepp will have the knee examined shortly after the season ends, and if he needs a second surgery, he could miss the next season. That would leave only senior Winston Brooks and redshirting freshman Josh Reisman to fill the void. Thus the interest in Clemons.

The Zags are back at practice again, and Few begins with a talk. Standing next to him is A.J., whom Marcy Few has brought to the gym for the early part of the workout.

"I guess you guys probably know Father Tony passed away yesterday," Few says, informing them of a memorial service in eight days. "One thing he did was cherish relationships. I guess if there's a message, value your relationships, live each moment. I spent time with him those last days, and he was happy. He was excited about where he was going."

Few moves on to a status report on his team.

"We need to improve our offensive execution and our team defense," he says. "Just like in the Pepperdine game, we wanted to make 'em shoot jump shots. They hit 'em in the first half, but the heat wore off and they were missing 'em in the second half. The third thing we've gotta do is hit the glass. We've gotta win the glass by 10. And the last thing is, improve our zone. Do those things, and we can play with anybody in the country.

"A lot is going to be said tomorrow about seeds. But don't get caught up in that."

Few steps forward two paces. A.J. steps with him.

"I want you to play aggressively. The team that plays aggressively and smart, that's a dangerous combination."

In the Zags' three-year, 10-game NCAA run, one thread has been common to their success. They have attacked every time out, taking the fight to the opponent, the antithesis of the tentativeness that often marks teams in the tournament. They have shot relatively well—45.5 percent overall and 42.4

from three-point range—suggesting a devil-may-care component to their March play.

Almost immediately, the practice is better than Thursday's return from the WCC tournament. The communication is louder; the execution is sharper.

"I think they got over the lull," says Jerry Krause with a smile. "That was a wake-up call Thursday."

Again, the workout is structured, centered on fundamentals without being overly regimented. Players get to their stations and work crisply amid the coach jargon: "Zone up, trap the ball screen." As the Zags work on press offense, Few chides Anthony Reason: "Listen, presses want to live off the jump pass. Every time we've thrown a jump pass, we've turned the ball over."

But the message is delivered positively, not in a pejorative fashion. There is precious little profanity, from coach or players. About the most off-color thing from Few's mouth is: "We're becoming too perimeter-oriented instead of getting our ass down and sealing somebody!"

They slip in free throws during the workout, at one point closing eyes just before the release. It's a good free throw shooting team, at 72.5 percent.

Two hours and 25 minutes after they began, the Zags have completed practice. Today they can feel they accomplished something.

Back in his office, Few is mulling the day's tournament results and wondering aloud about seeding. He's something of a bracketologist himself, checking out websites and analysts' projections. Connecticut is about to lock up with Pitt for the Big East title. Arizona has just won the Pac-10 tournament, launching its candidacy for a No. 2 seed. Who knows? That could crowd out Gonzaga's bid for a No. 2.

"There's a big difference between a two and a three," Few says. "At three, you could get somebody like Utah State."

Sunday, March 10, 2002

This is the day, Selection Sunday. It's a little bit of Christmas for college basketball fans—a day of thick anticipation—and it's never been more intense around Spokane. One moment it's speculation all over the map, and the next, CBS is flashing your team up on the screen and your immediate assignment is outlined. For players, told all year that they hold their fate in their hands, it's a day when somebody emerging from a hotel meeting room in a distant city dishes their future out to them.

In the late morning down at Arny's, a classic spinning-stool diner near the Gonzaga campus, they're serving up huge pancakes, garlic hash browns, and white gravy over biscuits to the sounds of "Venus," "The Stroll," and "At the Hop." A line forms for seating, which is understandable, given that there are only 17 seats in the place.

"Two eggs, hash browns, and a national championship," one GU student says, joshing a buddy.

"No problem. Got one of those in the back."

At noon, Gonzaga has a 90-minute practice. It's a workout heavily laced with fundamentals—catch-and-shoot jumpers, left-handed shots by the big men. Another one-on-one drill puts the ball in the hand of a wing on a fast break, contested by a single defender retreating down the middle. Everything seems a tiny part of a great template, to reveal itself in a basketball game.

At 1:30 P.M., Few ends the workout and the team gathers round. He contemplates the rest of the day's schedule when Zach Gourde interrupts.

"*Season on the Brink* at 7:00," Gourde reminds, referring to the endlessly promoted ESPN movie based on the book detailing coach Bob Knight's stormy times at Indiana.

Few ponders that and then agrees to accommodate.

"I want you guys to watch it," he says, grinning. "See how good you've got it."

Up in his office, Few is clicked into the Internet again.

"Oregon's got Santa Barbara," he says. Well, not exactly. Joe Lunardi's mock bracket on ESPN.com has the Ducks playing UCSB, a team Few thinks might be matched up against Gonzaga.

~ ~ ~ ~ ~

At the West Coast Grand Hotel less than a mile from campus, it's the next thing to bedlam. Maybe 1,000 fans are on hand for an autograph party/selection viewing with the Zags. After being thrust basketballs, T-shirts, and notebook paper, Gourde is asked how many autographs he has signed. "Over 400," he says.

CBS tantalizes the revelers by announcing three other regions before the West. By then, there are still heavyweight teams unaccounted for—Cincinnati, Oklahoma, Arizona, Ohio State. In itself, that's ominous for the Zags.

"We're getting screwed," a man tells his companion as they crane necks toward a big screen.

All those teams come up on the board, and so does Miami, as a No. 5 seed. Now it's a done deal. Shockingly, Gonzaga is a No. 6 seed, matched against No. 11 Wyoming. Not only is the seed a mind-bender, but the Zags are also sent to Albuquerque, not Sacramento. For the fans, it's a travel double whammy: it's too far to think about driving, and most flights to the New Mexico city cost double those to Sacramento.

CBS cameras, accustomed to shots of players on campus whooping it up at their selection, pan in on the Zags. Few has a look that would bore holes through the Division I basketball committee chairman, Lee Fowler.

Few handles it in as diplomatic a manner as he can muster for CBS and ESPN, but the Zags are clearly deflated over the assessment. Accurate or not, it probably represents the greatest disparity in seeding over what was popularly forecast in the history of the event.

"I guess we have to be perfect," Few says a couple of hours later. "And even then, what does it get you, a five seed?"

National reaction will be sharp. Dick Vitale goes on an impassioned rant—now there's a story—on behalf of the midmajor schools and their scheduling woes. Andy Katz of ESPN.com discusses a litany of questionable moves by the committee and concludes, "The worst error is the No. 6 seed for Gonzaga. Does the committee really believe there are 20 better teams than the Bulldogs?" And author John Feinstein, a former president of the U.S. Basketball Writers Association, calls it, "The single worst thing a committee has ever done to a team in this tournament."

Wednesday, March 13, 2002

Gonzaga is on the floor at University Arena, known more famously as "the Pit." It's New Mexico's dugout court—outside, a nondescript brick building that hints little of its purpose; inside, a lively barn that hosted North Carolina State's stunning climax in the run to its 1983 national championship.

The Zags have the mandatory one-hour practice for the public, something scorned by the competing coaches. Most teams will have their regular workout at a high school gym and save the froufrou for this session.

Through a coaching friend of Jerry Krause, the Zags have already put in a solid practice session at Valley High School.

"In the barrio," says Krause, smiling. "Perfect for our mentality."

In the locker room, Bill Grier talks about the recipe for beating Wyoming: deny penetration, negate transition, rebound.

"Statistically, they don't shoot it well," he says.

What an eerie observation that will be in a little more than 24 hours.

"They go to the glass almost assuming they're going to miss," Grier says. "It's almost as if their offense is: get it up on the glass and go get it."

Dan Dickau and Cory Violette are brought to the interview room, where a reporter asks Dickau if he ever asked for No. 12, John Stockton's old number, when he got to Gonzaga.

"It's kind of an unwritten rule, you're not going to get No. 12," Dickau says. "Our trainer, Steve DeLong, he's basically best friends with John Stockton, and he's not going to think about releasing that number. If anyone wrote it down, he's going to scribble it out."

Moments later, the Wyoming delegation would arrive on the dais.

"I don't think there's any question," says the Cowboys' fourth-year coach, Steve McClain. "We're going to walk onto the court thinking we can win."

Thursday, March 14, 2002

The game is done. The season is done. One minute, there is breathless anticipation, the next, utter melancholy.

Gonzaga shot 26.8 percent, worse than Pierce or anybody else can remember in years. Dickau, who was 7 of 24, handles himself well on the interview dais, his basketball career now an itinerary of NBA tryout camps.

Few talks about the void coming, the days when it seems natural to practice but there's nothing to practice for. And he contemplates the bigger picture.

"These kids have developed quite a following across the country, not only for the way they play, but the way they handle themselves," he says.

"It's good, because it's right."

Hours later, in room 1102 at the Old Town Sheraton, Few and a handful of family members are quietly putting the season to rest. Below, the lights of Albuquerque glisten.

Few's close friend Ray Giacoletti, the head coach at Eastern Washington, calls to commiserate. Just five days earlier, Few was offering his own shoulder for Giacoletti to cry on after Eastern's loss to Montana in the Big Sky tournament.

Few had been leery of the Wyoming matchup. The Cowboys had won a respected conference, they were Gonzaga's equal on the boards; they were athletic enough.

But it's history. It's a loss. It's the way of the NCAA tournament. Maybe someday Gonzaga's guys will come to put it in its proper perspective.

"Now they've got to go back and bury Father Tony on Monday," Few sighed. "But that'll be good for them."

~ ~ ~ ~ ~

A little more than three days later, they filed into the Martin Centre among 3,000 people, young men in suits and ties. The gym was a muted contrast to the raucous nights they have known there.

Slowly, they would edge back into the necessities of their lives, attending classes and playing hoops. And they would know that the excellence of Gonzaga basketball and the message it spreads are as Father Tony always used to say: To be continued. . . .

Afterword

Although I spent nineteen years at Michigan State University, in the seven years since my retirement most Spartan fans have come to feel that my greatest contribution to the team was not the national championship of 1979 but using my influence to have Tom Izzo named my successor.

The same could be said of the Gonzaga program. It started with Dan Fitzgerald, who named Dan Monson his successor before he retired; Monson in turn set the stage for Mark Few, who succeeded him when he moved to Minnesota. This has enabled the Gonzaga basketball program to maintain continuity, which eludes so many programs when there are coaching changes.

One of the first things I did when we retired to Spokane in 1995 was purchase season tickets to Gonzaga basketball. I did this because of my long association with Don Monson—who was my former assistant at Michigan State—and his family, as well as my respect for Dan Fitzgerald, a longtime coaching friend.

I still remember the first game I attended at the Kennel. It was during the Thanksgiving break against Central Washington. The students were gone and there were probably no more than 2,500 fans scattered in the stands. My wife, who was used to sold-out Big Ten arenas, asked, "Is this Division I basketball?" I said yes. She said, "There is no atmosphere." After watching five minutes of play, I turned to her and said, "There may be no atmosphere, but there are three players out there that could start on most of my Michigan State teams." They were 6'2" Kyle Dixon at point guard, 6'8" Scott Snider at power forward, and 7' Paul Rogers at center. I have been impressed with the talent level of the Zags ever since.

A couple of my many coaching clichés are "Be a guard, not a garbage," and "If you've got good guards, you'll have a good team." Gonzaga has been blessed with a number of really good guards. As you read this book and appreciate the great success of the Zags and the number of quality big men they have had, don't underestimate the contribution of the guards. They have been terrific.

I would be remiss if I didn't comment on the uniqueness of the Gonzaga program. The players like each other. The players like the coaches and the coaches like the players. Every player checks his ego at the gym door and buys into the team concept.

Perhaps Dan Dickau said it best at this year's Gonzaga banquet when he talked about his senior teammates, Alex Hernandez and Anthony Reason. "They have a different ethnic background than I do," Dickau said. "They have a different lifestyle than I do. But when we go to practice or play in a game, we share one common goal: to help each other prepare and to win. I'm proud and honored to have both as friends and teammates."

Gonzaga's phenomenal success has been built on the idea of putting team first, individual second. It started with Dan Fitzgerald and has been carried on by Dan Monson and Mark Few. Each coach has put his own stamp on his teams, but the common thread has been individual sacrifice and the team approach.

It is unbelievable to me that in the last five years, each Gonzaga team has been better than the one before. This is not supposed to happen in college basketball. The Zags do not rebuild or reload—they just repeat. The future looks bright with a new arena on the horizon, several good players, and great coaches. Believe me when I say that the best is yet to come.

As you read about the great teams, players, and coaches in this book, I hope you enjoy and appreciate Gonzaga basketball as much as I have.

—Jud Heathcote

Index

195